Long Live the Child

Long Live the Child

DEVOTIONS DESIGNED *for* DAUGHTERS OF PROMISE

CHRISTINE WYRTZEN

ZONDERVAN™

GRAND RAPIDS, MICHIGAN 49530 USA

ZONDERVAN™

Long Live the Child
Copyright © 2003 by Christine, Inc.

Requests for information should be addressed to:
Zondervan, *Grand Rapids, Michigan 49530*

Library of Congress Cataloging-in-Publication Data

Wyrtzen, Christine.
    Long live the child : devotions designed for daughters of promise / Christine
Wyrtzen.
       p. cm.
    Includes bibliographical references.
    ISBN 0-310-24652-0
    1. Christian women — Prayer-books and devotions — English. 2. Devotional
calendars. I. Title.
    BV4844 .W97 2003
    242'.643 — dc21

                                        2002015569

Interior design by Tracey Moran

Printed in the United States of America

03 04 05 06 /❖ DC/ 10 9 8 7 6 5 4 3 2 1

To my mother
Gertrude Theresa Hughes-Hewitt
1919–1984

AN INTRODUCTION TO CHRISTINE

*C*hristine Wyrtzen is the founder and director of Daughters of Promise, a national ministry for women. She is also a recording artist, author, speaker, and host of the nationally syndicated radio program *Daughters of Promise,* heard daily on many hundred stations. Christine's passion is to awaken women to the extravagant love of God and equip them to live as children in his kingdom.

A musician with fourteen albums and two books to her credit, Christine has been in ministry for twenty-seven years. She's been nominated for a Dove Award and long admired for her ability to communicate to an audience. She is an artist with words, and her poetic bent is evident in whatever she creates.

Highlights of her public ministry include a song she wrote in 1981 that celebrated the release of the sixty Iranian hostages. She sang "They've Come Home" in Washington, D.C., on the eve of their homecoming and received a standing ovation. Her best-known musical project is an album called *For Those Who Hurt*—a collection of songs meant to encourage those who suffer from the hardships of life. Her voice is soothing and brings peace within the first few moments of listening.

Christine has an ability to connect with people quickly by offering herself as a friend and wounded healer. Her desire to share her pain and her triumphs provides a platform that touches others profoundly. Her success in helping women discover the heart of God is due to her warmth and transparency.

She has been married for twenty-nine years to Ron Wyrtzen, and they have two adult children, Jaime and Ryan.

Become more familiar with Christine's ministry by visiting her website at www.daughtersofpromise.org.

DEVOTIONS AND THE CHILD OF GOD

The child is presented as a spiritual model throughout the Gospels. Why is this? Perhaps it is because a child has an innate ability to understand kingdom principles. Perhaps it is because a well-adjusted child lives empowered, as one who knows intuitively how to be creative, resilient, and discerning. Or perhaps it is because a child knows how to trust with complete abandon.

Many Christian women *believe* that they are God's daughters, but have somehow lost the wide-eyed wonder of a child. The ability to create, play, or receive love and affection has been compromised or lost altogether. Through sheer grit and determination, many try to live up to impossible expectations. Sadly, the result is often anger and confusion. I know. I've been there.

It took me many years to begin to discover my rich spiritual history and birthright. Until I embraced it as mine, my life's "house" was constructed with some destitute building materials. Because I had not seized the meaning of my spiritual adoption and understood the full ramifications of God's radical love for me, I worked for his approval. I labored too long in a travail that took its toll. It was self-abusive. I didn't know much about grace. Living the "victorious Christian life" meant "impeccable performance." Now I know it means "living life loved."

The kindest thing my Father has done in recent years has been to give me the choice to cooperate with him in the dismantling of my impressive-looking but diseased internal world. It's been painful to examine it all in the disassembly. I discovered what was missing. I did not know that I could build my life on the Father's foundation of love, security, and the joy of obedience. Instead I had built it on sheer grit, framed it with impossible expectations, and nailed it together with anger and loneliness.

Perhaps I've just described your existence. You *think* you know what it is you're supposed to be doing. You perform tirelessly, hoping to find joy and fulfillment as an outgrowth of your service to others and to the church. But you secretly admit that something, somehow, isn't working and that you live with a palpable emptiness. Much of what has passed for your Christian experience has amounted to little more than grand exercises in behavior modification.

Long Live the Child is for you. The devotions will help you connect with the heart of God. I have intentionally presented Scripture as the living revelation of God rather than some abstract textbook. Biblical passages have been personalized as a result of my decision to be authentic. In these pages I will share how I'm learning to live as a much loved daughter. I'll be up-front with personal obstacles such as cynicism, the difficulty of obedience, and the propensity each of us has to distrust God's ways. I'm hoping my transparency will give you the courage to join me on the journey.

As you spend this next year with me, know that our Father will cheer us on as we grow in stature as his daughters of promise. He will be delighted to see us discover the truths he knows will bring freedom. (I can see him rubbing his hands in anticipation at the thought that we might discover another secret of his heart.) Each day he'll offer us a new lifestyle option: a life fueled by the spiritual energy of his love, a life that promises to put a carefree innocence back on our face.

How to Read the Devotions

The Perfect Reading Environment

Meeting with God every day is not a formal occasion. You don't have to dress up, sit up straight, fight to stay awake, or say the right things to impress him. It's not about getting a Christian education and expanding your intellect. God is not a person to be studied but a Father to be known. Meeting with him is all about feeding your heart by spending time with the one who cherishes you. You are changed and enriched by his love language. Oh, daughter, he is calling you home. He invites you to dwell in the place where you can be yourself, take your shoes off, and curl up in your favorite chair.

The Cabin

I'm tired and drained to the core. I pray, "Jesus, show me where I can rest." I close my eyes and I can see it clearly. A log cabin, secluded in the mountains, with a gurgling stream making its nearby presence known. I see myself at the end of the walk that leads to the front door. It is a mild summer day and a man is bent over the flower bed, his back to me. He wears work clothes and his hands are dirty from working in the soil.

He turns at the sound of my footsteps and doesn't seem particularly surprised to see me. I continue to approach him, feeling a little shy. "Hello," he says. I stop two feet from him, look up into his face, and hear him softly call me by my first name, closing his eyes as he does. He is pleased to see me.

"Come on in," he says, leading the way into the cabin. As he pulls open the screen door, it squeaks like the one that graced my childhood home. Once inside I see that he has created the cabin just to my liking. He's been expecting me. I am enveloped by all my favorite colors.

The summer breeze follows me in through the screen. I breathe deeply of freshly mown grass and cultivated soil. I'm also aware of another wonderful aroma. My eyes search the room to find the source, and finally spot a table in front of the sofa. There, inside a huge vase, is the most extravagant arrangement of fresh lilacs I've ever seen. Few people allow themselves to clip so many blooms, but he has indulged himself with the pleasure. "My goodness, did you leave any lilacs on the bush?" I ask. Apparently, my delight is worth it, for he chuckles with deep satisfaction.

"Come sit with me," he says as he settles on one end of the sofa and pats the seat next to him. Without thinking, almost instinctively, I curl up next to him. I'm struck by how completely at ease in his presence I am.

"Welcome home," he says, as if this is the moment he has been waiting for. "You'll notice there are no clocks. Tell me your story, and there is time for me to hear all of it. I've waited so long for this."

I sigh with discomfort and wonder where in the world to start. He hears my painful hesitations, finally interrupts and takes over with an unexpected suggestion. "Tell you what," he says. "Let me tell *you* your story."

I settle against his shoulder more deeply, relieved that I won't have to find the words. His version takes a long time. As he finishes, I am relaxed and satisfied, having a more complete understanding of my life. I am at peace because someone knows me so well.

I feel like a little girl. I'm not sure when the change occurred. It was effortless and without intention on my part. I do not point it out to him, nor does he embarrass me by drawing attention to it. As if by second nature, I move into his lap. Curling up in his arms, I can hear his heart beat and am lulled by its rhythm into a semiconscious nap. I hear my own shallow breathing, am aware of my childlike mannerisms, but I'm struck by the realization that I am content. He holds me so securely that my every muscle goes limp.

I'm rocked to sleep by the sound of my name woven by the Master Musician into the most creative of melodies. Yet somehow it is also predictable. It's as if my heart already knows the song. Before entering a deep sleep, I hear him whisper, "Come back as often as you want. I'll be here waiting for you. You need this more than you even know. But you know what? This is important to me too. I created you just for moments like this."

(See the appendix for biblical principles of the cabin experience.)

January

January 1

New Paint, New Brushes, and a Fresh Canvas

In the beginning God created.

GENESIS 1:1

*B*eginnings are wonderful things. There's a fresh canvas on which to paint. Possibilities are endless. Dreams are born. Imaginations are the most fertile. Hope is alive because nothing has yet stood in the way of success. Yesterday is over and failures are behind me. All that lies ahead are vistas of opportunity. Optimism is at an all-time high.

Who has the best chance of creating something valuable? I am a creative person, but the best of my gifts are merely a shadow of God's genius. He is the ultimate Creator. He who fashioned the world in seven days could have done it in one! Only heaven will begin to reveal the extent of his capability. Today I only see a speck of his brilliance.

If it's a choice between him carving out this next year or me shaping my own future, I have only to look at my track record to see that I've made a mess of many years. Give me a clean canvas and sooner or later I'll end up distorting the very thing I began to sketch well.

The best choice I can make is to allow God to "create" through my life this coming year. I can decide to be the canvas on which God paints his dreams. His purposes existed long before my birth and will be carried out long after my death, but I can be a part of it while I'm here. When I choose to submit to this higher calling—a plan far bigger than the one I would have designed for myself—I will be the most fulfilled. And best of all, in December I'll look back and see God's fingerprints, not mine.

Oh, Creator, I'm yours this year. Amen.

January 2

The Qualities of Light

[John] was not the light; he came only as a witness to
the light.

JOHN 1:8

John was called by God to bear witness to the Light, who was
Jesus. John was influenced by the Light, changed by the Light,
and even radiated the Light. How much am I like John today? God
answered my question as he reminded me of some of the qualities of light.

Light warms. Our dog, Freska, loves to lie close to the fire in the
fireplace. So close that her fur gets too hot to touch. We cannot believe
she's not in pain. Light brings warmth to whatever is exposed to it.
Can I feel Jesus' warmth in my soul? Do others experience me as a
warm person? A "cold as ice" Christian should be an oxymoron. As
the light of Jesus' love washes over my soul, the cold places in my heart
will melt.

Light illuminates. Anyone who's done any camping knows the
power of a flashlight on a black night in the woods. How reassuring to
flick the switch and be able to see the trail. Time with Jesus brings
clarity and focus. It brings depth of understanding about issues,
people, policies, and the mysteries of spiritual truth. My life should be
marked by daily illumination.

Light radiates. Do others tell me that my faith is contagious? If so,
I know that my countenance is radiant. I will be as John, casting the
light of Christ's love on others and bringing them to an awareness of
their spiritual thirst.

*Jesus, I want the warmth of your love to melt me, and the clarity of
your truth to illuminate my path. After Moses spent time with you,
his face shone brilliantly. Whatever that spiritual phenomenon, I
petition it for myself. Amen.*

January 3

No Room for the Real Me

He came to that which was his own, but his own did
not receive him.

JOHN 1:11

*A*s you read the Gospels, are you frustrated for Jesus? Do you find it inconceivable that he received such harsh treatment from his own people, the ones he came to reveal himself to? So few recognized him as the Messiah, the one for whom their ancestors had waited. The irony is that the ones most blinded to his identity were the students of Scripture, the religious. Oh, the pain he suffered over not being recognized. Did he ever question whether his coming was worth it? I wonder, for pain can make us second-guess the most holy calling.

Our own flesh and blood often fail to receive us, too. The story of Jesus is repeated again and again. Except now we know where to go to find comfort for the emptiness in our soul. Jesus, who intercedes for us at the right hand of our Father, knows how to pray for us. He ached from abandonment and understands our longings.

For this reason his Father promises, "Though my father and mother forsake me, the LORD will receive me" (Psalm 27:10). God knows that family systems are flawed in varying degrees. He understands completely as we bleed from the open, gaping wounds of familial misunderstandings. He sees where our emotional growth was stunted as a result. We look like grown-ups, carry the responsibility of adults, but feel like children.

Jesus offers us the acceptance we crave. He can repair the breech. He stands in the gap between parents and children, offering wholeness to whoever seeks it. We who are born into his family need never fear rejection. We hold out our arms, he picks us up and never lets us go.

Jesus, you are my healer, credible by your own wounds. Amen.

January 4

He's Perfect!

We have seen his glory, . . . full of grace and truth.

JOHN 1:14

The better we get to know someone, the more their weaknesses are exposed. Just ask newlyweds who have discovered that the honeymoon is over and their two carnal natures have finally collided. What transpires at that point reveals their character.

John knew Jesus well. He ate with him and lived in his company for years. He watched Jesus under stress and beheld him under the eye of criticism. He saw his responses to false accusations. The honeymoon stage had long passed, and John got to know Jesus more and more intimately. Instead of learning that Jesus had a carnal nature, he increasingly saw the glory of his perfection! Ah, it is this that makes me run unafraid into a relationship with Jesus. I know I can't be disillusioned.

The true message of Jesus is revealed to us as grace and truth. John makes a strong statement that both frame the portrait of the gospel. Take one away and it's no longer the message of Jesus.

I can recall times when I saw grace but no truth. Sin abounded and compassion excused it. But more commonly the opposite was true. Many years I lived in an atmosphere where truth was declared, void of grace. There men, women, and children hid their true selves. We were the masters of disguise, never bearing our burdens to one another for fear of condemnation. We missed the joy of supporting one another with our prayers and tears.

Let's celebrate Jesus today and gift wrap his gospel in grace and truth.

Help me learn from you, Jesus. I might blurt out truth in a condemning way. Forgive me for the ways I misrepresent you. Make my words gracious and truthful. Amen.

January 5

State Your Name, Please!

"I am the voice of one calling in the desert, 'Make straight the way for the Lord.'"

JOHN 1:23

*H*ow would I answer if someone casually asked, "Who are you?" Would I answer, "I am a mother, wife, artist, musician, and founder of a ministry?"

What might my reply be if I was interrogated in a hostile setting and asked, "Who do you think you are!" Would I scramble to list my credentials, putting to rest the insinuations that I was a nobody? And would doing so add weight to my credibility?

John the Baptist was a priest from the line of Aaron. Strong credentials! Yet when the priests and Levites from Jerusalem investigated him—the equivalent of an inquisition by the Vatican—I am amazed at his answer. The question was posed, "Who are you?" The one who had impressive credentials divested himself of them all for a bigger purpose.

He revealed that he was simply a voice through which God communicated his mind to the people. It reminds me that I'm not called to teach my own wisdom. I am bankrupt. God wants to communicate his mind and heart through me.

I'm so glad he didn't say, "I am one teaching" or "I am one telling." One cannot cry out without passion and intensity. His description makes me ask myself if I ever talk about Jesus void of feeling. Do I teach in dry, sterile tones? Or is there a magnetic quality to my words because they are laced with earnestness? Would *heartfelt* describe others' experience of me?

Who am I, Lord? I am a voice you are using, one who speaks with passion, one who hears your mind in the wilderness, and one whose goal it is to make the way for you straighter today than it was yesterday. Amen.

January 6

My Home Is Yours

Turning around, Jesus saw them following and asked,
"What do you want?"

JOHN 1:38

Two men are so drawn to Jesus that after hearing that he is the Lamb of God, they change the direction they are walking and follow him. Jesus, sensing them behind him, asks, "What do you want?" Jesus notices the first motions of a soul turning toward him!

Their answer is vulnerable. "Where are you staying?" In other words, "We want to know where your home is, because we want more time with you." Jesus wasn't put off. He told them to follow, that he would take them to where he was staying. He was accessible then— and still is!

Christianity is the only faith that is personal. Other founders of religion develop a leadership style that keeps their followers at a distance. The bigger the movement, the more out of reach they become.

As one in public ministry, I am challenged to remain accessible to the people. Sometimes the most important ministry happens not from the platform but in one-on-one encounters beforehand or afterward. Performers and speakers who run out during the closing prayer, body-guards in tow, miss the point and harm the model of leadership Jesus instituted. Making themselves inaccessible, they distort the truth of God's accessibility.

Jesus invites us home with him. He inspired the writers of Scripture to underscore the personal nature of his interest in us. We are told he has numbered the hairs of our head, kept every tear close to him, and engraved each of us on the palm of his hand. How much more intimate could he be?

Jesus, I can see you crook your finger and invite me home. I'm coming. I need to be intimate with you. I'm empty unless I take you up on your invitation. Amen.

Dealing with Skeptics

"Come and see," said Philip.

JOHN 1:46

*D*o you have family members or close friends who are skeptical of your faith? That can be painful, making us feel we have little credibility with those who supposedly know us best. We feel powerless when we see that our words have such little influence. We often make a fatal mistake. We choose to talk more! We're too quick to try to prove a point and defend the work of God in our lives. Is there a better way to frame our testimony, a way that will draw others into the truth? I believe so.

The first chapter of John reveals the initial conversions of Jesus' disciples—how they heard, how they came, when they believed. Philip found his friend Nathaniel and said, "We have found him of whom Moses and the Prophets spoke, Jesus of Nazareth." Such wonderful news! Shouldn't Nathaniel have been ecstatic? Yes, but skeptically he asked, "Can any good thing come out of Nazareth?" Philip did not launch into rationales or lengthy discourses to try to prove Jesus was the Messiah. His answer was short but powerful. "Come and see!"

Let's face it! Not even parents, spouses, children, or friends are unanimously swayed by our powerful stories. They are blinded by the deception of their own hearts. I recognize the wisdom of Philip's challenge, "Nathaniel, come and see for yourself!" The story ends with Nathaniel hearing from Jesus things about himself that only God could know. Nathaniel trusted Jesus.

When we challenge others to try Jesus for themselves, we leave them in good hands. He who created their minds reads their objections, stills their fears, and dismantles the framework of their deceptive rationales.

Draw my loved ones to you, Jesus. May your love enlighten them. Change icy skepticism into passionate abandon. Amen.

January 8

Counting on His Mercy

"Do whatever he tells you."

JOHN 2:5

*T*he first miracle of Jesus' ministry takes place in the obscure town of Cana. Jesus and his mother are guests at a wedding. Mary, noticing that the hosts have run out of wine, turns to Jesus for help. However, his response is jarring. He is abrupt, reminding her that his time of ministry (and miracles) has not yet come. She is reproved not as a mother but as a child of a sovereign King.

I picture how I might have felt as Mary: put in my place, nursing hurt feelings. Not Mary! She knows Jesus well. Rising from the table, she says to the servants, "Do whatever he tells you." Wasn't she just told it was not time for him to act? Yes. Yet she knows Jesus well enough to know that his heart is moved by needs. Confident in his mercy, she sets the stage for him to perform the forthcoming miracle.

Many times my petitions were met by silence. I mistakenly concluded that God didn't care or he wasn't going to answer. But in reality delays in God's mercy are not to be confused with denials of prayers! We can know our Father's heart. It is outlined in the pages of Scripture, and it is showcased through the stories of his children, our spiritual ancestors. Like Mary, we can look for ways today to set the stage, internally and externally, for forthcoming miracles.

Has the wine been exhausted? Are you crying out in need? Rest in God's mercy. He has heard. He is moved. Look up confidently for new wine. You won't be disappointed.

> *I have doubted you, Lord. Forgive me. Your timetable is not mine. I rest in your mercy and your perfect timing. I await your arrival. Amen.*

January 9

The Icing or the Cake?

He did not need man's testimony about man, for he knew what was in a man.

JOHN 2:25

*J*esus knows people's hearts and how fickle they are. He knows not to depend on people for what only his Father can give.

Are you disillusioned with people today? Perhaps you live in a relationship in which you bare your soul and make your needs known, only to be ignored. Loving you would mean personal change, and perhaps the other person won't risk stretching out of his or her comfort zone.

As a result of growing up in a home where emotional needs were rarely expressed, I became a needy adult. Though I appeared poised, I looked to others for validation and love. Sometimes they were given. But in proportion to my need, the gestures were just crumbs. The insatiable hole in my soul could not be filled. Satan loved to point out my deep well of discontent, by the way. He can enhance the reality of our aching needs on a daily basis.

Did Jesus stop telling those close to him what he needed? No. When others reached out, he accepted their love with an open heart. When his disciples fell asleep, leaving him alone on the worst night of his life, his faith in his Father did not waver.

Is it okay to tell people what we need? Yes. Can we enjoy being loved? Absolutely! Meaningful gestures here on earth are icing on the cake, but they cannot be the cake. If I put my hope in people, I will experience inevitable disappointment and disillusionment.

Father, no one around me is perfect. I'm so glad my heart is safely with you.

Though I am sad today, I don't despair. You fill my soul when others fail. Amen.

January 10

Void of Thirst

"Whoever drinks the water I give him will never thirst."
JOHN 4:14

*J*esus is thirsty and uses this as a springboard to highlight a spiritual truth. The Samaritan woman believes Jesus is a stranger, but he knows her and perceives her spiritual thirst.

He is also skillful in conversation. He knows how to turn a phrase and draw her into a deeper conversation from a subject as mundane as thirst. He can birth a succulent metaphor from something so commonplace.

He tells her something so simple: "Everyone who drinks of this water shall thirst again." She knows that! This is why she fetches water daily. Last night's drink doesn't satisfy. What is the point here? Jesus then tells her about a drink that lasts forever.

Just as my body needs water every day, my soul craves fresh sustenance. Every day I look for love. Yesterday's morsels may be memorable, but sooner or later my heart needs a new supply. Jesus knows that this world cannot be relied upon to give us our daily spiritual bread. He loves us too much to put us in a tortuous predicament. He deposited his Spirit inside us, from whom we can draw what we need, when we need it.

Living water is plentiful though circumstances are bleak. Spiritual truths are profound though interactions with others are often shallow. Jesus' love is unconditional though many look to me for what I contribute rather than what they can give.

Christianity is a sensual religion. Once aware of our needs, we're offered a means by which we can live internally satisfied. Our thirst need never cripple us again, causing us to drink from undependable sources. We can dip our cup and taste of him who empowers us to live eternally satisfied.

God, I look to you for what I need. Quench my thirst. Amen.

January 11

A Drink That Spans Time

"Sir, give me this water so that I won't get thirsty."
JOHN 4:15

*J*ust as my body needs food and water daily, my soul also craves fresh sustenance. Every day I look for expressions of love, physical affection, and affirming comments. Yesterday's nourishment may be memorable, but sooner or later my needy heart looks for a fresh supply.

Unwrapping the gift of Scripture is like discovering old love letters with my name on them. The tattered parchments quench my thirst. Each message is pregnant with meaning, no matter who penned it on God's behalf. I share some of my favorites:

Whoever touches you touches the apple of his eye.
ZECHARIAH 2:8

"I, the LORD, have called you in righteousness; I will take hold of your hand. I will keep you and will make you to be a covenant for the people."
ISAIAH 42:6

"Can a mother forget the baby at her breast and have no compassion on the child she has borne? Though she may forget, I will not forget you! See, I have engraved you on the palms of my hands...," declares the LORD.
ISAIAH 49:15–16, 18

Once I start reading, it's hard to stop. Such love is intoxicating. They are messages just for me, yet also just for you. Although we might have read these words long ago, in the delirium of the long hours of toil we might have never stopped to consider that they were authored for us. Often I am stirred so deeply by them that I choke back tears.

I've been known to squeeze my eyes shut, press his Word to my heart, thinking his love too good to be true. Never has water tasted this sweet nor been so satisfying.

Heavenly Father, your love, expressed in such beautiful words, quenches my thirst. I love you, too. Amen.

January 12

Crumbs at the Table

"You have had five husbands."

JOHN 4:18

*C*an you identify with the Samaritan woman, who married repeatedly, looking for love? I'm sure her reasons were very complicated, but we can imagine that with each man she dreamed she would find love.

When our relationships deprive us of the love we crave, we begin to suspect that we should adapt our personality to fit the expectations of others. Anything to be loved! We twist and bend, cry, even manipulate to get others to give us what we need. Sometimes it works, but we get crumbs instead of a feast. We rationalize that a little is better than nothing, so we set ourselves up for another disappointment.

Continuing to look to people for what only God can give is idolatry. Only Abba, Father, can fill our souls. But turning to a long list of others requires repentance: "Oh, Father, I'm so sorry for trying to replace you. I should have come to you with my needy heart. Forgive me." Repentance always unlocks the power of heaven.

I realize that this might seem unfair at first glance. You might ask, "I'm the one consistently deprived; now I have to repent?" Yes, if in your need you have looked to others for your wholeness. Our fallen nature drives us, even subconsciously, to choose God last instead of first. Seeking anyone before God is idolatry. We might not have known better, doing it out of ignorance, but sinful choices still ruled us. Falling on our face in sincere apology is easy compared with what Jesus paid to say, "I forgive you." When we feel too proud and humility is far from us, let's remember all he suffered compared with what he asks of us.

You alone can fill the hole in my heart, Lord. Finally I'm coming to you. Amen.

January 13

Moment of Decision

"Do you want to get well?"

JOHN 5:6

*J*esus, always seeking those in need, comes to the pool of Bethesda and finds a crippled man who has been waiting thirty-eight years for his healing. That's a long time to be crippled. You know only one way of life. Your handicap is normal. Expectations of living life whole have long been dismissed.

I know. This was my life. I believed my internal depravity and disease was terminal! We must hang on tenaciously to this man's story, especially any of us in midlife and beyond. Jesus can write new beginnings no matter how long we've been trapped in our situation. Jesus delights in making old things new. He relishes writing new chapters.

He asks the lame man a question, the same one posed to us today: "Do you wish to get well?" By forcing us to answer, Jesus opens us to the possibility that life can be different.

What happened next to this man? Jesus didn't reach out and heal him, making him whole as he lay on his mat. He told him to get up, roll up his bed, and walk. Healing is always a cooperative effort. Before the man could begin to rise, he had to climb a mental mountain. He had to decide to try. Inner healing always begins with submission of our will to the Lord's. He is the Physician. He gives the prescription, and no matter what sense it makes to us, our job is to say, "I'll do whatever you ask, whether I understand or not. I know you love me and this is for my best."

Who am I to think that you can't change my life? You're God, I'm not. I will choose the new life you offer and will do whatever you ask of me. Amen.

January 14

Gatitude That Leads to Obedience

"The man who made me well said to me, 'Pick up your mat and walk.'"

JOHN 5:11

A man, ill for thirty-eight years, gets his healing from a stranger. Jesus gives him a command that tries his new faith. "Take up your bed and walk," he says.

We miss the significance of this in our culture. If this man follows Jesus' order, he will invite controversy. This is the Sabbath, and on this day there is to be no work. Not even the lighting of a lamp. To carry your bed down the street would be considered burdensome and a direct violation of Sabbath law. Jesus knows it and tests his new convert with a difficult act of obedience.

I love it when Scripture tells us "the rest of the story." We find the man interrogated by religious leaders who are unable to catch the beauty of his miracle. They are more concerned that he carries a bed on a holy day. Wouldn't you think they would say, "Sabbath or nothing, who is this person who heals a paralyzed man? This is a wonderful thing he has done." But there is no rejoicing. They are indignant over a broken Sabbath rule. The man doesn't have to wait long for someone to rain on his parade.

How will you and I be able to tell when God's healing work has taken effect? When confidence is born and we no longer hide our story from others. When the man is interrogated as to why he is carrying his bed, he answers, "The man who made me well said to me, 'Pick up your mat and walk.'" We'll never know the inflection of his answer, but perhaps what he inferred was, "Someone who has the power to heal me can ask me to do anything and I will do it!"

Lord Jesus, I'm often afraid to share my story, considering the audience first before opening my mouth. Give me the courage of this first-century Christian. Amen.

January 15

Empowered by Relationship

"I tell you the truth, the Son can do nothing by himself; he can do only what he sees his Father doing."
JOHN 5:19

Jesus, interrogated by the Jewish religious leaders for the crime of
healing on the Sabbath, gave them an interesting answer. He told
them that he did nothing without the direction of his Father in heaven.
He didn't say, "I'm really God. I know what to do."

Aware of the presence of God, Jesus discerned from him what his
next movement should be. He only did what God revealed, modeling
a pattern of living. Knowing the Law and acting on it is not God's
plan. Jesus knew the Law—he wrote it—yet he knew living it out void
of relationship was unthinkable!

Never taught by anyone to hear the voice of God, I was told the
Christian life was simply using Scripture as a foundation for living.
Each day I endeavored to live a life of mercy, joy, patience, faith, etc.
My Christian life was reduced to a code of conduct, lived by rote.
There was no Father's voice, just duty.

I've come to understand that living a life based on spiritual principles
is spiritual immaturity! It's not what God intended. Real maturity is
learning to hear and obey his voice moment by moment, so we know
when, where, and how to apply our foundation of learning.

I'm in kindergarten, with spiritual skills still developing. Oh, the
rewards! God is never boring, never giving stale manna. There are new
words every morning, fresh to the soul, exquisite to taste.

*Father, I know the Bible is not a textbook to be studied. You gave me
your Word so I may get to know you. Help me remember that you live
in the pages. Amen.*

January 16

The Source of All I Need

"Where shall we buy bread for these people to eat?"
JOHN 6:5

*A*n enormous crowd follows Jesus up a mountain. They will be with him awhile because their curiosity and spiritual hunger are great. Jesus knows that meals will be an issue, so he asks the disciples a very practical question about food. He already knows that he will transform the five loaves and two fishes into an unending storehouse of food, yet he inquires, "Where can we buy bread?" They are on a mountaintop, and the Sea of Galilee separates them from the nearest town. In short, there is a crisis.

Why does Jesus raise questions if he already knows the answers? He asks the disciples to further their self-revelation and spiritual growth. Perhaps he hopes they will conclude that he, the Bread of Life, will make bread where there was none. But the disciples never arrive at this juncture of faith.

Today how many of us are faced with a need for which we see no supply? God asks us, "Where will you find what you need?" We respond by throwing up our hands and saying, "You, Lord, should know I have nowhere to turn." By prompting us with the question, God presents us with a crisis, a pivotal moment that can lead to faith. "Though it appears there are no options, Lord, you can do all things!"

We, like the disciples, sometimes forget Jesus' power. We know who he is, yet with each problem or dilemma we look for human solutions. May we learn to walk with the eyes of faith. Reality is made up mostly of what we can't see!

Why am I fretting? Nothing is too hard for you, Father. You are the source of all I need, and I await your provision. Amen.

January 17

More Food Than We Thought

"Gather the pieces that are left over. Let nothing be wasted."

JOHN 6:12

*J*esus fed a crowd of five thousand with one boy's lunch. Each person ate until they were full. What a miracle, but we often miss that there was food left over!

After the meal was served, Jesus told his disciples to gather the pieces that remained. It was important that nothing be wasted even though he supplied in extravagant amounts. With what others might have considered waste, twelve baskets were filled, enough to feed the twelve disciples, who had probably not yet eaten.

Perhaps this lesson can be applied metaphorically. Whenever I was spiritually fed and felt satiated, was there more food available than I knew at the time? Perhaps God would have me retrace my steps and look for the missing pieces.

I'll consider the last time God allowed me to feast at his table. I'll recall moments when I was touched with spiritual insight. I'll then retrace the experience. I'll ask the Holy Spirit to "gather the pieces," to pull together any missing nuances of my spiritual meal. It might mean revisiting a journal entry or listening to an old sermon tape. Perhaps I'll reread a portion of Scripture (and the notes I made in the margin) that was pivotal in my life. "There's more food than you thought," God is telling me.

Wherever God takes us today in review, may we discover that scriptural stories are multidimensional. Each time their truth is exposed to the Light, it sparkles and glistens, revealing greater clarity and depth. God gets mileage out of everything, even a story about a boy, his fish, and some bites of bread.

What a tragedy to waste spiritual food. I need all that you desire to give me, Father. You supply my nourishment extravagantly. Amen.

Misjudged Kingship

Jesus, knowing that they intended to come and make him king by force, withdrew again to a mountain by himself.

JOHN 6:15

*A*fter Jesus fed five thousand people, he was so extremely popular that the crowd wanted to hail him as king. But Jesus, knowing he had come to die and his kingdom was not yet of this world, had to withdraw to a private place to escape this public ceremony.

Only hindsight and the full disclosure of Scripture gives us the advantage of knowing the crowd was out of line. They were thousands of years premature in their understanding of God's timeline. Put yourself in their shoes, though. Can you imagine how they felt when they wanted to celebrate him but Jesus was nowhere to be found? How frustrating.

The crowd saw Jesus as their deliverer. He who had the power to calm seas and heal diseases would overthrow the current government, put evil in its place, and set himself up as the righteous king they sought. What a wonderful plan, except Jesus withdrew. Oh, the disillusionment!

We still ache to see Jesus display his kingship in our earthly kingdoms. When he doesn't exert his influence in ways we expect, we are frustrated. When he chooses to allow cancer to eat away the body of one we love, we cry out, "Don't you care?" When children are abused in their own homes and his holy anger does not stop it, we wonder at his claims of love.

What the crowd didn't know was what lay ahead. Jesus' love and power would never be more visible than when hanging on a Roman cross.

You are sovereign, I am not, Lord. When it appears you have deserted me, give me the faith to know that your greatest work of love is in the process of being accomplished. Amen.

January 19

A Welcome Voice

He said to them, "It is I; don't be afraid." Then they
were willing to take him into the boat.

JOHN 6:20–21

*J*esus' disciples are in a boat in the middle of the sea. The opposite shore is nowhere in sight. It is dark and the sea is churning
with a brewing storm. Uncertainty and nervousness overtake them. At
that moment, Jesus appears, walking toward them on top of the water.
They have just seen him feed five thousand people with one small
meal, yet this sight is beyond comprehension. His power continually
surprises them.

Jesus, knowing their fear, says, "It's me. Don't be afraid." As soon
as he gets into the boat, they are immediately at the opposite shore!
Like the fears of a child whose parent shows up to take care of everything, their worries subside. Consider how elements of the story live
on past the disciple's time.

All of us are navigating our lives. Often there's no light to guide
us. Wisdom for the right course to steer is completely elusive. The
shore is behind us. Everything familiar is out of sight. We are in
uncharted waters, feeling inadequate. The sea is beginning to churn.
Passages are difficult enough without storms complicating things. Fears
intensify. Rational thought decreases. The roar of the waves bombards
our senses. Normal functioning ceases.

Jesus is on the horizon and asks to be invited into the boat. His
words resound more powerfully than the sounds of the storm. "It's me.
Don't be afraid." We realize we don't have to make the voyage alone. The
one controlling the storm with a mere whisper can be our companion.

*Never has a voice been as sweet as yours, Lord, heard above the noise
of my life. You have not abandoned me. Take me safely home. Amen.*

January 20

The Danger of Miracles

"Rabbi, when did you get here?"

JOHN 6:25

*J*esus intends to go to Capernaum. Getting there means crossing a body of water. The only boat available for passage, however, left hours ago with his disciples in it. Jesus is not trapped. He simply walks on water to join his disciples in the middle of the sea. Meanwhile the crowd, fed the day before with five loaves and two fishes, goes to search for him. When they find him in Capernaum, they are puzzled and ask, "Rabbi, when did you get here?"

This would have been a perfect opportunity for Jesus to talk about his power. Instead he circumvents their question by making the observation that, tragically, people seek him because of his miracles. Jesus does not desire this outcome, because his miracles are only intended to showcase his love for people. Miracles are not meant to be an end unto themselves. Jesus seeks people because he loves them.

We can watch revivals on television that emphasize miraculous acts of healing by God. Whether or not these displays are legitimate is not my point here. Why do we not hear more about his love being celebrated? Too often people get on the Jesus bandwagon because his gifts wow the crowd, the same love-struck followers who proclaimed him king one week, abandoned him the next. Jesus has never trusted a popularity that stems from miracle seekers. I believe that the fervent devotion of one who embraces him, even in secret, is what catches his eye and warms his heart.

My love for you can be so selfish, Lord. Help my love grow out of immaturity. I want to love you for who you are rather than what you can do for me. Amen.

January 21

Consuming the Bread

"I am the living bread that came down from heaven.
If anyone eats of this bread, he will live forever."
JOHN 6:51

I consider some of the things I have consumed in my lifetime, things that arrested my heart and dominated my thinking. As a teenager I lived and breathed the music of the Carpenters. Studying every aspect of their music, I "ate" of them to the point where I could mimic everything they did. I sang along with Karen and had every bend of her voice down pat. Their music became a part of me—so much so that when I recorded my first few albums, I heard, "You are the Christian version of Karen Carpenter." That should have been no surprise to me, for they had been my daily food. To eat of anyone or anything, there has to be appetite.

"I'm just not very hungry," you might say. "If that's the key to being full of God, I'm sunk." Every person is born hungry, but hunger can be dulled by lack of eating. I have heard that extremely malnourished people lose their appetite completely. You have to coerce them to get them to eat again.

The same is true of spiritual food. We have to force-feed ourselves to reawaken our hunger. Before long we discover that we are ravenous. Our preoccupation with Jesus arrests us to the point where our thinking, feelings, and behaviors change. Just as food is consumed, digested, and applied to every living cell, so is the life of God applied. He becomes part of us on a cellular, spiritual level.

Jesus, grace me with the discipline to spend time with you every day. Awaken my hunger. May I consume you and be forever changed. Amen.

Rivers Instead of Trickles

"Whoever believes in me, as the Scripture has said,
streams of living water will flow from within him."

JOHN 7:38

*W*hat an amazing truth. The core of my soul can slowly be transformed into a source of life-giving water. The process begins when I allow God to empty his life into mine. He slowly infuses my heart with his love, his wisdom, his character, and I become more of a channel through which he can flow.

The key to the success of this phenomenon is making room for him. If I am filled to the brim with my unredeemed self, my distorted mind-set, my limited perspective, and my fears and irrationalities, my heart is like a full cup into which nothing else can be deposited. Only to the degree that I make room for his Spirit, to not only move in but have the elbow room needed to function, will I begin to notice his profound expression through my life.

Every day spent with God needs to result in spiritual housecleaning. As I spend time with him and find myself overcome with his beauty, my own inadequacies become apparent to me. At that point I can choose to avoid his company because it's too convicting, but how tragic that would be! When I'm willing to see what needs acknowledgement, confession, and then redemption, I make more room for God's Spirit. Being the house of God is the greatest joy I know in this life!

The results are tangible to those around me. Instead of offering occasional drips of living water to others, my words and actions give them an opportunity to bathe in the rivers of his Spirit.

Show me where I'm filled with myself and have failed to make room for you, Jesus.

I won't run from my need for you. Amen.

Losing Life to Find It

"I am the light of the world. Whoever follows me will
never walk in darkness, but will have the light of life."
JOHN 8:12

I look back over the course of four decades and see that though I
had Jesus inside, I stumbled in darkness! My countenance was
sad. I knew little insight. Joy was elusive. Passion was unknown. I put
one foot in front of the other, robotically. I spent a lifetime wondering
how I could house the Holy Spirit, know so much Scripture, but have
no life.

It's amazing to me that the answer lies in Jesus' statement, which
is really a conditional promise. He said that if we follow, we will have
light. What is involved in following? "If anyone would come after me,
he must deny himself and take up his cross and follow me" (Matthew
16:24). Taking up my cross means that I must give up rights to myself.
This sends me into panic. Why would I dare do something so
ludicrous? Because Jesus told me that I am self-deceived. Left to my
own self-made plans, I will crash and burn.

I choose to take Jesus at his word on all issues. I believe that his
principles are life-giving, even when I cannot understand them. I
follow them wholeheartedly, by faith! Such moment-by-moment
harnessing of my thoughts and desires brings the promise of this verse
to my experience. Freedom appears to be slavery, but only through
such focused obedience do I find the opposite to be true. To the
human mind it makes no sense, but the ways of the Spirit never do. I
can tell you firsthand that it works.

*It's a paradox, Lord. I give up my life to you, and you'll give real life
back to me. I cannot understand your ways, but I trust them. Amen.*

Exasperation

"Your testimony is not valid."

JOHN 8:13

When Jesus told the Pharisees he was the Light of the World, they were incensed. He told them God, his Father, endorsed his witness, but no explanations opened their eyes. Throughout their long, personal encounter, they continually asked, "Who exactly are you?" Jesus kept answering, "What have I been telling you?" It's hard to imagine he was not exasperated.

Jesus said his real identity was hidden for two reasons. First, they judged him in ignorance. Second, they judged him according to the flesh.

God's work in us is misunderstood, often for the same reasons. Others did not live in our skin when we received his life-changing call. They were not there when our inner world shook with significance as his words penetrated our thinking and feeling processes. They were not present when God wiped our slate clean, rewriting our identity. They did not feel the cataclysmic effect of our personal paradigm shift.

Our words have little effect with some people, usually among those who have known us the longest. They think they know us. We look the same, with familiar personal idiosyncrasies. But they cannot read our soul that has been rewritten. They cannot see our spirit, seated with Jesus in heavenly places, ingesting truth with earth-shattering ramifications.

Jesus, who created language, came up against barriers of man's free choice. He who defined charisma could not force truth. When we are prone to condemn ourselves for our lack of persuasion, may we remember that others judge in ignorance, according to the flesh. May God give us the courage to live out our faith with authenticity and endurance, even amid skepticism.

If you were misunderstood, Jesus, why don't I think I will be? Help me in my loneliness. Amen.

Making His Word My Home

"If you hold to my teaching, you are really my disciples."
JOHN 8:31

I love our present home in Georgia. My mind spun with possibilities the first time I saw it. I decided to showcase the hardwood floors. I contemplated color schemes and elected to weave hues of lavender throughout. It is now a warm and wonderful place to live.

Jesus says that we can make Scripture our home. For years, though, I missed the joy of moving in. I never unpacked. The walls stayed white, pictures were never hung, and I never painted my name on the mailbox. I walked around in a cavern, feeling like a visitor looking for the rest room. Searching for a particular passage was as awkward as trying to find the silverware drawer in an unfamiliar mansion.

Once it hit me that the Lover of my soul was the Author of Scripture, I began to see it differently. I marked up the pages. The margins now chronicle my journey: dates I last read the passage, how it impacted me, and answers to prayers. My Bible has become my heart's home. The platform is no longer intimidating, since my Bible graces the lectern. Speaking becomes a vehicle from which to talk of my Father, the one who lives and breathes in the pages of the book in front of me.

I still feel as if I'm moving in. There's so much more to decorate. So much more wall space to adorn. So much more renovation to be done in me, but this will be my life's project.

Forgive me, Lord, for all the years I treated your Word as a textbook rather than a living, breathing revelation of you. Now I treasure it. Change me with the power of your words. Amen.

Bondage-Blind

"We are Abraham's descendants and have never been
slaves of anyone. How can you say that we shall be
set free?"

JOHN 8:33

*J*esus has just spoken of how knowing the truth will make people
free. Who was his audience? The religious people! Often the lost
know they're in bondage. It is God's children, the ones who are
supposedly enlightened, that fail to understand this reality. Jesus'
comment left these religious leaders flustered. See their response? Can
you hear the arrogance in their question?

Freedom in Christ is a seeming paradox to human reasoning.
Never are we so free as when we are walking within God's parameters,
but the world calls that enslavement. The agenda of heaven is making
men and women free in Christ. When we're not, Jesus longs to speak
to us and show us where we're still enslaved. The key is whether or not
we're listening.

Am I free from my spiritual enemies, or do I feel oppressed? Am
I freely enjoying the privileges of being God's daughter, or is my heart
plagued with insignificance? Am I free from lust, or is my mind
completely tangled in sexual preoccupation? Am I free from failure, or
am I wallowing in yesterday's choices? Am I dull to spiritual hunger,
or is my life marked with vitality and passion?

The rewards of answering such questions are tangible. Once we
embrace the truth, we have taken the first step toward freedom. The
heart that lives in confession, trust, and obedience is unencumbered
and fully free to soar.

*Jesus, I can always count on you to tell me the truth. Help me hear
your voice, for you want to show me where chains of darkness still
bind me. I will cooperate with you to do whatever it takes to turn
from evil and walk in your ways. Amen.*

Sudden Understanding

"Rabbi, who sinned, this man or his parents, that he was born blind?"

JOHN 9:2

Two people can witness the same scene yet perceive it differently. Jesus encounters a blind man, and though Jesus is running for his life, he is moved with compassion and stops to heal him.

The Jews see the same man but are analytical about his condition. They use his story as a platform for empty posturing and vain discussion. He becomes their object lesson. He is useful only to the extent that he serves their agenda of appearing clever. While the man gropes in darkness to feel his deliverer's robe, curious onlookers are theologizing about the possible reasons for his blindness.

Have you stood in the blind man's shoes? Perhaps there were a few who had compassion on you, but you also knew that others made you the subject of discussion. They spoke eloquently of your plight, but their hearts never pulsated with mercy.

How many times did the psalmist David cry out, "Have mercy on me, O God!" Too numerous to mention here. David knew where to find mercy. He didn't seek it in empty places, among those who should have given it but turned up empty hands! He knew that if he stood at the gate of heaven, God would be moved with compassion. Never was he disappointed. "I trust in your unfailing love; my heart rejoices in your salvation" (Psalm 13:5).

I doubt that any of us who have stood at the gate, in the place of the blind man, will ever forget the pain of others' detachment or the exhilaration of being noticed, and touched, by the Author of mercy.

Show me, Lord, if I ever use others' tragedies as a springboard for intellectual bantering. Forgive me. Mold my heart to yours. Amen.

January 28

Religious Voyeurism

"Neither this man nor his parents sinned," said Jesus,
"but this happened so that the work of God might be
displayed in his life."

JOHN 9:3

*W*ebster's dictionary defines a voyeur as a person who is obsessed with sordid or sensational subjects. We would call this person "nosey," someone without regard for the welfare of the person they victimize.

Religious voyeurism is alive and well. The religious crowd is accompanying Jesus on a walk. They meet a man blind from birth. The religious men's motives become clear when they pose their opening question: "Who sinned, this man or his parents?" Actually, it's none of their business. Jesus' answer surprises them, and he gives the blind man the gift of a lifetime. Validation. Absolution from those who misjudge him because of his misfortune. Jesus makes it clear that the man's blindness happened so that he, Jesus, might prove himself to be the Light of the World.

Can you imagine the blind man's enlightenment? "Ah, now it all makes sense! I've been blind all my life so this one moment in time could take place."

It's a wonderful thing when suffering makes sense. I remember such a moment for me. It occurred on a morning when I told God that I doubted there could ever be a future for me. God's answer to me was, "Your life has been such so you could experience my healing and redemption. Everything until now has been the wilderness, preparing you for your true ministry." Like the blind man, at that moment I understood my life story. Through it God would showcase his healing power.

I understand now. My life has not been a waste. You have arrived, Jesus, to show your power and glory. Amen.

January 29

Blindness and Enlightenment

Jesus said, "For judgment I have come into this world, so that the blind will see and those who see will become blind."

JOHN 9:39

*J*esus is saying that he came to give sight to those who are spiritually blind. And to those who are conceited in their own wisdom—wisdom that contradicts divine wisdom—he seals them in ignorance.

The Pharisees were looking for a Messiah. They just could not bear to think that Jesus was he. His teaching was so contrary to their traditional laws. The spiritual worship he prescribed overthrew their manmade formality. Though they saw miracles firsthand, they would not believe that Jesus was anything other than an imposter. In their commitment to disbelieve, they worked to find holes in his credibility. They said, "This man is not from God, because he does not keep the Sabbath."

The work of God is hampered today in similar ways. We have our traditions, our preconceived beliefs that God only works in ways with which we're comfortable. Our minds put him in a box, leaving little room for him to be God. Often we are not free to worship. Our arms are stuck to our sides, as if with Velcro! Our praise can be stingy, whispered only by rote. A shout of joy is often inconceivable to those of us who have been raised in a religiously stoic environment.

I want divine sight. I know there are areas where I am still spiritually blind. May Jesus expose my blindness so I can see. May I be freed from anything traditional or generational that seems right but is not of him. If I cling tenaciously to error, the Holy Spirit may stop speaking and allow blindness to mark that area of my life. I will have forfeited truth and joy.

I openly praise you, God, for the ways you are shaking up the religious corners of my soul. Do not give up on me. Amen.

January 30

Leadership Styles

"When he has brought out all his own, he goes on ahead of them, and his sheep follow him because they know his voice."

JOHN 10:4

*H*ave you ever worked under an umbrella of authority that was characterized by insensitive leadership? Orders were given without care for proper development. There was little instruction. There were high expectations, but you were abandoned while you labored at the task.

When I was twenty-one, I was asked to orchestrate an entire musical road production. I expressed my concern that I wasn't trained or experienced. I buckled under the pressure to do it anyway. A deadline was given, but no offers were made to network me with professionals who might help me through the process. The leadership style of the person who delegated the task to me was, at that moment, poor.

What kind of leader is Jesus? He describes himself as the shepherd who goes before his sheep. This was not the way shepherds usually worked. They were known to drive out the sheep from the pen. They sent them out in front. Not Jesus. He goes before. He's already checked the path for stones and tree roots. He marks the way and is known to say, "Don't step here or you'll get hurt" or "Watch me; I'll show you how to do it." There's security and safety for all who follow him.

Are you a parent, a teacher, or a pastor? There's nothing that feels worse to those under our care than for us to give an order and expect a performance for which there is no training. We need to be considerate, giving others a taste of what it's like to serve a God whose intentions toward his children are always laced with loving-kindness.

You've shown me how to follow you, Lord. Make me a leader like you. Amen.

January 31

False Shepherds

"All who ever came before me were thieves and robbers, but the sheep did not listen to them."

JOHN 10:8

To whom was Jesus speaking when he gave this speech? He was speaking to the Pharisees, the ones accusing him of heresy because he claimed to be God! The Pharisees saw themselves as true spiritual leaders, elevated to judges of spiritual truth. It's unsettling to realize that thieves and robbers are in the church. According to Jesus, they are self-deceived leaders.

It is reassuring to notice that Jesus says the sheep are never really comfortable following them. In their hearts they know the truth. It may take some time, but eventually God's sheep will know they're being robbed. Self-proclaimed shepherds always steal from the sheep, leaving any who try to follow them and Jesus at the same time in great conflict.

- *False shepherds steal our peace.* They set up impossible spiritual standards for us to meet, causing us to live in torment, never feeling we measure up.

- *False shepherds steal our childlike trust.* How can we trust a God who, we're told, is never pleased with us? We become like anxious children knowing that when they round the corner into their parents' room, they'll experience more disapproval.

- *False shepherds steal our affection.* How can we love a God with a cross face? Because God is sorely misrepresented as the unreasonable Father, we miss the joy of knowing we can be as dearly loved children, throwing our arms out in abandon, proclaiming our affections.

If we can't run home today with joy, or even limp home with high levels of confidence, chances are we've been robbed blind. Discover what's missing. Start looking in places where peace, trust, and affection should abide.

Am I following a shepherd of yours, Lord? Show me. Amen.

February

February 1

A Courageous Question

> "Lord, . . . if you had been here, my brother would not
> have died."
>
> JOHN 11:21

Mary and Martha's brother, Lazarus, is dead. They sent for Jesus but he hasn't come. Now it's too late.

Martha, hearing that Jesus is finally arriving, leaves to meet him. Mary does not. Scripture says she stayed at home! Hear her thoughts? *He's coming now? Where was he when I needed him?* She nurses her questions privately.

Finally seeing Jesus, her heart dares voice the question haunting her. "Where were you?" Then we read the shortest and one of the most powerful verses in all of Scripture: "Jesus wept."

I know how Mary felt, crying out for help and having no one come. I know what it's like, sitting for days plagued with nagging doubts. I've nursed questions, fearful to admit I even had them.

Nonetheless they festered in secret. "Where were you, God, when this happened? If you had intervened, I would have been spared!"

We often fail to remember Jesus' response, straining to hear his voice instead of looking at his face. There may be no words of explanation, but listening, we hear the sound of weeping.

Where was God when we suffered? Where was God when Jesus was crucified? Weeping over the choices people were making with his gift of free will. His Son suffered just as we do.

However, Jesus' tears are not laced with hopelessness. After sharing Mary's grief, he brought Lazarus back to life. He will regenerate places of death in our lives, too, but in the meantime, in our questions, he weeps.

God, giving people free choice was a courageous thing. With it they crucified your Son, and all your children have been hurt. Before I look for miracles, help me see your tears. Amen.

February 2

Wrapped in Graveclothes

Jesus said to her, "I am the resurrection and the life.
He who believes in me will live, even though he dies."
JOHN 11:25

*P*eter and John ran to the empty tomb, looked in, and found the limp graveclothes. Then they went home. They did not believe a miracle. There were no songs of victory. There was no rush to find the other disciples and declare the good news. They witnessed the power of Jesus firsthand yet hovered between faith and unbelief.

I understand that, don't you? In my past opinion, miracles were always for someone else. When it came down to Jesus changing the very core of me, I doubted. Sure, Jesus can raise people from the dead, but can he heal my broken heart? Yes, he can turn a turbulent sea into a sea of glass, but can he change the nature of an angry son or daughter? I was skeptical.

Resurrection power is ours today. In many respects yet to be revealed by the Holy Spirit, I am still dressed in graveclothes. The stone has been rolled away, but this is not reality yet to all parts of me.

Just as Jesus called Lazarus out of the grave, he calls us from death to life. Death for us may be lies we believe. It may be addictions we are powerless to change. It may be labels of worthlessness with which others have defined us. It may be an inward rage that rots our bones. Our hope today lies in hearing Jesus' declaration, "The tomb is empty. Come forth to new life!"

Why would I ever turn down your power, Lord? I want it. I want to experience the fullness of all you have for me. Show me where I need your powerful touch of resurrection life. Amen.

February 3

A Breathtaking Good-bye

Mary took about a pint of pure nard, an expensive perfume; she poured it on Jesus' feet and wiped his feet with her hair.

JOHN 12:3

*A*fter Jesus raises Lazarus from the dead, the controversy heats up. Those who had been enraged against his claims of divinity band together, forming an evil core of power. Intent on killing him, they have the power to do it. They are evil men, making those under them the instruments of their unrighteousness.

Knowing the time of his coming death is premature, Jesus retires to the home of Lazarus, Mary, and Martha for dinner. Lazarus sits at the head of the table. Martha serves and Mary, having a rich history with Jesus, is also there. She has had moments of disbelief and disappointment, but each time she and Jesus worked it out. Their friendship is deep and solid. I wonder at Mary's thoughts. I imagine she is in conflict, tormented, knowing Jesus is hunted as a criminal.

Mary says good-bye to Jesus, expressing love in an act so beautiful, we scarcely comprehend it. Taking a full pound of the costliest perfume, she pours it over his feet! Oil was normally used to anoint the head. Outrageously, she anoints his feet, using her hair to wipe them dry! Her act of worship is performed with abandon. The eyes of her family do not sway her. She does not appear awkward, though Jesus' disciples watch and Judas voices his disgust.

She follows her heart and dares to love in a way others might disapprove of. This is good-bye, and she'll have no regrets.

Make me a Mary, Lord. She is my hero, for I want to love you with abandon, too. Make me less inclined to follow others' rules. Amen.

February 4

Tradition or Adventure?

"We would like to see Jesus."

JOHN 12:21

*J*esus made his way to Jerusalem at the time of the Jewish Passover Feast. We're told that certain Greek Gentiles came to take part in the Feast. Upon arriving, they encountered Philip and requested, "Sir, we would like to see Jesus." The Gentiles came to the Feast to worship the God of Israel and knew that unless they saw Jesus, the ritual would be meaningless.

Traditions without the breath of the Holy Spirit are empty. So I ask myself some tough questions today. I sang hymns on Sunday. Did the words and music resound with the presence of the Holy One? I took Communion. Did my spirit tremble in wonder of the remembrance? I taught a small group at church Wednesday night. Was our time touched profoundly by his presence, or was it religiously dry and predictable? I said a prayer before my meal today. Do I recall its reverence? I will attend a church business meeting next week. Will the business of the church reflect God's agendas and be directed by his Spirit, who is present?

Traditions can become robotic. I know because I was a robot for many years. My faith lacked passion and I was spiritually bored. It wasn't until I hungered for Jesus that dead things began to fall away. What I had previously performed through religious programming gradually became alive and acquired meaning. At what moment did it change? When I opened the Scriptures one particular day and, like the Greeks, asked, "I would like to see Jesus." Nothing has been the same.

Nothing has been the same since I prayed that prayer, Lord. I'm so glad I did. Never allow me to pay you lip service with a cold heart. Make sure I keep my heart close to you. Amen.

February 5

Time for Honor

"My Father will honor the one who serves me."
JOHN 12:26

*H*ave you ever been honored? Perhaps you recall the circumstances. It was your birthday party. Many of your friends came. Some wrote notes of appreciation that now grace a scrapbook. Others recalled difficult parts of your journey and recounted how they admired you from afar for your tenacity and endurance. A special teacher, grandparent, or mentor showed up unexpectedly. Their presence made that shining moment even more significant.

Can you even imagine God honoring you? His hand is on your head. His eyes are full of love. His presence is bathing you in light and glory. Will anything here have been too hard? Will we be preoccupied then with all the things that weigh us down today? I doubt it. The wonderful thing is, we can begin to experience that moment even now. There are times when I sense God's nod of approval, his hand on my shoulder in appreciation, and the warmth of his delight. I stop and take it in, grateful for the infusion of strength it gives me.

When we intentionally make the things of this world of lesser importance than the real kingdom to which we belong, Jesus tells us our reward ahead of time. He takes joy in seeing his Father honor us, just as he was honored. Through his death he made us his brothers and sisters. That means as coheirs we will inherit his kingdom. Oh, may the vision of his Father bowing over you in reverence give you courage, friend.

Dear God, serving your Son is my privilege. Walking in his footsteps is my joy. Honoring me is proof that your heart overflows with gifts of undeserved favor. Amen.

February 6

Embracing All of God

Jesus cried out, "When a man believes in me, he does
not believe in me only, but in the one who sent me."
JOHN 12:44

*J*ust days before Jesus' death, he withdraws from public ministry.
His last days are spent in the company of his disciples. Once alone
with them, he cries and expresses his heart. He grieves that many
people seem to want to embrace him as man but cannot grasp that
they must embrace him as God. He and his Father are one.

If Jesus were a sinful man, he would love the chance to be adored,
but he came to point the way to his Father. He protests that he is the
object of their worship, while Abba is overlooked.

We must be careful that we embrace and worship all of God.
Much of Christendom is one-sided. Churches can be guilty of
centering their worship on the Dove, when the Holy Spirit's role is to
reveal the Father's heart and mind. People do what the crowd did in
Jesus' time; they center their attention on Jesus. They appreciate him
as friend and wounded healer but conveniently ignore the righteous
God who sent him.

I had to ask myself this morning if this issue was important to me.
I had to admit it seemed like a small technicality. Not to Jesus. It was
enough to cause him to shed tears among his friends.

*God, you are most holy and righteous. I worship you as Father. Jesus,
you are divine. I adore you as the crucified Son of God. Holy Spirit,
the Dove sent from heaven, I bow to you as the one who comforts
and enlightens me. I embrace you, Trinity, in all your holiness.
Amen.*

February 7

Sad to Leave

Jesus knew that the time had come for him to leave this world and go to the Father. Having loved his own who were in the world, he now showed them the full extent of his love.

JOHN 13:1

*J*esus loved his own and loved them till the end. He was partial to friends and family. Though Jesus bonded with a few outside this group of fishermen, the disciples were his heart mates. While some betrayed him, he never gave up on them or withdrew from their close-knit circle.

I find the quality of his love amazing and humbling. Can I even imagine being God and choosing to spend a small chunk of time on earth? Can I perceive what it might be like to leave perfection and live among the fallen? It would be admirable enough if the text revealed, "Jesus had grown quite fond of them—but was now anxious to go home to his Father." We would understand that and not hold it against him. After all, they had been anything but easy to live with. They had tried his patience on more than one occasion. I marvel that he wasn't counting the days till heaven's alarm clock signaled his release from their presence.

But we find Jesus sad to leave, clinging to fallen humanity. His love is, once again, beyond our ability to grasp. He loved till the end. What he began well, he ended well. His final act of love was yet to come and would be the most difficult, stretching out his arms on a wooden cross to embrace those who had loved him imperfectly.

Lord, I will never love others as perfectly as you love. Never let me forget that understanding and receiving your love is my most profound spiritual lesson. Amen.

February 8

Humility in the Extreme

Jesus knew that the Father had put all things under
his power.... he ... took off his outer clothing, and
wrapped a towel around his waist.

JOHN 13:3–4

These are dark days. There is something sad in the air. Jesus talks of
dying. The disciples' dream of his kingdom coming to pass in
their lifetime is shattered. Their group is fractured by the revelation
that Judas is a traitor. There are eleven left. They are stunned and sad.

Jesus, the ultimate communicator, doesn't need words. Sometimes
words just fail. He connects with their hearts through an act that will
astound them for years to come. He washes their feet.

In Jesus' time only the lowest servant in a household was given the
chore of washing a guest's foot. Was Jesus ignorant of his divinity? No.
"The Father had put all things under his power." He is from eternity
past and will inherit eternity future.

With keen awareness of his deity, he chooses to love in the most
humble way. Can you close your eyes and feel the wonder? The men
are incredulous, awkward, awed, and touched. The sound of water
lapping over the tops of their feet is the only sound in the room. Jesus
takes his time. In the minutes it takes to love these men, perhaps time
stands still.

This is the way Jesus says good-bye. He chooses this act to say,
"I love you." Little do they know that a greater act will follow on a hill
called Calvary. But for now they partake in something earthly
made holy.

*Jesus, I need a lifetime to comprehend how low you stooped in
loving me. Give me courage to receive your love as you gently wash
my feet. Cleanse me from the soil of my earthly journey. Prepare my
feet for eternity. Amen.*

February 9

Whom Can You Trust?

The devil had already prompted Judas Iscariot . . .
to betray Jesus.

JOHN 13:2

One disciple out of twelve is about to defect. Not bad odds, really, but it won't ease the pain of betrayal. Though heartbroken, Jesus will not lose perspective. He won't write off the other eleven just because one turned bad. He will not resort to rhetoric and say, "Who can you trust these days!" In contrast our human, sinful nature can cause us to throw up our hands, overgeneralize, and say, "The church is full of hypocrites." We allow one or two to color the whole lot.

Instead of withdrawing, Jesus takes care of the remaining disciples. He knows that the betrayal will wound eleven individuals, and he anticipates their disillusionment. He demonstrates his love for them by washing their feet. His tenderness will help soften their impending wounds. Matthew Henry wrote, "Antidotes must be stirring when the infection has begun." What is Jesus' antidote in this setting? Love.

Has a Christian leader let you down? Has your pastor lost his credibility? Has your best friend done the unthinkable? Often our first instinct is to withdraw and never trust again. Before we pull the covers over our head and back away from Christendom, may our response be to draw close to Abba for the healing of our wounds. Then let's take the Source of comfort to others who were also affected. Just as the remaining disciples needed Jesus' touch, so do today's believers who teeter on the brink of cynicism or disillusionment.

Lord, I want to be fully alive. I don't want to retreat emotionally at the first sign of evil. Help me. Heal me. Make me an agent of comfort and restoration to those feeble in faith and wounded in spirit. Amen.

February 10

Conditions for Intimacy

"No," said Peter, "you shall never wash my feet."

Jesus answered, "Unless I wash you, you have no part with me."

JOHN 13:8

*H*ave you ever been offered a gift that seemed too extravagant to receive? Perhaps it was intimacy and it seemed too threatening, or it cost too much and you didn't feel worthy.

I've known such gifts. I remember wanting to hide rather than receive them.

I understand Peter's response. Jesus wanted to not only touch his feet but also wash them. How preposterous. Peter probably thought he was being noble by refusing. Perhaps he anticipated hearing, "Peter, how wise of you. I should never stoop to wash another's feet. Mine are the ones that should be washed, as an act of worship."

Isn't it shocking to read Jesus' response? "If I do not wash you, you have no part with me." No intimacy without receiving. Our shame makes it hard for us to receive. Often we'd rather give to "work off" our shame. If we do something honorable enough, we can raise our concept of ourselves. God's message to us today is, "You can't elevate yourself. It's not about doing; it's about receiving. Though you don't deserve it, I love you and proclaim you to be worthy. Though you want to shrink back in shame, will you dare receive my gift of love? If you won't, you can have no part with me."

We raise our heads, look into his eyes, and submit to his plan, and our shame is replaced with a joy we never knew existed.

Jesus, though I want to run from you, I won't. I will let you love me, though I squirm. I'm undeserving but that's the point. I need and I receive your love and mercy. Amen.

February 11

Blind Obedience

When he had finished washing their feet, he put on his clothes and returned to his place. "Do you understand what I have done for you?" he asked them.

JOHN 13:12

*H*as God ever asked you to do something preposterous? There was no explanation with the command. It seemed convoluted and you obeyed in faith. Later God revealed why the act was so important.

Many giants of the faith have walked before us in this. Abraham was told to take his family and move to a far-off place. Joshua was told to march around Jericho seven times. Naaman was told to dip into the dirty Jordan River seven times. No coddling, no explanation.

Our Father desires implicit obedience yet few of us comply. We desire equality in our relationship with him. We want to be "in the know" and have full disclosure about his every expectation. Otherwise we'll ignore what seems unreasonable. We rail in our immaturity, "That makes no sense to me. Why should I do that?" Our Father, whose plans for us are good, says, "Obey, child. Later you will understand."

How awkward it must have been for the disciples to engage in the foot-washing ceremony. Perhaps they felt vulnerable, thinking it was they who should have washed their Master's feet. Nonetheless, the love with which Jesus performed this act must have moved them. Did they let down their guard and enjoy it? It must have taken a while for Jesus to wash the feet of these men. Yet they sat on their questions. I applaud them. I don't know if I could have done as well. I might have dared whisper, "Jesus, why are you doing this?" Oh, that I might grow up and be childlike in my trust.

Father, I'm on a journey home. You know the way; I don't. When you tell me which path to take, I'll go. No explanations needed. Amen.

February 12

Entertaining Angels and Traitors

"'He who shares my bread has lifted up his heel
against me.'. . . Whoever accepts anyone I send
accepts me."

JOHN 13:18, 20

We are often confused about traitors in the church. Can wise disciples avoid being tricked? Jesus is foretelling the betrayal of Judas in the presence of his family. These twelve men have accompanied him for three years, sharing his bread, viewing his miracles, and knowing the thrill of being chosen to be his friends. Each has been welcomed into social situations as Jesus' disciple. That was their identity. What is Jesus' message now to the Eleven as they learn the true heart of their brother Judas? "You received him as your own because he was chosen by me."

We are not privy to the disciple's thoughts, but we suspect that they did what we do when we're deceived. We second-guess ourselves, agonizing over possible blind spots. We feel foolish for having trusted, but Jesus would have his disciples understand that they received Judas as their friend because Jesus chose Judas as his!

We must receive those who come in the name of Christ, until information surfaces that proves they are traitors. To do otherwise is to potentially turn away true disciples and forfeit sweet communion. In this world doctors, plumbers, friends, children, and even clergy will burn us. Jesus' spirit was troubled as he made the announcement about Judas. So is ours when we learn the true nature of the one we trusted.

As Jesus delivered this sad news, John was reclining against his breast. That is the best place to deal with tragedy.

Jesus, you were the perfect friend yet Judas betrayed you. I received some people who came to me in your name, and they betrayed me. Heal my heart so I may trust again. Amen.

Pain and Glory

"Now is the Son of Man glorified."

JOHN 13:31

*J*esus speaks these words about himself on the last night he is to spend with his disciples. In his sovereignty he knows that everything has been put in motion for his arrest, trial, and death. He shares these words that must astound his friends. Hasn't he been glorified all along? At his birth angels sang. Because of his miracles the sick were healed. Because of his love for his friend, Lazarus came out of the grave. What does Jesus mean?

Have you ever been to a perfect vacation spot and proclaimed, "Now, this is living!" Does that mean you never lived before? Or upon seeing the perfect fall sunset, "Now, this is beauty!" Was nothing beautiful before? We make such statements to emphasize a point. In essence Jesus is telling us, "You think I was glorified before? Wait until you see what happens next!"

Jesus will be more glorified in his death than he was through any other event. This is true of our sufferings. Winning the Nobel Peace Prize may be small in comparison with allowing God to shine in our darkest hour. When tragedy happens, we tend to think that life is over. But since we were born to glorify God, our real purpose has just begun.

The greatest spiritual tools I possess are those that have resulted from the things I thought would destroy me. In them and because of them, God radiates and others are drawn to his heart. It gives new meaning to Jesus' words, "When I am lifted up, I will draw all men to myself."

Jesus, I want to run from pain and often think it's wasted. But our greatest hour of collaboration waits. Fractured, I turn to you. Glorified, you shine through me. Amen.

February 14

Babes, Toddlers, and Adults

Simon Peter asked him, "Lord, where are you going?"

Jesus replied, "Where I am going, you cannot follow now, but you will follow later."

JOHN 13:36

*J*esus is on his way to the cross and announces to his disciples that this is good-bye.

Peter protests. He proclaims his love for Jesus, even unto death. His love is sincere but his faith is weak. Jesus knows this, and when arrested, he intervenes for the safety of his disciples. "Let them go their way," he says to the soldiers detaining him. The faith of his closest friends is not strong enough to endure death. Not yet. Peter will be crucified, years later. By then, though, he will be ready.

Jesus is considerate of our maturation level. What he requires of us today is congruent with our level of spiritual growth. Forty years separated the parting of the Red Sea and the conquest of Canaan. Four decades in the wilderness were needed to bring the children of Israel to maturity. At the Red Sea they had no faith, so God performed miracles for his infant people. Time was needed to grow them up. They became toddlers, then adolescents, and finally grew into spiritual adults. By the time they faced the giants in the land of Canaan, they were seasoned warriors.

God never sends all his children to the front lines. Young lambs are not sent to slaughter. Only the experienced are called. Are you a spiritual baby? God will handle you tenderly and protect you fiercely. According to your faith, so shall your calling be. We have a kind Father.

Oh, Father, thank you for not expecting something impossible of me today. You are the perfect leader. I follow you and therefore I walk in safety. Amen.

February 15

Bravado

Peter asked, "Lord, why can't I follow you now? I will lay down my life for you."

JOHN 13:37

*P*eter's profession of love and fidelity is beautiful to read, but unrealistic because he fails to understand his own limits and depravity. He is young and his faith has just been birthed. Not capable of laying down his life for Jesus quite yet, Peter will soon deny his knowledge of Jesus three times.

Barroom brawls are built on bravado. Alcohol fuels the ego, causing people to boast beyond their capabilities. The alcohol of pride does the same. I am reminded of the times I thought myself above certain behaviors, only to discover I wasn't. I fell flat on my face, admitting that I was the worst of sinners. I became aware that under the right circumstances I'm capable of doing most anything vile.

When we see ourselves through God's eyes, we succeed in understanding our own hearts.

We are the beloved, but also the depraved without application of God's grace. Many of us never come to this realization. Instead we take our place on a self-made pedestal. Looking down on the poor souls who enter our sanctuaries and admit their vices, we see ourselves as counselors and messiahs. In our minds we are above them. Our self-proclaimed spiritual status leads to disaster. Pastors wipe out, marriages of thirty years fracture, and at the very least ministries are stagnant because those they serve live in perpetual condemnation.

Humility is becoming. It is cultivated in an atmosphere of truth and tears. The genuinely changed life is one in which the nature of God has been applied to the depravity of the human heart.

I want my life to be all about your mercy, Lord, not righteousness I have to pretend to possess. Amen.

February 16

Jesus Addresses Hopelessness

"Do not let your hearts be troubled."

JOHN 14:1

*L*et's put this verse in context. Jesus has tenderly washed the disciples' feet. They are vulnerable. His words of comfort come on the heels of bad news. He has announced that he is going away in a cloud of suffering. They are stunned and sad. Judas has been exposed. They are disillusioned. Jesus has just revealed to Peter that he will betray him. Everyone is unsettled. Yet Jesus does not deliver bad news without caring for their hearts. He knows the secret wounds of each one. He is a tender shepherd who does not shy away from his followers, no matter what they feel.

What does your face look like today? It may be sad. Family members and friends may choose to ignore this; they're too busy, uncaring, or uncomfortable in the skills of comfort. Jesus is not. He never fails to notice and extends hope if we turn to him. Nothing escapes his intuitive understanding of us. Nothing is hidden. That can be both threatening and comforting to us, can't it?

Jesus touches his disciples' grief with hope. "In my Father's house are many mansions. I go to prepare a place for you." Lest they think Jesus will die and leave them to suffer hopelessly, he assures them that he goes before them to prepare their new home.

Today whether we are in touch with it or not, we ache for his kingdom. We strain to see fairness, mercy, tenderness, rewards for our labor, and our tears wiped away. We are like the disciples, who receive one piece of bad news after another yet are not without hope. Jesus' words are intended for our ears. Hear him whisper, "Don't let your heart be troubled."

I hear you, Jesus. I lift my eyes to my new home. Quiet my heart. Amen.

February 17

The Power of Asking

Thomas said to him, "Lord, we don't know where you
are going, so how can we know the way?"

JOHN 14:5

*J*esus is telling his disciples that he is going to a place where there
are many mansions. They do not know such a world. Home for
them has been one temporary dwelling after another. Mansions mean
permanent, elaborate homes and connote a lifestyle none of them has
ever known. It is natural to inquire where this place is, but Thomas is
the only one who asks. He owns his confusion.

I don't ask enough questions. When I'm lost, I like to try to
figure out my own way with a map. Sometimes this doesn't work,
because the map is wrong or outdated. I used to be so insecure that I
could not admit what I didn't know. If I were in a meeting, I would
nod my head in agreement because that's what everyone else was doing.
It's only in recent years that I can say, "Please explain that. I don't
understand what you just said."

Jesus said, "You have not because you ask not." Jesus cares about
what we need but does not give it until we ask for it. Why? Because
there is power in asking. Admitting our need acknowledges him
as provider.

I have an upcoming meeting and as of yet do not have a clear
agenda. I've already told God, "I called this meeting and I do not know
why I am going. Show me the way." Jesus hears our sincere questions, and
that's comforting today to us who know we're lost without his wisdom.

*I often think I know how to run my life, Lord. I don't. I need you
to show me the way. With each step infuse my thoughts with your
light. Amen.*

How Well Do I Know Jesus?

"Don't you know me, Philip, even after I have been among you such a long time?"

JOHN 14:9

*W*hen Philip met Jesus, he acknowledged him as the Messiah. But he also asked Jesus in ignorance, "Show us the Father!" How preposterous! The Father had been with Philip continually in the person of Jesus, yet he did not recognize him.

We can know people for decades and still be surprised by them. I've been married twenty-eight years and feel I know Ron well. However, there have been times when he has reacted to a new experience in ways that surprised me. In times of distress I saw a strength I hadn't seen before. I said to myself, *Wow, I never would have guessed he'd do that!*

I've had a relationship with Jesus for a lifetime. Still, I feel I'm just beginning to know him. At age seven I made him my Savior. Yet he continues to save me from the lies and distortions that have controlled me. I have sung songs about Jesus as my deliverer. Yet every day I am openmouthed at his deliverance. Today I know him as friend, but tomorrow I will be shocked by his tender expressions of friendship.

I feel like the disciples, who preached of Jesus' power yet shook with fear when he walked on the water, thinking him to be a ghost. Perhaps through the revelation of the Holy Spirit we can speed up this process of intimacy. I want to make knowing Jesus my passion, not a hobby. I don't want to miss anything of him.

Lord, do whatever it takes for me to know you better. I want the intimacy of our relationship to define who I am, what I believe, and how I'll choose to live today. Amen.

February 19

Dad's Still Here

"I will ask the Father, and he will give you another
Counselor. . . . I will not leave you as orphans."

JOHN 14:16, 18

*J*esus' relationship with the disciples was multifaceted. He was
their shepherd, their friend, and soon would be their Savior. Just
before he leaves them to go to the cross, his words take on a paternal
ring as he promises not to leave them as orphans. His care of them has
been physical, emotional, and spiritual. Jesus knows their growing
sense of abandonment, knows how deeply they've come to depend on
him. Thoughts of saying good-bye send them into panic.

Notice that he doesn't say, "I will not leave you friendless." He
remembers that they have left father, mother, and family to follow him.
He naturally fills familial voids.

If any of you have lost both parents, you know that moment when
you suddenly realize you're an orphan. You're no one's daughter
anymore. There is no one here to look after you.

I'm near that place as my father battles cancer. My mother died in
1984, and as painful as that was, I was comforted that one parent was
still left. "I'm okay," I said. "Dad's still here!"

Jesus, anticipating his disciples' grief even before they feel it, makes
provision before the need. His Spirit will reside in them and their
descendants till the end of time.

Whatever you need today, Jesus already knows it and has talked to
his Father about it. Nothing takes him by surprise. Within the
functions of the Trinity we have everything needed to live in peace,
comfort, and total security.

*I'm still okay, Jesus, because you're still here. Thank you for your Holy
Spirit. Allow me to feel the comfort and security of your presence.
Amen.*

Love the Son and You Will Be Loved

"He who loves me will be loved by my Father."

JOHN 14:21

*I*f you are married, you remember the day you met your in-laws. You probably felt as if you were on trial. Your future parents were going to see how well you loved their son. Whether or not you were "family material" depended on it. As a parent, that is the critical thing. If others love our children, we're drawn to them.

God's measuring stick is no different. He sent his Son to earth to love people and to ultimately die for them. Yet he knew that few would love him in return. Worse than that, his Son would be blatantly rejected and falsely accused. Imagine how joyful the Father's heart must have been when one person on earth saw the beauty of his Son!

When Mary carried Jesus in her womb, nurturing the hope inside her, God loved her tenderly. When Joseph took Mary as his wife despite the scandal and adopted her newborn Son, God regarded him with favor. When the wise men traveled great distances to find a baby in an obscure place and then fell to their knees to adore him, God looked at them with gratitude.

When I adore a Savior whom I've never seen with my eyes, God looks on me tenderly. When I place all my hope in his promises, share in his sufferings, and ache for his coming kingdom and reign, God delights in me. Each obedient act earns the favor of Jesus' Father. Each cry of faith in spite of the darkness of our times brings God pleasure. Any friend of Jesus is never without hope. The light of his Father's love warms his back for a lifetime.

God, I love your Son. I'll live out my remaining days for his honor and glory. Amen.

A New Teacher

"The Counselor, the Holy Spirit, whom the Father
will send in my name, will teach you all things."
JOHN 14:26

*B*efore Jesus goes to the cross, he takes care of his own. The eleven disciples are not just his closest friends but also future leaders. Each will have a ministry, some of staggering proportions. Jesus wants them equipped for the task. He has been their teacher but soon he will be gone. Who will carry on in his place? The Holy Spirit will come to teach them privately.

Jesus knows you cannot address ministry issues without first addressing the hearts of the ministers. So he gives no strategic plan for the successful expansion of the church. Instead he gives the promise of a personal teacher. His message is this: a ministry is built on the transformation of the minister.

Daughters of Promise is growing slowly. A solid ministry can't be built on musical talent, a good song or two, and a slick marketing campaign. It won't have power unless I have a deep connection with the Spirit and am engaged in personal change. If I am in spiritual crisis, the ministry can look flashy but have little substance. Eventually the shiny veneer will dissipate and an empty shell will remain.

You may teach a class, serve tea to neighbors, or hang out at the coffee machine during an office break to impact fellow workers. The principle is the same. If we are to have anything life-giving in our hands, it will come out of a heart that feels the breath of the Spirit. A day without his touch is a day without true power.

My ministry begins with you, Holy Spirit. Teach me, change me, and fill me with all that you are so my touch on others will be your touch. Amen.

February 22

Less of a Target

"The prince of this world is coming. He has no hold
on me."

JOHN 14:30

*J*esus warns his friends that Satan is on the loose. He tells them to
be careful because Satan's activity will increase. But he also reveals
that Satan is no threat to him because there is nothing internal for
Satan to latch on to. Jesus is without sin. He is perfectly tied to his Father.
His identity is secure. Therefore all of Satan's schemes have no effect.

The truth that Satan had no hold whatsoever on Jesus causes me
to take daily, spiritual inventory: "The ruler of this world is coming.
Is there anything in me that makes his work successful?" Anything
internal that is not of God can make Satan victorious. Any unresolved
emotional issue is targeted. Any habit controlling me marks me as
Satan's prey. Any lie I believe about myself serves as a bull's-eye for the
Evil One as he contemplates where to shoot his arrows. He is merciless, using even the smallest doorway to enter and work his destruction.

If I struggle with an addiction, Satan will do whatever necessary
to make sure I am incurable. If I continue to be defined by the lie that
I am only as good as what I do, Satan will set up cruel standards for
me to try to meet. If I am imprisoned by fear, he will do whatever
necessary to exaggerate the dangers and enhance the feelings. Fear that
cripples children of God is Satan's delight.

As I grow up in the perfect child-rearing environment of my
heavenly Father, I want to more fully resemble his Son. If I ask, Jesus
will shine his light on anything inside giving Satan an advantage. I'm
not left defenseless in this battle.

Jesus, am I an easy target? Show me where. Amen.

To Whom Am I Grafted?

"I am the true vine."

JOHN 15:1

For a vine to produce fruit, it must first be planted in the earth. God knew that and placed his Son here. Jesus lived, laughed, wept, made friends, and was betrayed here. Through it all he became our friend. If we cultivate a relationship with him, we will enjoy spiritual riches.

Because he was planted as the Vine, he made it possible for us to be grafted to him. When we are, we flourish and begin to bear the spiritual fruit for which we were born. This brings a profound sense of well-being not found anywhere else.

If we are grafted to any other vine, the fruit may look good but will eventually be revealed as counterfeit. Time spent attached to the wrong vine will result in a river of tears when its fruit is finally exposed. We will grieve over wasted years and suffer disillusionment.

The vine of other relationships will leave us wanting, for other people cannot give all that our soul needs. The vine of prestige will be satisfying momentarily, but the fickle public will replace us with someone newer and better. The vine of materialism will offer us trappings that look good, but they will become obsolete or wear out over time.

Only the true Vine can nourish us with everlasting life. "I will betroth you to me forever; I will betroth you in righteousness and justice, in love and compassion. I will betroth you in faithfulness" (Hosea 2:19–20). Such connection to Christ will bear fruit identical to his. We will be righteous, just, loving, compassionate, and faithful. If we lack anything of Jesus, we may be grafted to a wrong vine. Time to do some gardening.

Jesus, I want in all ways to be grafted to you. Amen.

February 24

Abiding and Bearing Fruit

"As the Father has loved me, so have I loved you. Now remain in my love."

JOHN 15:9

I can only begin to imagine the grief God feels hearing his Word communicated with the wrong spirit. Many teachings I have heard based on the principle of Jesus as the Vine have been harsh. Mean faces bear the message while fingers wag at the congregation. "Are you bearing fruit? Jesus says if you are abiding in him, there will be some!" The emphasis is on the fruit, but there is no instruction on abiding.

Tragically, many have been led to believe that bearing fruit consists of doing works generated on our own. We get up in the morning with a list of good deeds that, when accomplished, will be the fruit that proves we are Christians.

Not true. Good deeds can be fruit, but not all good deeds are fruit. What sets spiritual fruit apart from carnal works? Those marked by the Spirit of Christ. Bearing the sweet fruit of the Vine is the result of abiding in Jesus' extravagant love. The effortless overflow makes guilt-producing sermons obsolete.

I must understand that abiding is not rigorous Bible study and prayer. Jesus tells me it's about living in his love. I talk a lot about love, but I have spent too little time basking in it. Today my abiding skills are equivalent to how deeply I receive God's love for me. To the degree that my allowing him to fully embrace me is compromised, abiding and bearing fruit is minimized. There is no greater prayer we can pray than this:

Jesus, it's all about love. That's why you were born. That's why you lived and died. I need to receive more of you. Show me how. If I'm afraid of such intimate love, heal me. Amen.

February 25

The Root of Joy

"I have told you this so that my joy may be in you and that your joy may be complete."

JOHN 15:11

Is Jesus referring to the kind of joy that comes on a day when everything goes well or when we're at that perfect vacation spot? When he speaks of a soul filled with joy, I think he means a joy we can feel on days when nothing is right with our world or when pressures and demands would otherwise drain us of peace. A joy tucked securely in our soul.

He doesn't promise joy in stingy amounts, for he says we can be full of joy if we follow his teaching on abiding, given earlier in John 15. This passage teaches that the spiritual keys to victorious Christian living are wrapped up in "living in love."

At our last family gathering someone suggested taking pictures. I didn't feel like it, but you know what happens on the count of three. Everyone says cheese and smiles for the camera. However, there's a world of difference between a pasted-on smile and a face that radiates with joy.

I wore a counterfeit smile for years. The sermons I'd heard on the commands "Be joyful" and "In everything give thanks" were delivered out of context. This just produced more guilt and further attempts to put on a happy face. This is not what Jesus wants.

Over the past few years I've been learning how to abide. I now know the joy of being loved, secure, and significant to my Father. No matter what storm beats at my door, my joy is strong enough to weather the elements.

Joy is a response, Jesus. I see that clearly. Because you love me, I am overcome with joy. Remind me to focus on your love every day. Amen.

Unthinkable Love

"Greater love has no one than this, that lay down his life for his friends."

JOHN 15:13

I may sacrifice now and then for those I love, but I have not been called to give my life for them. Would I do it? I'd like to think so. Who isn't moved by a story of a father giving his life for his children, or a man taking a bullet to save his friend, or even a dog lunging toward an attacker to save his master from harm?

Jesus didn't give his life for friends; he gave it for enemies. His love is not of this world but is unmistakably divine.

Let's put this in perspective. Who is my enemy? Someone who hates me, everything I stand for, and everyone dear to me. If atrocities were committed against me or those I love, would I be willing to embrace the offender and offer to take his punishment? It would be like asking a member of any family affected by the World Trade Center disaster to give their life for Osama bin Laden.

We often think Jesus died to save good church people, and forget that he died to take the punishment of the very people who drove the nails into his hands, spat on him, and gave him vinegar to drink instead of water. In the face of such cruelty and suffering, he died in their place and asked his Father to forgive them. It will take a lifetime to understand that my worst deed has been paid for by a love I can only begin to imitate.

Jesus, I'm not like you. But the more time I spend with you, the more you rub off on me. Do a divine work in me. Amen.

February 27

Afraid of Friendship

"I no longer call you servants. . . . Instead, I have called you friends."

JOHN 15:15

*M*any of the slaves freed after the Civil War returned to their former owners. Not knowing how to handle their freedom, they chose to continue living in slavery. They had been given a rare gift, but fear of the unknown was too intimidating.

Through his death Jesus made us free. Yet many of us have never left the front porch of our old habitations to investigate the new life he offers. We continue to see ourselves as we have been seen by others. Our life view is that of a slave. What could be more frightening for a poor maiden who thinks she's worthless than to look in the eyes of a prince and accept his love? Yet doing so is her ticket to new life.

Jesus paid for our freedom with his life! Can you imagine his grief when we continue to think and act like slaves and expect to be treated like slaves? He's calling out to us, "Come out of the slave quarters. Move into the big house with me. Sit at my table. Let me serve you. Oh, by the way, I've put you on the deed. Everything I have is yours."

It takes humility to accept such a gift, for I did nothing to earn it. Will I initially squirm when he washes my feet, and shift in my seat at the banquet table? Will it take some time to dance in the reality that I'm rich? Oh yes, but I'm on the journey. Every day there is a greater sense of joy over my new inheritance.

I lay down my pride to accept your gifts, Jesus. I don't want to miss one! Amen.

February 28

Real Persecution

"If they persecuted me, they will persecute you also."
JOHN 15:20

Not all Christians who suffer are suffering for the cause of Christ. Many claim to be, but it's important for us to understand the difference between persecution and the pain that is derived from other sources.

First, all humanity suffers. Hardship is inevitable to anyone born to this world. Death, disease, and the wounds inflicted by imperfect people will visit a young child and accompany him throughout his lifetime. This is not the persecution Jesus describes.

Second, all humanity suffers the pain due to the consequences of their choices. Where we have intentionally or in ignorance conducted ourselves outside the spiritual guidelines God prescribes for our happiness, we shipwreck. We live with the painful results, but this is not the persecution Jesus refers to, either.

Third, Christians often seek sympathy for what they perceive as "persecution for Jesus' sake." Martyrdom is written across their countenance. "Poor me, I'm being criticized because I'm a Christian!" Quite possibly they experience the scorn of unbelievers. Lest we assume it's the persecution Jesus spoke of, let's be spiritually intuitive. Spiritual arrogance often marks the church. The elite club we represent, which excludes sinners and makes them feel unworthy of our love, repels them.

Jesus, however, was humble and reached out to receive the worst of sinners. Hanging on a Roman cross, he still loved. He was a true martyr yet never sought sympathy. He forgave those who crucified him. I must understand that unless I suffer as a result of living my life under his control, I am not suffering persecution for Jesus' sake.

Jesus, if I'm disliked because I've sinned against others with my self-righteous attitude (and called it persecution), give me the courage to ask them for forgiveness. Amen.

February 29

Preparation Is Everything

"You also must testify, for you have been with me from the beginning."

JOHN 15:27

Jesus was speaking to his closest friends to prepare them for his departure. He was readying them to disperse and head out on their own.

I'm reminded as I read this of what high importance Jesus places on preparation for ministry. Before any disciple was launched to do kingdom work, he spent three years in the company of the Teacher. Each had to develop his own relationship with Jesus and weather the tenuous beginnings of a new friendship. Each had to work through his own issues via interaction with the Master. They came to understand his thoughts, how he loved, and how he was sustained by his relationship with his Father. Jesus showed them how, just as he communed daily with Abba, they would eventually relate to him when he was in heaven.

I am sobered as I think of my many years in ministry. In some ways it was premature. I had not spent time in the company of Jesus. I didn't know him well enough, and therefore I didn't know myself. I sang songs and spoke of things by hearsay and Bible study only. Personally I knew little of what I communicated.

I cannot give away what I do not first possess. My love for others is anemic if I have not first been loved. My wisdom is shallow if I have not spent time at Wisdom's feet. My compassion is composed of platitudes if the Comforter has not first held me in his embrace. May our touch on others be fueled by experience. If Peter or John weren't sent out unprepared, I don't have a chance of winging it.

I hunger for you, Jesus. Not for study of you but for experience of you. Amen.

March

March 1

Authenticity

When Jesus saw Nathanael approaching, he said of him, "Here is a true Israelite, in whom there is nothing false."

JOHN 1:47

*M*inistry to others is powerful when built on a foundation of transparency. I know that now but I used to believe the opposite. I thought I needed to portray a woman who had her act together. I put pressure on myself to appear picture-perfect. When the spotlight was turned on me, my response was automatic; an unreadable yet pleasant Christian countenance appeared.

I'm so glad that God stepped in one night and challenged my paradigm. He encouraged me to cease perpetuating the myth of perfection.

I was giving an evening concert for three thousand university students. No one would have known by the first half of the performance that my mother was dying of cancer. But when I started the second half, I struggled. I tried to sing numerous songs about suffering and death. I became so choked up that I feared I wouldn't be able to finish the concert. Afraid that I'd have to quit and walk off in embarrassment, I heard the Spirit of God speak to me. "Can't I be glorified if your voice is choked with emotion?" "If you speak from your heart, isn't that better than planned eloquence?" "If you're honest with them, they'll find the courage to be honest with me."

I decided to be vulnerable and bridge that illusory gap between the person on the platform and the audience. I decided to show the students that I was human. I admitted that I was afraid of what lay ahead, that I was not equipped to handle my mother's death without the resources of my heavenly Father. By showing my need for him, I gave them permission to stop playing pretend with each other.

God asks his people to walk authentically, and for any who lead, that responsibility starts with us.

It's frightening to be real, Lord, but you will help me. Amen.

March 2

Surprising Enemies

"They will put you out of the synagogue; in fact, a
time is coming when anyone who kills you will think
he is offering a service to God."

JOHN 16:2

Jesus is a considerate leader. Following him holds few surprises,
for he tells us ahead of time what we will be facing. Unlike the
many leaders who woo others to follow, and then spring the unexpected, Jesus is up front. He lets us count the cost with our eyes open.

The disciples are warned that the truth they hold so dearly in their
hearts will be received poorly, mostly by the religious people. His words
are prophetic, for all the disciples will be martyrs except for John.

It's disconcerting that those who profess to know God can be the
real enemy of the truth. Satan's agenda has been accomplished through
the ages by many who claim to be doing it in God's name. The
atrocities of holy wars fill our textbooks.

You may not be facing death because of your faith. However, you
still may know what it feels like to be an outcast of the synagogue. You
have endured the fires of criticism and suffered under labels of
apostasy. Those who zealously claimed to be connected to God rejected
the tender but powerful workings of God in you. Jesus gives the
reason for this painful reality. He says, "These things they will do
because they have not known the Father or me."

If your character has been assassinated and you have been called
an enemy of God, may you rise out of your pit of self-doubt. Every
trailblazer for the Son of God, those who have encountered the
radical love of the cross, will cause lukewarm, intellectual faith to
squirm. It's a kingdom truth, and we who follow our spiritual
ancestors walk in their footsteps.

*Your disciples are my brothers, Lord. If they were controversial, I am
too. Strengthen me. Amen.*

March 3

Sorrow with Perspective

"None of you asks me, 'Where are you going?'"
JOHN 16:5

*I*t's hard to see beyond bad news. If the eyes of our spirit are not trained to see this life in the context of spiritual realities and our coming kingdom, we will be overwhelmed. Instead of finding troubles to be mere spiritual challenges, we will find them crippling.

Jesus' words are timely for us. He has been delivering the difficult news to his disciples that he's dying, and suffering also awaits them. But Jesus tells them that their hearts are sorrowful because they fail to ask him where he is going. In his absence he will send someone greater who can live inside them. While they live out the rest of their days on earth, Jesus will be in heaven, interceding for them and preparing their future home. Little do they know that their sorrow is only misplaced hope.

A friend of mine told me about a journalist who traveled to Kosovo and interviewed a small girl who had lost her parents in brutal acts of ethnic cleansing. The journalist asked, "Are you angry with the people who killed your family?" With a voice free of malice, she said, "Oh no, that's just what war is." She had no illusions about this life. Her answer, though tragically void of hope, is truthful and reminds me that I should also be realistic about my expectations of life here. However, this should not lead to hopeless resignation. The best awaits God's children.

Unfortunately, the disciples temporarily placed their hopes in the here and now. If we're not careful, we can make the same mistake. We dream of the perfect house, adoring children, and obedient retrievers lying by the fire. It doesn't take long to become frustrated. Jesus is asking, "Why are you sorrowful? See where I am?" As we explore his kingdom, we ache for it. That's good, though. The aching raises our arms to heaven in expectation.

Help me lift my eyes to you, Jesus. Your love brings me comfort. The life you have waiting for me brings me hope. Amen.

March 4

Choosing the Best

"Unless I go away, the Counselor will not come to you; but if I go, I will send him to you."

JOHN 16:7

*J*esus had been accessible to people for thirty-three years. Their eyes could see him and their hands could touch him. They experienced him fully. Now Jesus tells his friends that it is to their advantage to say good-bye. They are to be weaned from his presence. Giving up one thing makes them ready for a greater gift.

No one likes to be weaned. Without mother's insistence, we would have nursed at her breast for more years. Yet it was for our good to move from milk to solid food. What felt like a loss was graduation.

From what is God weaning you today? Old, dysfunctional friendships may be straining for change. It may feel like death but the process is one of advancement. God may be pulling sources of security out from under you. People you've always counted on are distracted or misunderstand you. God may be allowing it, weaning you from a dependence on them to an absolute trust in him. He's calling you to the wilderness. It feels like a land of deprivation, but in reality it is a quiet place where God chooses to tenderly reveal himself.

Before God can build something new in our lives, he dismantles what is old and unhealthy. The richest spiritual gifts come at a great price. The disciples said good-bye to Jesus and were asked to count the cost. How tenaciously will we pursue the kingdom? How badly do we want new truth? How desperately do we want advancement to the next spiritual plateau? The answer lies in what we are willing to part with.

I trust you, Jesus. You never ask me to give up anything that is not for my good. Amen.

March 5

Good Guilt

"When he comes, he will convict the world of guilt in regard to sin."

JOHN 16:8

Jesus is teaching his friends about the Holy Spirit. His role is clearly defined. He will highlight our sin and convict us of it by bringing feelings of guilt. Jesus explains that the Spirit will open up the wound before coming in to comfort.

I pray diligently, "May your Spirit rest on me." Because God's Spirit is called "Comforter," I can want his company for comfort's sake or for the sweet manifestation of his presence. However, I forget that conviction of any unknown sin is his primary role. That will most assuredly happen as I give him permission to work freely in me.

There is confusion about the area of guilt today. Many conclude that all guilt is bad and is from the enemy. Not true. When God's Spirit reveals sin, feelings of remorse follow. Guilt is an emotion God instituted, providing a road map for confession and repentance. But Satan steals things of the kingdom and distorts them. He creates false guilt, the kind with no resolution, causing people to live in torment. Many live with feelings of guilt but are unable to tell you what they've done wrong. This is not of God. The Spirit pinpoints our sin, leading us immediately to freedom through the cross.

God's Spirit may have been showing you a sinful pattern in your life, but because you felt guilty, you assumed it wasn't God speaking. Your guilt is evidence of his voice. He won't rush in to dry your tears too quickly. Your guilt and need of a Savior will drive you to repentance and change.

Feeling guilty isn't pleasant, but if it leads me to repentance and new life, I thank you for it. Reveal my own heart to me, Spirit of truth. Amen.

March 6

Considerate of Our Maturity Level

"I have much more to say to you, more than you can
now bear."

JOHN 16:12

*T*hroughout Scripture God refers to us as his children. He invites us
to grow up in his perfect child-rearing environment. Under his
care, he never gives tasks that are incongruent with our maturation level.

Because of a mentally unstable mother, a dear friend of mine was
made the matriarch of the home at a young age. Living on a farm, she
was responsible for chores before school, meals, laundry, and then
additional chores after school. She had little time for homework and
no time for play. When she was sixteen, she nearly cracked under
the pressure.

There is so much more Jesus could tell his disciples before he leaves
earth, but they are not able to handle the information yet. As Creator
of the world, he could tell them more of how things operate. He could
enlighten them about the kingdoms of light and darkness, and the
battles ahead that will ultimately end in Satan's defeat. But this might
overwhelm them.

Jesus could also reveal what joy and sorrows are ahead for them.
But think about it: aren't we glad we don't know what tomorrow
brings? If I knew what Daughters of Promise would look like ten years
from now, as happy as I might be, I might throw up my hands and
declare myself inadequate to lead it.

Each of us is given one day at a time to manage. God is faithful to
reveal himself in that day. He builds us up, precept upon precept,
experience upon experience, preparing us for tomorrow. Never has a
parent been so kind.

*I understand your words now, Jesus, that your grace is sufficient for
me. You are so considerate. Amen.*

March 7

Unity of the Spirit

"When he, the Spirit of truth, comes, he will guide
you into all truth. He will not speak on his own."

JOHN 16:13

The Trinity, though three distinct parts of God, acts in perfect unity.
No one who experiences the Spirit will come away feeling
differently than if he experienced Jesus. Beliefs, words, and emotions
are all consistent within the person of God.

Not so with us. The Fall in the Garden fractured the internal world
of humanity, and we've been divided ever since. Because we're divided
and inconsistent, we're unstable.

We're also self-deceived. Without the help of the Spirit, we will
fail to really know ourselves. Who we think we are is often radically
different from what we portray to others. Hidden parts of our subconscious really rule our thoughts and feelings about life, while our
words can sound so impressive.

Oftentimes I can say one thing but convey another. My words
don't match my face. I have chuckled at family vignettes in which a
parent says to a child, "I'm not angry!" but their yelling and their
cherry red face betray them.

Growing into the image of Christ is all about allowing the Spirit
of God to show us where we are sinfully divided. It is giving him
permission to bring every corner of our soul into the light of his grace
and then working with him to change each part so we also may live in
unity. Self-disclosure empowered by the Spirit can be painful, but the
rugged introspection pays off. No longer will our testimony reveal that
we know the truth but we feel the opposite. We can live in peace and
harmony with ourselves and with the God who lovingly created us.

Work in me, O Spirit, to make me unified with you. Amen.

March 8

I Can't Hear You!

"What does he mean by 'a little while'? We don't understand what he is saying."

JOHN 16:18

*J*esus has been a considerate friend to his disciples. He's been preparing them repeatedly for his coming absence. However, in spite of his many speeches about leaving, they cannot hear. Again they ask one another what he is talking about. They refuse to give up their belief that he has come to establish his kingdom in their lifetime, and the truth can't stick. Error and truth cannot coexist. When a falsehood preoccupies our mind, the truth of God cannot nest and develop.

This lesson is humbling. How many falsehoods dominate places in my heart? They are destructive, preventing the rich word of Christ from taking root. I consider all the ways in the past in which I forfeited the joy of being loved by clinging to lies about myself.

The foundational truth of Christianity is "Jesus loves me." Yet as long as I thought he loved everyone but me, the real truth had no place to reside. I became one of his disciples who asked incredulously, "What did he say, he loves me? I don't know what he is talking about."

As I'm writing, I'm taking mental inventory. Where might I still disbelieve Jesus cognitively and emotionally? He makes some radical predictions about any child of his who fully embraces him. He says we will live abundantly, live loved, walk free of shame, rejoice over our inheritance, and know the riches of his calling. If I fail to know any of these realities, chances are there are lies embedded from my past or present experience that are blocking the work of God.

There are beliefs I need to let go of, Lord. Show me what they are so I can hear your words and be transformed by them. Amen.

March 9

There's More to Life Than This

"Now is your time of grief, but I will see you again and you will rejoice."

JOHN 16:22

Jesus is at the home of Mary, Martha, and Lazarus. They are close friends. Curiosity seekers from Jerusalem—namely, the religious elite—come to get a glimpse of them. Can you hear their whispers? "Let's go see the man who was dead but now is alive." At the root of their interest is malice. To be blunt, Jesus threatens their power; Jesus and Lazarus are enemies of the organized church.

The religious council arrives to satisfy their curiosity about Lazarus and then calls a meeting. Their intention is to put Lazarus to death! Perhaps Lazarus thought, *I was brought back to life—only to face this?*

Ever been there? You endure hard times. You turn a corner by God's gracious intervention. You think you've seen the worst. But then something unforeseen occurs that is worse than what you survived. You wonder if the journey is worth it.

While the plot against Lazarus fizzled, the scheme against Jesus heated up. In a few days Jesus would be arrested and crucified. If our attention remains on these few days in the life of Jesus or his friends, we will feel futility. In light of eternity the events are cradled in the story of redemption. Jesus will live again and sit at the right hand of his Father. His friends will tell the story of his humanity and divinity, and ultimately live with him in heaven.

Lack of vision can be the ruin of many. Vision fueled by faith is marked by hope and joy.

This is not all there is. Help me not get lost in distress today, Lord. I look forward by faith to my glorious future. Amen.

March 10

Ask for What?

"Until now you have not asked for anything in my name. Ask and you will receive, and your joy will be complete."

JOHN 16:24

*J*esus says we don't ask for enough, or at least we don't ask for enough in his name, which is the critical distinction. I'm not surprised; I'm often confused about knowing what I can ask for. The secret is learning what petitions can be attached to the name of Jesus.

It would be wrong to ask God to give us a more luxurious house in the name of Jesus, or a bigger church so we can compete with the biggest and the best. We know better. We shouldn't petition for something carnal and attach Jesus' name to it. God will not honor that.

Praying for a larger home for the purpose of using it for the kingdom is another matter. Laboring in prayer for the expansion of our church because our hearts are broken over the needs of our community is also in line. We need to discover the motives behind our prayers. If it serves me, I ask in vain. If it serves God and the principles of his kingdom, I can ask without hesitation.

It astounds me that Jesus has to tell us to ask for more. We were born self-centered, with hands out to receive everything we could. But somewhere along the line our idealism was shattered. We came up against the imperfect love of others. That for which we longed was given in stingy amounts. Awakening our spirit to the love of the Father reawakens our desires. As I grow to be more like Jesus, I want what God wants and I can ask for it with great expectation.

I come in Jesus' name, not my own, Father. Make me wise enough to distinguish the gifts in your hands. Amen.

March 11

Teaching So Others Can Hear

"Now you are speaking clearly and without figures of speech. Now we can see that you know all things."
JOHN 16:29–30

*B*iblical principles are deeper and more mysterious than we can ever comprehend yet simple enough for a child to understand. Jesus, speaking to his disciples on the eve of his arrest, condenses his message and his mission to short and clear statements. The disciples respond with relief: "Ah, now you're talking so we can fully understand. We get it!"

Communicating the things of God so the brilliant are engaged and the uneducated are enlightened is a task far too big for any of us. It is only the Spirit of God who can enter our mind, select a personal experience with which to illustrate a teaching, and then express himself through "our" words to touch a listener. When it is left to us, we tend to make it too simple or too complicated.

I've sat under simplistic teaching in which clichés were handed out like candy. This form of teaching promises victory and peace for every situation and reduces God to predictable behavior. In short, God is put in a box. I have since learned that God's Spirit rarely resides where there are no expressed needs. Self-sufficient Christianity, as perpetuated by legalistic churches and organizations, is ill-equipped to explore or ease human needs, depravity, and longings.

I've also sat under complicated teaching. You know the kind. Abstract scriptural principles and fancy elevated language. While it may stimulate the mind, it circumvents the heart entirely. Truth must always be a heart thing. The Spirit of God is most anxious to help us understand it and communicate it that way.

My heart is a clean slate upon which you can write your truth. Teach me, Spirit. Amen.

March 12

Peace in Spite Of

"I have told you these things, so that in me you may
have peace."

JOHN 16:33

*J*esus intends each of us to know peace. Not the peace felt sitting
by a lake or taking in a sunset from a back porch swing. Most
anyone can experience peace in these settings. Jesus makes it clear that
the peace he promises can coexist with tribulation. A distinguishing
mark of a Christian is a soul at ease though troubles have marched in
the front door.

How is this possible? By not allowing pain to define us. In the
thirty-three years Jesus lived on earth, he could have been adversely
affected by the pain he endured. But he wasn't. His identity and
purpose were never shaken.

When Herod's army set out to destroy him as an infant, he never
owned their hatred. When his parents scolded him for using his gifts
at age twelve, he never second-guessed his calling. When the religious
elite criticized his methods, he never owned the shame they intended
to inflict. When his own disciples wavered in their belief as to who he
claimed to be, he never embraced rejection. And when the world hung
him on a cross, he did not exact revenge. He extended forgiveness instead.

Whatever tribulations I face today need not define me either. My
soul need not succumb to destructive messages that accompany my
trials. My identity is secure no matter what my circumstances say. Who
am I today? A beloved daughter of God. The cherished bride of Christ.
The one he calls lover and dearest friend. The one whom Jesus looks
on tenderly. How can I not have peace?

*I've been looking for peace in my circumstances. It isn't there. That's
because it's found in who I am with you. Change my expectations,
Jesus. Amen.*

March 13

The Prayers of Jesus

"I pray for them."

JOHN 17:9

When we want to learn to pray as Jesus prays, we usually go to the Lord's Prayer. However, the seventeenth chapter of John is Jesus' longest recorded prayer. Even though facing the cross, Jesus prays not just for himself but for those closest to him. He aches for the welfare of those he loves. He wonders what will happen to them in his absence. He hopes that the truths he taught them will be remembered.

It is comforting to know that Jesus needed to pray. He needed what we need: comfort, assurance, and confirmation of God's purposes. He taught us that it's okay to ask for what we need and that we won't get it unless we ask specifically. His prayer of twenty-six verses is one request after another. It is a prayer for spiritual prosperity. It resembles what we pray for our own children and provides a wonderful prayer model.

"Keep them and care for them.... Unite them together as you and I are knit together.... Keep them safe from the Evil One.... Fill them with my joy.... Make them pure and holy by teaching them your words of truth.... May they be entirely yours.... May they know that you love them as you love me."

Jesus finishes with words of commitment: "I have revealed you to them, and will keep on revealing you. I will do this so that your love for me may be in them." Praying for others only profits them if my own faith is authentic. If others see me pray and respect the way I live my life, my prayers benefit them and encourage them to regard God with honor.

Empower me to live authentically, Lord. May my life and my prayers bring you honor. Amen.

March 14

Eden Redeemed

There was an olive grove, and he and his disciples
went into it.

JOHN 18:1

*R*edemption permeates Scripture. God's Word reflects his most treasured agenda: exchanging things of death for gifts of eternal life.

Gardens are objects of redemption. The Garden of Eden, that
utopian, idyllic environment destroyed by Adam and Eve, was the
birth site of God's plan for redemption.

Jesus, on the last night of his freedom, entered another garden.
Arrest and crucifixion awaited him. Preparing himself, he entered a
garden on the Mount of Olives. Here tears were heard and Jesus taught
his disciples how to handle persecution and submission to God's purposes.
This garden played host to the Priest paying for the sins of Eden!

Look inside. What is God redeeming today? Perhaps you once
enjoyed facets of Eden but you or others corrupted it. Childhood
marred by an alcoholic parent, a good marriage ruined by infidelity, an
idealistic view of life shattered by too many disappointments. The
destruction of Eden is never the end of the story for God's child. Your
garden can be restored by God's gift of new life to the soul. Hope can
live again. Your idealism can be firmly rooted in God's kingdom and
heavenly expectations. Jesus paid with his life to redeem our places of
sin and death.

Jesus was buried in a garden. But the garden that cocooned his
mortal body was also redeemed, becoming the garden that would
showcase the empty tomb.

*Raise my expectations, Jesus. I've adjusted my eyes to the fallen world
of Eden rather than choosing to look for your redemption. Begin to
show me where you want to exchange death for life. Amen.*

March 15

Waiting in the Garden

Now Judas, who betrayed him, knew the place.

JOHN 18:2

*I*t is late in the evening, already dark. While most of the world has retired, Jesus takes his disciples and goes to the garden where he will spend his final night of freedom. Judas will arrive shortly with a mixed band of officials to arrest Jesus. Judas knows where to find Jesus, for he has been to this garden many times. Previously he came as Jesus' friend. Now he intrudes upon this formerly intimate place as a traitor.

Infidelity is always excruciating, for it is composed of the betrayal of someone who knows us intimately. They have eaten at our table and accompanied us to our favorite hangouts. They know how we like our coffee, and they can reveal our deepest secrets as well. They might call us by endearing nicknames. No wonder we are sent reeling.

Jesus knew ahead of time what Judas was going to do, but he comes to the garden anyway. His suffering begins now, hours before he will carry his cross. It is born with the kiss of a friend who has witnessed the most sacred spiritual acts firsthand. Tragically, Judas' own quest for power and prestige has grown to such proportions that his affection for Jesus is annihilated.

The disease of self-interest also resides inside me. How many times have I told Jesus one day that I love him, only to do something the next day which looks like a retraction? Jesus must have winced, but he kept coming to the garden, hoping I'd come back. He'll always choose intimacy, even at the risk of our unfaithfulness.

Jesus, I cannot fathom your friendship. You wait for me, always, in the garden. May I come with fidelity in my heart. Amen.

Our Cross Versus Satan's Mirage

Jesus, knowing all that was going to happen to him, went out.

JOHN 18:4

*T*he time for the cross is upon Jesus. He knows it and surrenders willingly to the authorities coming to arrest him. This is not the first time his life has been in danger. Numerous times before, he fled to retire for a while to some obscure place because he knew the timing for his death was premature. Satan would have loved to tamper with God's timetable, but Jesus never allowed it.

We're told that we'll be called upon to take up our cross and follow Jesus. However, knowing the proper time is as critical for us as it was for Jesus. Satan brings crisis after crisis meant to overwhelm us and bring us to destruction. Often unaware of his tactics, we mistake painful scenarios as our time for bearing our cross, rather than treating them as the mirage of the Evil One. When we should be engaging in spiritual warfare, we retire instead and carry our counterfeit cross on the shoulders of immature, feeble faith. Not able to withstand the pressure, we crumble in defeat and wonder why God wasn't faithful to give grace in our time of need.

On the flip side, there are conflicts we should excuse ourselves from. There are illnesses to pray against. There are blows to our character needing a tough-love response rather than a turning of the other cheek. Knowing when to retire or resist is critical. God can show us what is needless pain meant to harm us and what is his cross, the cross that allows us to share in Jesus' suffering.

If I face suffering that is in your perfect plan, Lord, I surrender. To all else I take up a sword against the plans of our enemy. Amen.

March 17

Looking Silly

Jesus commanded Peter, "Put your sword away!"
JOHN 18:11

*P*eter once made a declaration to Jesus of his love and loyalty. "I will die for you," he said. Now when Jesus' life is threatened, Peter makes good on his promise and draws a sword. The problem is, though Peter acted to defend Jesus, he was actually standing in the way of Jesus' road to the cross. His intentions were noble but because his action was initiated without direction from his Master, he tainted heaven's purposes.

We cannot depend on our own hunches when making spiritual advances. How many times do we thwart the cause of Christ when we believe we're helping it? We evangelize by using intellectual arguments rather than winning others to God's heart through acts of friendship. Our need to be right, coupled with our sincere desire to defend God's truth, is a deadly combination. Hence the label "Bible thumpers"! We dispense truth without love and assassinate the nature of the gospel.

Each time we try to change someone by harassing and nagging them with the truth, we potentially ruin the soil that could grow good seed, were it cultivated through prayer. Truth and love must be wedded. Truth is incomplete unless it is delivered in an atmosphere of love.

We have good intentions. We want to handle the message of Jesus with integrity. We want to reflect his character. We want our words to be laced with wisdom, yet I'm vividly reminded that I cannot generate any of this on my own. The way of the cross is a mystery. When I react against others and the trends of society according to my own passions, I end up looking like Peter rather than Jesus.

My influence is powerless without your direction, Lord. Show me how to use it. Amen.

March 18

Giving Peter Grace

Simon Peter and another disciple were following Jesus.
JOHN 18:15

When Jesus was arrested and led away, the disciples fled, except for Peter and one other. They followed Jesus and the officials at a safe distance. Peter had openly declared his love for Jesus. He made a commitment to put himself in harm's way should the need arise. Now when most of his friends have retreated in fear, Peter trails Jesus to the house of the high priest. Although it will be here that Peter will deny Christ, let's give him credit for hanging in there this far.

He has earned an unfair reputation. When we remember Peter, we often think of his act of betrayal. We recall his temper in cutting off the ear of the high priest's servant. We even snicker in discomfort over his public proclamations of love to Jesus. Why is it that a few eccentricities and one mistake became Peter's defining characteristics? After all, the rest of his life was lived admirably. He was eventually crucified, upside down, because of his devotion to Jesus.

This is human nature. One sin potentially erases a hundred good deeds. A person walks circumspectly for fifty years, falls once, and is remembered for that one misdeed. If I were merely running the race for others' approval, I'd throw up my hands and quit.

I'm glad Jesus does not reject us because of a few blemishes on our spiritual resume. Our scars make us wise. Our failures become our greatest teachers. The applause of heaven is not reserved for those hiding behind model behavior. It is extended toward anyone who admits depravity, walks in the joy of daily forgiveness, and then puts forth another good-faith effort.

I need grace today, Lord. When others start throwing stones, you extend a second chance to me, just as you did to Peter. Amen.

March 19

Half-Truths and Watered-Down Messages

The high priest questioned Jesus about his disciples
and his teaching. "I have spoken openly to the world,"
Jesus replied. . . . "I said nothing in secret."
JOHN 18:19–20

I am a quiet person. I think before I speak, and my mouth rarely
gets me into trouble. However, I'm sure there have been occasions
when God wanted me to share, but anticipated rejection locked up
my words. The challenge for me, even today, is to offer insights and
opinions freely, without counting the cost. I'd rather contribute something when asked.

Jesus spoke openly. He never told half-truths. While he might not
have welcomed the adverse reaction his words caused, he shared them
nonetheless. Angry Pharisees didn't cause him to retreat behind a safe,
stoic facade. He bore the wrath of their arrogance. Though his words
brought sadness to the rich young ruler, Jesus didn't touch his sadness.
The gospel beseeches others to count the cost, and the young ruler
decided it was too great, for Jesus had hidden nothing of the truth
from him.

Jesus' openness creates a model that is difficult for us to follow.
We are prone to be secretive, choosing to whisper truths to some while
withholding from others.

Do others really know the Jesus in me? Is my story the same
regardless of who asks? Is my spirit free enough to radiate my passion,
or am I more apt to water down my excitement, for fear of being
labeled a radical? Oh, that I would become more like my Savior. He
risked his life for me. I can certainly risk a few authentic words.

*You made me to live freely in you, Lord. May I not quench your
Spirit by sitting on my passions. May I speak, sing, and dance with
my words. Amen.*

March 20

How Dare You?

When Jesus said this, one of the officials nearby
struck him in the face. "Is this the way you answer the
high priest?" he demanded.

JOHN 18:22

*W*hen Jesus was questioned by the high priest about the nature of his teaching, he said, "Why do you question me? Question those who have heard what I spoke to them. They know what I said." That answer incurred the wrath of the guard, and he reached out and struck Jesus, saying, "Is that the way you answer the high priest?"

Can you imagine hitting deity and accusing him of impertinent speech? Jesus, who knew this guard when he was formed in his mother's womb, was struck by his creation? We all perish for lack of knowledge. In our ignorance we strike out. In our fear we become enraged by anyone who threatens us and say things we regret.

Can I identify with the guard who objected at Jesus' words? Unfortunately. Though I used to be polished at appearing pious, my thought life accused me. During times when faith would have been spiritually becoming, I railed against God. I have been known to cry out in anger, "How can you say that? What else do you want from me?"

I cringe, remembering how easily I elevated my thoughts above God's. How arrogant. Yet he loved me in spite of it all. I understand that I have not only been the hotheaded guard who struck Jesus, but I also helped those who drove the nails through his hands. That knowledge brought a season of grief, but I was then bathed in the joy of forgiveness. Imagine being washed clean of such deeds!

You always speak the truth, Jesus. My thoughts are foolishness apart from you. I trust everything you say and bow my will to yours. Amen.

March 21

Gross Hypocrisy

The Jews led Jesus from Caiaphas to the palace of the
Roman governor. . . . The Jews did not enter the
palace; they wanted to be able to eat the Passover.

JOHN 18:28

he chief priests and Pharisees wanted Jesus out of the picture. He
threatened everything their appetites desired. They could have
taken Jesus into an angry mob for him to be stoned, as Stephen had
been. But that didn't serve their purposes. They didn't want the
scandal of that resting at their front door. They would use the justice
system of the Roman government.

Jesus was delivered to the Praetorium, where Pilate sat in power.
But instead of going in to Pilot to make their case, the Jewish leaders
stayed outside so they could go to the Passover!

I am incredulous. They didn't want to defile themselves by
publicly participating in the death of the Son of God, yet they would
defile the Passover? They dared hide behind a ritual so sacred? They
presumed to celebrate all that the Passover meant, by plotting to kill
the very one whose blood would be applied to the doorposts
of humanity?

I look for my own incongruities. Am I hiding behind religion?
Do I defile the very things I say I believe in, by acting in ways that
contradict them? Do I mock the crown Jesus wears, by donning an
insubordinate attitude? Do I call Jesus "Master" and then use
Christian freedom recklessly?

He who put his life on the line to win our freedom is still looking
for those who will embrace him in the public courtyard, regardless of
the cost.

*I'm sorry, Jesus, that you stood alone before Pilate. May I not be so
busy playing church that I think I am excused from the real business
of being salt and light. Amen.*

March 22

Watch Out

One of the high priest's servants, a relative of the man whose ear Peter had cut off, challenged him, "Didn't I see you with him in the olive grove?"

JOHN 18:26–27

When a car passes us, there is a moment of time when we experience a blind spot in our side mirror. We may feel safe enough to change lanes but we're not. We have a false sense of security. What looms just behind us can kill us.

Peter is in a precarious place. He warms himself by a fire in the midst of bad company. He has already been asked if he is a friend of Jesus. He denied it. Instead of removing himself from this place that holds further danger, he is lulled by the warmth of the fire. Like the car that nears our rear bumper, Satan stalks Peter. He heard Peter's first denial and will now double his efforts to trap the disciple who has already started faltering. If only Peter would flee the presence of evil.

Satan is merciless. He knows every blind spot I have. Every lie I believe about myself he will try to confirm, destroying my sense of belovedness. Every myth I embrace about God he will cement, leading me to conclude that God cannot be trusted. Only as I allow God to show me my blind spots can I anticipate the danger, expose Satan's schemes, renounce his lies, and allow my soul to reside in the safety of truth. Just as the driver of an automobile can't afford to get drowsy at the wheel, I must be diligent to guard my heart on this perilous journey in foreign territory.

You have 360-degree vision, Lord. Lead me in paths of safety and freedom. Amen.

March 23

The Day the Rooster Crowed

Again Peter denied it, and at that moment a rooster
began to crow.

JOHN 18:27

Roosters are God's creation. They were made to crow and therefore none of those in the court of the high priest were surprised
to hear it. Their lives weren't interrupted at the sound of it.

For Peter, though, the sound was the voice of God. He went away
weeping because he had denied three times that he knew Jesus, and at
the conclusion of his words the rooster chimed in. Jesus foretold this
event the night before. Peter had been incredulous, having just proclaimed undying love for his Master. However, Jesus knew that Peter's
faith was still immature and would not stand firm through adversity.

There is only one God and Scripture reveals him. However, God
relates to each of us uniquely. He speaks through the most bizarre
circumstances: through dreams, a line in a movie, or a seemingly
insignificant phrase spoken by a stranger. The point is, once we hear his
voice, our world is never the same. A simple crow of a rooster changed
Peter's life, and I imagine that the sound of it held meaning for the rest of
his days.

How many of us will hear the voice of God resound today in a
private revelation? It might be the answer to months of tearful,
heartfelt prayers. It might be a sound we alone recognize. There may
be a kindred spirit who will be able to hear our story and discern the
power of it, but for the most part the only one whose world is shaken
with significance is the one to whom God speaks.

*You know just how to speak so I can understand, Lord. I am moved
to know you love me enough to talk to me. Amen.*

March 24

Not Here, Not Yet

Pilate replied. "It was your people and your chief priests who handed you over to me. What is it you have done?" Jesus said, "My kingdom is not of this world."

JOHN 18:35–36

*T*he kingdom to which I belong is not of this world. Jesus is a King but his kingdom is one that is set up in the hearts of people. His children live in this world but are not of it.

It is sad when I transfer my hopes from the kingdom of God to the world in which I live. I set myself up for failure by my unrealistic expectations. Jesus looks on with frustration and sadness as he sees me foraging like a pauper throughout the earth for the things of heaven. They won't be found. Yet I will keep doing it anyway without rigid self-check.

I am one who craves immediate rewards. I think life should be fair. I want wrongdoers to be exposed and punished so the underdog will win. Without conscience effort to nurture the truth that my citizenship is elsewhere, I will try to pat my world into place. I'll burn out trying to build the perfect life: picture-perfect marriage, two kids, house by a lake, and a couple of retrievers running freely on the property. When anything stands in the way of this utopia to which I feel entitled, I get angry with God.

But he never promised bliss here. Living in heaven awaits, but the emotional and spiritual reality of his kingdom is mine today as I dance as a child before my King in worship. I celebrate my future by faith. I am expectant, radiant, and joyful.

Forgive me, Lord, for feeling entitled to a perfect life on earth. You didn't promise that. I ache for heaven but I am already a child in your kingdom. Amen.

The Nature of Truth

"What is truth?" Pilate asked. With this he went out again to the Jews and said, "I find no basis for a charge against him."

JOHN 18:38

*J*esus wanted to offer Pilate the truth that would set him free. But after Pilate asked the question, he left without waiting for Jesus' answer. He's like so many of us who go to the right person for advice but don't end up taking it to heart, because we don't like being thrust out of our comfort zone.

Truth always does that. It grates against the voices of the times. It contradicts our own logic and pathways of reasoning. It seems too simplistic somehow. Only years of adherence to God's precepts reveal that simple is also profound. Truth usually leaves us openmouthed. Pared down, it resembles the clear thinking of a child.

To really appreciate the truth Jesus offers, I recall the relationships and institutions I've been a part of that were ruled according to untruth. Quickly cobwebs of distrust were spun. Insecurity flourished. Good ethics were replaced by relativism. Interaction was political.

The prodigal son shipwrecked when trying to run his life apart from the blessing of his father. I know some of his heartache, for I've tried to live facets of my life according to my own brand of truth. Without exception there was a tragic end.

I am resolved not only to discover truth but to align my beliefs and behavior accordingly, even when the ways of Jesus seem backward, costly, and inconvenient. If Pilate had chosen to alter his life according to Jesus' truth, his soul would have prospered.

I need wisdom in many areas of my life today. But as you give it, Lord, may I trust you enough to embrace it and act on it. Amen.

March 26

An Impotent-Looking King

The soldiers twisted together a crown of thorns and
put it on his head.

JOHN 19:2

*J*esus was mocked. Though truly a king, he didn't look like one. He
appeared impotent. Those who fashioned Jesus a crown believed
he faced the end of his reign of influence, but in reality he only
manifested the power of restraint. He would soon march against the
gates of hell and win.

Jesus is still King but things haven't changed much as far as
public perception. How much of that is my fault? I hail him as King
but I can make him appear impotent by the choices I make. I am often
a traitor, paying homage to the King of heaven with my lips but
embracing the god of this world with my heart.

When I fail to honor the poor, the widowed, and the
feeble-minded, I make a mockery of the government of my King.
When I obsess over the details of my life and fail to entrust each one
to the King who creates life with his very breath, I belittle his position.
When I secretly dream of how those who wronged me should pay for
their sins, I take the scepter of justice out of the King's hands and
become a corrupted judge and jury.

Unless I have abdicated all rights to myself and given complete
power over me to the King of the Jews, I am little different from the
soldiers who taunted him. When others see me live my life today, will
they behold my quiet confidence in a King who is unlimited in power,
or will their view of God be injured by my preoccupation with
self-preservation?

Jesus, in every way today, I honor you as my King. Amen.

March 27

Which Robe Am I Wearing?

They clothed him in a purple robe.

JOHN 19:2

*T*he soldiers put a mock robe over the shoulders of Jesus. How different it was from the one we'll see Jesus wear one day: "On his robe ... he has this name written: KING OF KINGS AND LORD OF LORDS" (Revelation 19:16). The Roman soldiers dressed him in the first (and it was even the right color), but God will adorn him with the last. Derision accompanied the Roman robe, but God will bestow honor when he outfits his Son in glory.

Who we allow to dress us makes all the difference. Whose robe am I wearing? There are plenty of choices available. They're pleasing to the eye and tailor-made to fit perfectly. They feel right around my shoulders, so it takes a while for me to understand that I wear a counterfeit.

Recognition and honor feel good. They ought to, for God has promised both to his children. But as soon as I seek them from sources other than my Creator, I've signed myself up for a dose of disillusionment. Because the world's robe may look right, it takes a while to discover that it's the wrong garment. Only as the robe is torn from my shoulders because someone better came along will I understand that I bought into a fickle system of recognition and rewards.

Nothing can rival being chosen by God. To know that he sees me and wants me is a truth so beautiful that it takes a lifetime to internalize. He crowns me with honor, with loving-kindness and tender mercy. Though I was previously an orphan in Satan's kingdom, he adopted me into Jesus' royal family. When God put that robe around my shoulders, it was permanent and satisfying.

No one loves me like you, God. Expose the counterfeits. I want all of the real thing! Amen.

March 28

Just a Man

---

*When Jesus came out wearing the crown of thorns and
the purple robe, Pilate said to them, "Here is the man!"*
JOHN 19:5

*P*ilate's strategy is quite impressive. He brings Jesus, scourged and
bloody, out to the chief priests and officials who have been so
enraged by his claim to be God. He assumes that once they see him
emerge looking like a common criminal, their anger will abate and
they will cease to be intimidated. He proclaims, "Behold the man!" In
other words, "Look who you've allowed to get under your skin. He's
just a man!"

There have been leaders in my life to whom I've given too much
power. When they were self-impressed and wielded their influence
with a sense of recklessness, I backed away and deferred. I tiptoed in
fear, lost my voice, and forgot that they were merely people.

I was ruled by fear but only because I had committed idolatry. My
significance failed to rest in the One who had all authority and power.
My identity was not rooted in being the daughter of a righteous and
wise King, for if I had but known that, I would have been able to say
of those I feared, "Behold, they're merely people!" I would not have
accommodated every request. My sense of self would not have shrunk
if they had failed to recognize me. My future would not have been
threatened if I had been overlooked.

Today I can look at people—as people. To each who acts
pompously I say to myself with a wry smile, "Behold the human
being!" My purpose today is unshaken. Unlike Pilate, I look up and
say, "Behold my King!" There's only room for one person on the
throne, and who better than Jesus?

*Oh, the joy of no longer being afraid of people. You are the one who
defines my life, Lord, the King on whose palm my name is carved.
Amen.*

March 29

Forgiveness for This?

The Jews insisted, ". . . He must die, because he claimed to be the Son of God." When Pilate heard this, he was even more afraid.

JOHN 19:7–8

*I*t's one thing to be responsible for giving the order to crucify someone who claims to be a king, but can you imagine the responsibility you'd feel for crucifying the Son of God? Pilate trembled over the weight of this dilemma. The stakes had just increased considerably.

He ended up making a decision to save his skin. He should have saved his soul. He pacified the bloodthirsty Jews. (I have often made decisions to pacify others.) Pilate was intimidated by their anger and aggression. (I have also allowed myself to be ruled by others' anger and aggression.) Jesus, who was innocent, got hurt. (Someone suffered because I also acquiesced. Often that person was I.) God's Son was crucified and Pilate was left with blood on his hands. (I have done things for which I feared there could be no possible forgiveness.)

Is there an unforgivable sin? Amazingly, the answer is no if sin is repented of. Pilate might have stood at the foot of the cross, beholding his prisoner, watching the life ebb from Jesus' body, and been granted full absolution. The power of Jesus' blood, the blood of Pilate's sacrificial lamb, was enough to forgive him of even killing deity.

Over what am I walking in guilt today? What scene gets rehearsed in my memory like videotape I choose to rewind over and over again? What have I done that causes me to walk in perpetual self-condemnation? What punishment have I inflicted upon myself instead of believing Jesus and receiving his forgiveness? If Pilate is a candidate for forgiveness, surely I am, too.

If I think I am beyond forgiveness, Jesus, then I minimize the power of your death. Thank you for your unfathomable love. Amen.

March 30

Putting My Neck on the Line

From then on, Pilate tried to set Jesus free, but the Jews kept shouting, "If you let this man go, you are no friend of Caesar."

JOHN 19:12

*I*f there is anything in me that will bend to please others, I am an easy prey for the enemy, who waits to sabotage my allegiance to Christ. He knows that with pressure I'll betray the Spirit who wishes to direct me down narrow paths, not highways of popularity.

Pilate knew Jesus' innocence. Pilate was commendable, declaring to the chief priests that he found no fault in him. He held fast through several rounds of debate. But as soon as the Jews intimated that Pilate would set himself up as Caesar's opponent if he freed Jesus, he crumbled under the weight. Caesar was his superior. Would Caesar try him as a traitor of Rome for freeing a man who claimed to be a king? He couldn't risk it.

Many times I have allowed the confident voices around me, who are more than happy to tell me what I should do, to drown out the whispers of the Spirit. I caved in to their pressure and forfeited blessing and peace.

I am learning that God's plans for me are unique. Conceived in God's heart, they cannot be second-guessed accurately by people. As God restores my sense of childlikeness, releasing my creativity, my place in the kingdom is unpredictable. God always paints with unexpected colors, and the world is wide-eyed at his revelation through you and through me. It's worth any risk to walk with Jesus.

God, I give you permission to release Jesus in my life. I want to live authentically. I will follow his voice and his plans, even if it means charting a course that surprises everyone who knows me. I seek your pleasure. Amen.

March 31

My Indignant Heart

"Here is your king," Pilate said to the Jews.
JOHN 19:14

*P*ilate tried everything to pacify the rage of the Jews. He presented Jesus to them beaten, wearing a crown of thorns and a pretend royal robe. In this context Pilate declared, "Here is your king." In other words, "This is the man who so threatens you? Does he look as if he would be dangerous to the government?" Yet their anger would not be assuaged. This was spiritual war, and nothing but the annihilation of Jesus would suffice.

Jesus is truth and truth is powerful. A few simple words from the Spirit of God can prick the conscience of the most hardened heart. Something deep within us that is adversarial to the person of God rises up to take offense at his words. We are threatened at the very core of who we are.

I understand the indignation of the Jews. I have been that resistant to change. Jesus brought a sword before he offered peace. My security in myself was cut in two. My sense of goodness was severed. His precepts sliced through my beliefs and I ended up seeing my own depravity. True spiritual power came through the doorway of spiritual poverty.

Why go through this arduous process? Ah, because peace with God is worth any sacrifice. When I no longer need to wear a crown and seat myself on the throne, I find that he is a much better King than I. No longer ultimately responsible for myself, I can live as a child in his kingdom, trusting him to rule righteously. The one who once threatened me can become the Lover of my soul. Capitulation is the beginning of joy.

I know the joy of submission to you, Lord Jesus. If there is any place in me that still fights you, show me. Amen.

April

April 1

Beyond Calvary

Carrying his own cross, he went out to the place of the Skull.

JOHN 19:17

The suffering of Jesus began before his crucifixion. He lived with the knowledge that death was coming. He always knew his purpose and functioned under the weight of it. That any laughter marked his life was a miracle! No wonder God is kind to us, not letting us know what tomorrow holds.

Jesus was made to carry his own cross through the streets. His shoulders, which were torn and bleeding from the scourging he'd just received, bore the weight of this heavy cross. Can I begin to imagine how painful every step was? No.

If we saw our dearest family member extracted from our home and beaten out on the street by a gang of thugs, we would be traumatized for a long time. Seeing one member take the wrath for our entire family would bring a mixture of reactions. Anger. Grief. And guilt that we were spared while our loved one suffered.

Is it any wonder that I haven't thought about Jesus' death too much? It's macabre material to begin with, and to know that he was innocent and did it willingly, just for me, makes me cringe. How do I properly receive such a costly gift? Not feeling worthy, I can shut down emotionally and just say my token thank-you during Communion. I miss out. As I foster an intimate relationship with Jesus, I no longer look at his crucifixion forensically. I am emotionally involved because I am connected to him. As each nuance of his death overwhelms me, I reach out to embrace it. It takes courage but there are two outcomes: humility and gratitude.

Jesus, I will enter into your pain. Help me fully receive the gift of your sacrifice. Amen.

April 2

A King from Nazareth? Really!

Pilate had a notice prepared and fastened to the cross.
It read: JESUS OF NAZARETH, THE KING OF THE JEWS.
JOHN 19:19

*I*t is said that Pilate designed the sign as a reproach. The hidden meaning was, "Can you imagine anyone from Nazareth claiming to be king?" Earlier in Jesus' ministry, when his humble beginnings were discussed, some had said, "Can any good thing come out of Nazareth?" The place of Jesus' upbringing had been a stumbling block to many in believing he could be the Messiah.

God will exalt whomever he chooses. None is disqualified for lack of breeding. God is found in unsuspected places. His face shines through unexpected vessels. After all, Jesus was born in a stable. Who thought to find God there?

I am convinced that I have looked too hard for God in places in which I assumed he would be showcased. The larger the church, the more of God you'll find, right? Not always. Christian entities might be well funded, utilize the latest marketing strategies, and offer everything from self-help groups to aerobics, but the system can be carnal. While size *can* be a sign of blessing, we must not forget to look for the face of God in Nazareth. He may be found behind a shabby storefront.

Finally, what if you are from Nazareth? You feel discounted. Your calling is not taken seriously. Your confidence is marred by your lack of credentials. Jesus died beneath a sign of reproach, but no one was laughing three days later when he rose from the dead. If God chose you to do great things, no birthplace and wrong last name can thwart the purposes of our sovereign King.

Jesus is my brother, from Nazareth. Use my life, God. I'll do my part.
I'm confident you will do yours. Amen.

April 3

Expectations and Anger

> Those who passed by hurled insults at him, shaking their heads and saying, "... Come down from the cross, if you are the Son of God!"
>
> MATTHEW 27:39–40

*T*he majority who saw Jesus crucified thought he was weak. If he had exerted his power by saving himself from the cross, they might have spoken of his strength. But we wouldn't have a Savior! His accusers' perception of what is weak and what is strong was entirely wrong. They were living life in the moment. They were not able to see that the power was in the cross, the thing that looked pathetic.

God has appeared feeble to me. Like those who hurled insults, I cried out, "If you are God, come down and change this." Yet the sources of pain that caused me to demand deliverance have become the very things through which the power of the cross has been showcased. Where I was weak, through Christ I am strong. Where my heart bled, through Christ my scars bear the handiwork of his grace and glory. The things I thought would destroy me have in essence saved me. All of them have been the doorways that brought me to the end of myself and to the beginning of new life.

We cannot live in the moment, daughter of promise. Things are not as they appear. We cannot judge whether or not God is powerful by looking at our present circumstances and setting up a criterion by which God must prove himself. We need only look back to see that he has already done that. We need only look ahead to see that he is a King who will rule throughout eternity. What could be more powerful than the cross and future glory?

Your plan for me is redemptive, Lord. I trust you with my life today. Amen.

April 4

Investing for the Future

About the ninth hour Jesus cried out in a loud voice,
"Eloi, Eloi, lama sabachthani?" — which means, "My God,
my God, why have you forsaken me?"

MATTHEW 27:46

At the pinnacle of Jesus' suffering Scripture came from his lips. He chose the very words David spoke in Psalm 22 when David expressed his own anguish. Jesus was tied to David just as we are joined with our spiritual ancestors. Their lessons of faith become ours. Their life experiences serve as part of our curriculum. Their heroic moments inspire us. Their stories of failure warn us, and their stories of despair comfort us when we've lost our way. Their voices resound with clarity for any of us committed enough to read their stories.

If Jesus quoted Scripture during his darkest hour, I see that it's possible for me to do the same. How embarrassing to realize that for many years everything but Scripture erupted from my tongue. My words were laced with fear, bitterness, and hopelessness. My spiritual well was dry.

I've learned the hard way that if the only time I turn to God's Word is when times get rough, I'm not preparing for inevitable time in the valley. I'm putting myself in a position where there'll be no reservoir of spiritual sustenance in the wilderness.

I'm finally immersing myself in the words of God. I missed the thrill of it for a decade or two. I was shortsighted, for I failed to see the cumulative effect of such a discipline over the course of years. Now that I've changed my ways, his words run through my heart like a gentle waterfall, bringing continual refreshment and wisdom. Living water is filling up my well. There is nourishment that enables my soul to prosper, no matter what.

Nothing is more critical than making your Word my own. Remind me of this, Father. Amen.

April 5

You're Still My Father

"My God, my God, why have you forsaken me?"
MATTHEW 27:46

*H*earts are broken every day. Parents are mocked by their child's behavior. Children are abandoned by their parents. Friends betray friends. If the wound is severe enough, there can be such a degree of severing that there is a disowning of the relationship. "You're no longer my friend!" "I disown you as my son!" Such statements reflect the depth of the hurt and a heart that has turned the other way. The well of mercy has dried up.

There was no darker moment in Jesus' life than when his Father turned his face away from his Son. Jesus took our sin upon himself, and since God cannot look on sin, he turned his back on his Son—momentarily. Jesus cried out with a loud voice, "My God, why have you forsaken me?" Though his body was weak, his voice was strong. Though his spirit despaired of his Father's posture, Jesus didn't give up on the father-son relationship.

Have you ever been tempted to walk away from God? Perhaps you concluded that much of the pain you were experiencing, he caused. While God gets blamed for things he never did, there are also times when he arranges a course of events that make no sense to us. In our distress we begin to wonder if he is a loving Father. Our feelings are in conflict with our theology. At that point we may feel like saying, "You're no longer my Father. I don't trust you anymore."

May I be like Jesus and never remove my small hand from my Father's providential grasp. While Jesus afforded himself the luxury of giving voice to his painful emotions, he never ceased to own God as his Father.

I don't always understand you. But you're Abba. I trust you. Amen.

April 6

What Will It Take?

When the centurion . . . saw the earthquake. . . , [he was] terrified, and exclaimed, "Surely he was the Son of God!"

MATTHEW 27:54

*B*ecause we can't see God, our relationship with him is built on faith. When faith is young, we are plagued with doubts. As you read this today, perhaps you fear that God has forgotten you. What would it take for you to believe?

For the Roman soldier who was guarding Jesus, it took an earthquake and other unnatural phenomena to shake him into a state of belief. The signs were enough that he exclaimed, "Okay, Jesus has to be God's Son!"

I've known seasons in my life, even though I was a Christian, when I was sure God had walked away from me for some reason. I no longer interested him. I couldn't see his hand nor hear his voice. It was as if someone had put a veil over Scripture and the power of it was hidden from my eyes.

The insidious nature of disbelief causes us to shut the door between us and heaven and stop asking for a revelation. This is the worst mistake we can make! God longs to be known and knows our tender and tenuous faith. And though his design for us is mature faith and trust so we never battle disbelief again, he recognizes the needs of infant faith. When he delivered his children out of Egypt, they were spiritual babies. God did it all for them. He swallowed up their enemies without requiring them to draw a sword. He even rained down food from heaven without having them plant a crop.

If your faith is small, what will it take for you to believe? Will you dare stretch out your hands and ask for it?

I can't find you, Lord. I need my own "earthquake." Penetrate my unbelief. Amen.

April 7

Cowards Become Heroes

> Joseph took the body, wrapped it in a clean linen
> cloth, and placed it in his own new tomb.
>
> MATTHEW 27:59–60

Nicodemus investigated the claims of Jesus by night so as not to incur the Sanhedrin's disapproval. Eventually he became a devoted disciple of Jesus, but it was not easy overcoming his fear of identification with him. When the Sanhedrin devised measures against Jesus, Nicodemus raised mild objection while still not owning that he himself was a believer. When the Sanhedrin ultimately decided to put Jesus to death, Nicodemus was quiet. It is said that he absented himself from that meeting!

Timidity was also a mark of Joseph of Arimathea, a friend of Nicodemus and fellow member of the Sanhedrin. After Jesus' death Nicodemus and Joseph surface, working in unity, strengthened by each other's company. It was customary that the bodies of those crucified be set out as garbage, or their family could purchase them for burial. In the absence of Jesus' family members, Joseph and Nicodemus appear before Pilate to beg Jesus' body. They confront their own cowardice. Originally they had come to Jesus by night. Now they come again, except this time faith is openly expressed. They prepare Jesus' body, wrap him in linens, and place him in the expensive tomb that Joseph had prepared for himself.

What is the personal cure for fear and timidity? John tells us: "Perfect love casts out fear." That must be what changed two cowards into brave men. Today no sermon or tongue-lashing will melt our cowardice, only a face-to-face encounter with the One who loves powerfully.

Jesus, I want to live out my love for you with abandon and declare my allegiance without reserve. Heal the coward in me with your love. Amen.

April 8

Intimate Access

At that moment the curtain of the temple was torn
in two from top to bottom. The earth shook.
MATTHEW 27:51

*A*t the moment Jesus died, the veil in the temple was torn in
two. This allowed intimate access to God. Before this event
God's children were prevented from entering the Most Holy Place in
the temple, the place where God's presence resided. People were
disqualified because of their sin. The high priest could go in, and then
only once a year after extensive ceremonial rituals. Only Jesus, the pure
Lamb who atoned for our sin, could tear the veil in two and bring the
rest of humanity into the presence of God.

Consider how the writer of Hebrews described this event:
"Therefore, brothers, since we have confidence to enter the Most Holy
Place by the blood of Jesus, by a new and living way opened for us
through the curtain, that is, his body, and since we have a great priest
over the house of God, let us draw near to God with a sincere heart in
full assurance of faith, having our hearts sprinkled to cleanse us from
a guilty conscience and having our bodies washed with pure water"
(Hebrews 10:19–22).

Jesus literally died to bring us to his Father. Jesus, who knew what
it was like to live in intimate relationship with him, considered it worth
any price to make this possible for us. He was willing to pay with his
own life to accomplish it.

Today there is no ceremonial law that prohibits me from having
access to Abba. I won't be struck dead if I dare to enter the place where
God lives. Jesus has opened the door. He bids me welcome and points
the way to God's arms, which are open to receive me with joy.

Without hesitation I'm coming, Abba. Amen.

April 9

Forced Exposure

When the soldiers crucified Jesus, they took his
clothes, . . . with the undergarment remaining.

JOHN 19:23

*T*heological truth is meant to engage the heart. I know that Jesus
was my high priest, having suffered as I suffer. But it is quite
another thing to consider that he, of all people, knows the specific
shame of nakedness. He suffered public humiliation through forced
exposure, and all this was just prior to facing the painful death of
crucifixion. Before nailing him to the cross, the soldiers took his
clothes, leaving only his undergarment.

Images come to mind of stolen innocence. Jewish mothers, fathers,
and children standing naked in large groups, about to enter the gas
chambers. Prisoners of war stripped and beaten, left shivering in a
stone cell. Young children abused in the presumed safety of their own
home, afraid of nighttime. I cringe at these scenes, knowing many who
have suffered the last. Yet I can celebrate Good Friday and handle the
suffering of Jesus so stoically.

I know the extent of what it means to be powerless against evil
(I lost my Pollyanna view of the world at the hand of it) and can come
to Jesus today with full confidence. I draw near, see his open embrace,
and hear him say beneath his breath, "I know." Two words have never
meant so much. He provides a safe place, for he understands
humiliation. He, the very person I need to run to, is often the last one
I seek. I live in hiding, with downcast eyes, overcome with shame,
failing to realize that he understands me perfectly. He is my "man of
sorrows, acquainted with grief."

*How you suffered, Jesus! You were powerful enough to stop it all, yet
you let people humiliate you so you could die and bring me home,
robed in white and fully healed. Amen.*

April 10

Not My Coat!

"Let's not tear it," they said to one another. "Let's decide by lot who will get it."

JOHN 19:24

*T*he soldiers took Jesus' clothes and ripped them into equal-sized pieces to take as souvenirs. Except for the coat, which they left in one piece. They decided which one would get that by casting lots.

It is said that the coat was one Jesus' mother made for him. Can you imagine the sentimental value? While Jesus amassed almost no worldly goods over the course of three decades, his coat was most likely his only possession. The soldiers even defiled that.

I have something that is precious and irreplaceable. A gold bangle bracelet that was my mother's. It's an antique, with beautiful scrollwork over the top half. Whenever I dress up, it is part of my outfit. I feel incomplete without it. It connects me to my mother, now in heaven, by the memory of it on her wrist. If someone were to desecrate it somehow, scratch it intentionally, or fail to see the value of it and toss it into the garbage, I can imagine my strong reaction.

Jesus' time on earth was about to end. Was it easy for him to part with his coat—and with his mother, who stood nearby? Did he hurt for her, knowing she had to watch him suffer? The agony he must have felt cannot be told in words. The taking of his coat, his possession from childhood, is certainly metaphorical. We who stand on the threshold of heaven open our hands to let go of everything here. Though this is difficult, nothing on earth can compare with the sentimental value of what awaits us.

Do you still think about your coat, Jesus? I wonder if you and your mother talk about that awful day? Like both of you, I consider my treasure to be in heaven. Amen.

April 11

My Child's Pain

Near the cross of Jesus stood his mother.

JOHN 19:25

I remember holding my children for the first time. I wrapped them up tightly in a receiving blanket and held them to my heart. This was significant. I wish I could always keep my children nestled at my side, tucked in safely, so nothing could ever harm them. But I am not God. Once outside of the womb, once severed from the umbilical cord, they started on a journey of independence.

Watching our children suffer is our greatest heartache. We would much rather bear their hurts than see them crushed by the grief of their world. The older they get, the less control we have in protecting them. When they were young, they cried over classmates who teased or a bully who ruled the bus. Now they suffer racial discrimination, abusive employers, and severe health problems for which there is no easy cure.

"Mary stood near the cross," Scripture says. So short a phrase but so vast the pain for Mary. A world of feelings exists in those few words. She did not cry out in agony or weep without hope. She stood nearby, true to the end. She watched her son being crucified but God was faithful. He gave her immeasurable amounts of grace.

We never know how much we can bear until the trial is upon us. Mary reminds us that we can count on divine grace to compensate for our weakness. God's unseen arms of support and his Spirit, which infuses our mind and heart with stamina and divine purpose, carry us through the darkest moments of our lives.

You see how my children suffer. I can't fix their world, Father. They are yours. Thank you for giving all of us the grace to finish our time here on earth. Amen.

Loving What He Loves

"Here is your mother." From that time on, this disciple took her into his home.

JOHN 19:27

John was the only disciple who appeared at the crucifixion site. He stood there with Mary, Jesus' mother. For whatever reasons, the other disciples stayed away. Perhaps what sidetracked them and prevented them from coming was fear of association, the grief of losing their friend, or disillusionment that their dreams for a king were dying with Jesus.

John, "the one Jesus loved," was nearby. His love for Jesus constrained him. Good thing, for Jesus needed the comfort of knowing that he could entrust the care of his mother to someone. Looking at his friend, he declared, "Here is your mother." In other words, "In my absence, treat my mother as your own." John did and started by taking Mary home with him.

Jesus is still looking for those to whom he can entrust his concerns and passions. Where are those who draw near to him regardless of personal cost and ask, "What do you love? Show me. I embrace your cause as my own!" Instead most of us are like the rest of the disciples, who never came close. I know, because for much of my life personal issues of fear and insecurity prevented me from being able to enjoy intimacy with Jesus. I was off nursing my wounds.

Healing from the inside out is critical. It enables me to get close enough to Jesus to hear his voice so I can love what he loves. I want to be like John, one to whom Jesus can say, "I want to tell you what's important to me. Will you embrace it as your own?"

I'm here, Jesus. I'm listening. Tell me what matters to you. Amen.

April 13

Vinegar or Water?

A jar of wine vinegar was there, so they soaked a
sponge in it . . . and lifted it to Jesus' lips.

JOHN 19:29

Oh, the cruelty of humankind! Would it have been so hard for the soldiers to give Jesus this one thing, in light of his extreme suffering? Was there no pity for a man who just carried a cross on his back a long distance and then lost massive amounts of blood? Certainly there was real water around. But even in this they mock him. "Here, want some water? Have some vinegar!"

Is your soul thirsty today? To whom will you go for water? Have you exposed your need to someone who desires to give you only vinegar? Perhaps they don't even know they offer a counterfeit. When you ask for compassion, your story is minimized and you receive a pep talk. When you express your fatigue, you get a sermon on making a lifestyle change. When you finally venture to ask for help, you're belittled because you can't seem to do it all. When you try to relate how you got your battle scars, people back away in disrespect. When you admit you're lonely, you're looked at like a loser.

I wish everyone were like Jesus. But cruelty, unfortunately, is found inside the church as well as out. It is often unintentional and ill-informed. "People perish for lack of knowledge."

Jesus said, "Come, I will give you rest" and "Come, if you are thirsty. If you drink the water I give, you will never thirst again." There are some wonderful people here and there who add water to my supply, but I come to the real source first. Jesus fills my cup to overflowing. I'll never find cruelty in the presence of the Holy One.

Let your living water wash over my soul, Jesus. Amen.

April 14

A Violent Death for a Saint

He bowed his head and gave up his spirit.

JOHN 19:30

All people must die. Whether we are Christians or nonbelievers, we have this fate in common. Jesus and the two thieves who hung on crosses to his left and his right were alike in some respects. All three suffered excruciating pain and all died in similar agony. Jesus' death was no easier than theirs.

A child of a dear friend of mine died this morning. Her last hours were terribly difficult. Should that be tormenting to her parents? Should they be angry with God because he didn't make her passing easier? After all, she was a child of his!

I know many Christians who hide the details of their loved one's death because they feel shame over the story. We have read and heard firsthand about the glorious endings of some saints. They died with a Bible in their hand, seeing a vision of what was to come. They passed with a barely discernible sigh, a smile on their face. While I don't doubt these accounts are true, I can tell you just as many stories of godly men and women who made the transition with great struggle, even facing a violent end. Did God love them less? Does living close to Jesus guarantee us a blissful transition?

Jesus' end was anything but peaceful. Death for him was, and is also for us, a curse. That will comfort my friend as she lives with the memory of her daughter's last moments. She and Mary, the mother of Jesus, have something in common. They both watched their child die. The nature of Jesus' death, and Mary's pain as she watched, should bring comfort to my friend.

Jesus, you know about the difficulty of death. Comfort us as we face life's final curse. Amen.

April 15

Nothing I Can Do

Jesus said, "It is finished." With that, he bowed his head and gave up his spirit.

JOHN 19:30

*E*ver climb a mountain? The first part is often easy as you walk miles along flat terrain until the ascent begins. The end usually requires supernatural effort as you push your muscles beyond their accustomed limits. Standing at the summit, you declare victoriously, "I did it!" There's exhilaration over what you've accomplished.

Jesus finished the redemptive work when he spoke the words, "It is finished." Heaven was exhilarated. God prepared for his Son's homecoming! There was nothing more to be done to accomplish our salvation. A spotless Lamb was needed to atone for sin, and Jesus was the only one qualified. Our efforts are nullified by our relationship to sinful Adam. His seed has corrupted our genetic makeup.

Yet I often treated Jesus' death as though it were insufficient, even though he stated otherwise. I worked zealously to make my contribution to the redemptive cause. I thought I could make it more complete. I declared some of my worst acts unforgivable and refused to believe Jesus when he said, "You're fully forgiven. Dance with joy!" Seeing myself as guilty, I labored feverishly to earn the rest of my salvation. I burned out for the cause of Christ, believing that he required it of me so my sin would be paid in full. What a tragedy, when radical forgiveness and complete restoration was mine to embrace.

You did it all, Jesus. You died so I wouldn't have to. Your blood was payment for all my sins. I can do nothing more for myself. I receive your gift with unspeakable joy and walk out of sin's prison as a free woman. Amen.

April 16

Unsuspected Heroes

> Joseph was a disciple, ... but secretly because he feared
> the Jews. . . . He was accompanied by Nicodemus, the
> man who earlier had visited Jesus at night.
>
> JOHN 19:38–39

*J*oseph and Nicodemus had two things in common: they both
loved Jesus, and their affection for him had been a secret until
Jesus' death. In the absence of Jesus' disciples, God raised up two
unlikely candidates to take care of the body of Christ. Nicodemus
brought the spices and Joseph provided the sepulcher. Two men who
worshiped Jesus in secret turned into the two who carried out one of
the most endearing roles in history. They took the dead body of our
Savior, washed it clean, and gave him a burial with honor.

If you know a timid Christian with anemic faith, don't give up on
him. At some unsuspected moment he may rise up to proclaim great
allegiance to Jesus. We often think that timidity will be worsened by
adversity, but pain is often the catalyst that sets people free from their
fears. God causes them to rise up with surprising courage.

Perhaps you are the timid one but are on the brink of being set
free. Christians have given up on you, so you might think that God has
also. Not so. He sees your faith, though barely a flame. While it was
nearly extinguished by the elements of your story, he protected it. The
Spirit of God cupped his hands around it and by his breath of mercy
it burns still.

As someone who used to be timid, and as someone others
considered frail and overly sensitive, let me tell you that the story is
never over when we decide to allow God to empower us.

*My heart is stirred by the hope that I can be different and do
something radical, Jesus. Amen.*

April 17

Single-Minded Mary

Early on the first day of the week, while it was still
dark, Mary of Magdala went to the tomb.

JOHN 20:1

*I*t's not easy to write about Mary Magdalene. There is much about
her to understand. She is deep and I really want to try to capture
on paper what she's like. She deserves that.

Many agree that Mary Magdalene was the prostitute who, to the
disciple's disdain, poured expensive oil over Jesus' feet, wept, and then
wiped his feet with her hair. When his religious companions were
appalled, Jesus said, "She loves much because she has been forgiven
much!" How true his words proved to be.

Mary's commitment to Jesus never wavered, no matter how grue-
some the scene, no matter how broken her dreams, no matter to what
degree she physically suffered. She was there at Jesus' crucifixion and
stayed till the end. She was there when Joseph of Arimathea took Jesus
off the cross and when he placed Jesus in the tomb. Now, as soon as
the Sabbath is over, the very earliest it's appropriate for her to visit his
grave, she does. She comes though it's still dark. Her love for Jesus
supersedes sleep and other distractions. She has a one-track mind
and heart.

I feel a connection with her. She found mercy when she deserved
none. She found forgiveness when others would have had her stoned.
She expressed exquisite love when those who claimed to love Jesus
found her display distasteful. But look at who is true to the end! The
tears that washed Jesus' feet are now poised to fall again at his gravesite.

*My heart is yours, Jesus. I wake thinking of you in the night. You are
first on my mind in the morning. Make me even more single-
minded. Amen.*

The Unlikely Disciple

Peter and the other disciple started for the tomb.
JOHN 20:3

*H*ave you ever let someone down? Perhaps you broke a promise, even a marriage vow, and you still struggle with guilt. The more severe the sin, the longer it takes for the relationship to experience stability. It's difficult to look the one we offended in the eye. Glances are fleeting. The sense of shame we feel can be overwhelming, and we feel unworthy of forgiveness.

In light of those realities, I'm shocked that it was Peter who ran with John to the tomb to investigate the missing body of Jesus. Wouldn't another disciple have been a better choice? After all, just days earlier Peter had stood in Caiphas's garden and denied three times that he knew Jesus. Hadn't Peter disqualified himself from leadership? Apparently not. John, the one for whom Jesus had a special affinity, let Peter accompany him.

Perhaps we have strayed too far from our spiritual predecessors. It doesn't appear that the disciples ever lost touch with their humanity. None of them would have had trouble admitting that Jesus picked the least likely of men to enter his mentoring program. Greed, pride, and other signs of spiritual immaturity were rampant among them. Gross sin still exists in our ranks. It exists in me. But perhaps we've romanticized biblical figures. As a result, we feel inadequate to fill their shoes, and we are forced to hide behind pretended piety.

I applaud Peter. When Mary told him that Jesus' body was missing, he took off to investigate rather than hide. He didn't abandon his faith. He knew Jesus. He had seen firsthand the power of repentance and forgiveness. He leads any of us who hide in shame to reenter the race after our season of tears has ended.

Jesus, you forgive seventy times seven. Thank you. Amen.

April 19

Hearing but Not Understanding

They still did not understand from Scripture that
Jesus had to rise from the dead.

JOHN 20:9

*H*earing has never been a problem for me. Understanding has. For
example, as a child, I heard that Jesus loved me, but I did not
understand the ramifications of that until midlife. I heard that Jesus
was powerful enough to perform miracles, leaving his spectators openmouthed, yet I didn't understand that he might perform one for me.
These truths weren't mine. I didn't claim them as "my messages."

I have since concluded that a person's greatest need is to take the
truth and make it theirs personally. We know too much. We experience
too little. We are saturated with information, while our hearts shrivel
from lack of application.

Jesus told his disciples repeatedly that he would die and three days
later rise again. Yet when Peter and John found the empty grave, they
were stunned. Why? Hadn't they been told? John relates the reason:
"They did not understand." They had heard the words but had failed
to internalize them into their experience.

What keeps our faith purely intellectual? Maybe we're afraid to
believe good news. That we're valuable to God. That we're lovable.
That fairy-tale love really does exist. That we matter. That we're created
to house the glory of God. What if we're wrong? Won't the despair be
overwhelming?

I ask you to step on the path behind me. I ventured out five years
ago on this journey of the heart. I dared to believe God and make his
messages mine. I am alive and free. I am resilient and strong. His truth
is for me and it's for you. Will you join me?

Help me carve a pathway from my head to my heart, Jesus. Amen.

Looking Where You Last Found It

As she wept, she bent over to look into the tomb.

JOHN 20:11

*J*esus was last seen in the tomb, so when Mary discovers that Jesus' body is missing, she begins her search there.

Losing someone can be frightening. Some years ago, my husband and I took our two children and Scott, the six-year-old son of some close friends, to a large amusement park for the day. I stopped to order drinks for all of us and dropped Scott's hand to pay for our refreshments. When I turned to hand him his soda, he had vanished. For the next thirty minutes, there was sheer panic. Scott had wandered to the other side of the park and had asked for help from someone in uniform. We eventually recovered him in the lost and found area, eating ice cream. But my point is this: The park employees suggested we begin our search around the area where he first disappeared.

This principle extends beyond what we can see. What are you missing? Perhaps it's the ability to trust. Where did you lose it? Go back to where you first learned to distrust. What happened? How did your beliefs about life change?

Oftentimes we get stuck in relational ruts and think we're doomed to live in emotional exile. Our distrust, our cynicism, our inability to receive or give love, keeps our hearts from thriving. God wants to heal us and he can with our cooperation. He wants to lead each of us on a search-and-rescue expedition.

We weren't born distrustful. We lost trust when life's experiences seemed to prove it invalid. As God helps us pinpoint on our individual timelines the events that caused us to lose trust, he holds us while we grieve, and then he slowly begins to realign our belief system. We can be whole people. We can be free of childhood vows of distrust that, though they protected us for a time, are no longer expedient or necessary with God as our Father. He designed us to live as much loved children in his kingdom. Where growth was stunted, limbs can heal and bear fruit.

Mary's weeping led to searching. May my tears be proactive, Lord. Amen.

April 21

By Faith, Not by Sight

At this, she turned around and saw Jesus standing
there, but she did not realize that it was Jesus.

JOHN 20:14

Nothing short of seeing Jesus would make Mary stop crying.
Two angels appeared earlier, and though she experienced a
conversation with heavenly beings, her weeping continued. She had a
one-track mind, and it was focused on Jesus' absence. She grieved that
he was not where she expected him to be. Yet he was there; she simply
didn't recognize him.

Mary had a crisis of faith, as I do when I'm tossed by the storms
of life. The roaring sound of the waves drowns out Jesus' whispers. The
fog and the mist obscure my sight of him. I think he's missing yet he
stands near. I weep for his absence though he has his arms securely
around me. I accuse him of abandoning me, when he has already
moved heaven and earth to give me intimate access to him.

King David reassured me of this. "The LORD is close to the
brokenhearted," he said (Psalm 34:18). I may rest in this certainty. If
I seek Jesus, he is near. My relationship with him is driven by faith,
not by sight.

Mary would have been comforted if she had recovered the dead
body of Jesus, but Jesus gave her more than what she asked for. He
appeared alive, not dead. We who seek heaven's treasures always find
riches beyond our wildest imagination. God gives us more than we
could have dreamed of. He is generous, extravagant, and delights in
giving lavish gifts. If we weep at our tomb of loss today, let's hang on.
Jesus is with us, and our sorrow will soon be turned to indescribable joy.

*Lord, I trust that you're here. You will reveal yourself, in your time,
by your mercy and loving-kindness. Amen.*

April 22

The Best Good News of All

Mary Magdalene went to the disciples with the news:
"I have seen the Lord!"

JOHN 20:18

I consider some of the best news I could receive in my lifetime: "Congratulations! You got the job." "Your child is this year's valedictorian." "Your father's cancer is in remission." "Your biopsy came back and it's benign." "You'll be getting a substantial tax refund this year." Any of these announcements would cause me to celebrate. However, they would only affect my life here on earth, which is only a brief moment on the eternal timeline.

The best news I could hear today is this: "Jesus rose from the dead, Christine!" Ah, my present and my future will be written differently because of this!

Mary knew the power of such news. She went to Jesus' tomb to grieve. She had watched him, the one she loved like no one else, suffer and die. He had seemed powerless, this one who had claimed to be King, had performed miracles, and had forgiven her of her sins. She was confused. Her tears most likely reflected broken dreams as she remembered the withered Jesus on the cross. She never expected to hear him say her name again. So imagine her reaction when he appeared and said, "Mary." Rarely has such pain turned to ecstasy so quickly.

Jesus' power to emerge from the grave changed everything for Mary. It changes everything for me. It redefines my whole existence. Whatever seems hopeless no longer entraps me. The One who holds resurrection power calls me from death to life. He has rolled the stone away from whatever entombs me. I need only the courage to rise up, walk out, and live my life in the light of such powerful love.

I hear you calling my name, Jesus. Amen.

April 23

Locked Doors

When the disciples were together, with the doors
locked for fear of the Jews, Jesus came and stood
among them and said, "Peace be with you!"

JOHN 20:19

The disciples are hopeless. They had grown to love Jesus. He said
he was King, but they watched as he was arrested, condemned to
death, and then crucified. The disciples had never faced a more desperate moment. Now they meet to comfort one another in their cor-
porate loss. To add to the grief they are experiencing over their Lord's
death, they also fear for their lives. They meet in secret. The doors are
locked. Anxiety and tension have peaked. Jesus enters the room that is,
to all others, off-limits. There is no obstacle that prevents him from
appearing. He is God.

I understand the disciples well in this passage. I know what it is
like to be locked away in fear. When life took one bad turn after
another, I retreated into a silent world and shut most everyone else
out. Not because I wanted to be antisocial but because the pain
rendered me speechless. The story was too long to tell, the need for
healing too desperate, and the ability to interact through everyday
chitchat was out of reach. I became an emotional recluse and felt that
I was destined to live the rest of my days in isolation. I didn't know
how to connect with God.

Are you hiding today? Is your heart sealed away in a tomb of
disillusionment or fear? Perhaps you're keeping your entire world on
the other side of the door, but you fear that even God cannot reach
you. He can! In your hidden place he calls your name and says, "I'm
here. Peace be with you."

I'm looking for you, Jesus. I need you. Amen.

April 24

The Breath of God

He breathed on them and said, "Receive the Holy Spirit."
JOHN 20:22

I wonder what this scene looked like as the resurrected Jesus breathed on his friends and said, "Receive the Holy Spirit." Wouldn't you like to see a reenactment of this event? I would. The disciples, who had been drunk with the vapors of fear and grief, became wonderfully intoxicated with the Spirit. Their fear met peace. Their grief kissed hope. Their earthbound perspective embraced God's eternal kingdom.

The spirit of others also breathes on us. What kind of impact do they have? Do they leave a residue of anger as they air their many complaints? Do they stir up anxiety as they openly obsess about their future? I feel the effects of others' spiritual halitosis all the time, don't you? I moan under my breath when I see certain people coming toward me, because I'm well aware of the outcome. It takes spiritual intensive care to recover from the worst cases.

But I have also felt the breath of the Holy Spirit on my face when a total stranger told me of their life-changing encounter with Abba. Their eyes danced, the story lived, and their words were born in me.

What a gift Jesus gave his friends. He offered them himself. That's all. He didn't move them to a secure location, post angels at the door for their protection, or even promise them deliverance from the political dangers they would face in the future. When I pray, I often focus on solutions that will offer relief from the cares which burden me. I ask for things, when the very best thing I can pray is:

Breathe on me, Breath of God. My soul will be well because you are enough. Amen.

April 25

Dealing with a Doubter

[Thomas] said to them, "Unless I see the nail marks
in his hands and put my finger where the nails were,
and put my hand into his side, I will not believe it."

JOHN 20:25

*D*oubt is a part of our rational thinking process. It occurs when there appears to be sufficient evidence to disprove what we have regarded as true. Unresolved doubt breeds fear and insecurity. Given enough doubt, there can be torment.

How other believers handle us when we are in that place is critical. If we are scolded, we take our thoughts and feelings underground. Many Christians work through their tortuous thoughts in isolation. It takes longer for them to arrive at a place of peace and resolution without the love and encouragement of spiritual siblings. Some are never able to work through it alone!

Jude, the half brother of Jesus, grew up in the presence of divinity, yet it took years for him to understand that Jesus was God's Son. In his short letter he writes, "Be merciful to those who doubt" (Jude 1:22). Jude knew that it was possible to live with Truth yet doubt his very nature and origin. He also knew, perhaps firsthand, that believers can be brutal with those who wrestle with their faith. Jude and Thomas were not Judas, after all.

If you are in a place of doubt today, Jesus reaches out to you with mercy, not condemnation. You are not seen as a traitor. Just as he eventually appeared to Thomas and revealed the wounds in his hands and feet to dispel Thomas's torment, he is accessible to you. What do you need to hear? Ask for it. Your doubt can give way to joyful security.

Show me who you are, Jesus. I feel doubtful but I'm committed to trusting you. Amen.

April 26

If Only I Had Believed Sooner

Thomas said to him, "My Lord and my God!"

JOHN 20:28

*T*homas came to be known as "Doubting Thomas." An unfair label, really. He only doubted for eight days. Once Jesus appeared and encouraged him to touch the scars where the nails had penetrated his hands just ten days earlier, Thomas believed. He didn't mutter under his breath, "Hmm, it really *is* you, I guess. Okay, you *are* alive." He passionately exclaimed with ownership, "My Lord and my God!" Thomas was convinced. There was no going back to a doubtful stance. He saw. He believed. Nothing would be the same again.

When the truth of Jesus is obscured, we cannot conceive that we will ever be sure of him. Our doubts are firmly entrenched. Their shadows infiltrate our entire belief system. We are shocked when God finally unlocks spiritual mysteries and everything becomes so clear. Suddenly we wonder why we couldn't see it before. It was so simple all along. There's no desire to turn back. Our entire being resonates with new truth.

My joy of finding that God was real, personal, and loving toward me is still sometimes tainted by my regret over the wasted years I spent in spiritual blindness. With an aching heart I have cried out, "If only someone had shown me these things sooner. If only I could live my life over with the faith I have now." Yet as soon as the feelings are expressed, I understand that it was the pain and emptiness that drove me relentlessly to the arms of God. The years were anything but wasted. Wisdom is birthed in the desert. Living water springs from a parched landscape.

I can't go back, Lord, so don't waste a moment of the pain. Turn those years into nuggets of wisdom and understanding. Amen.

April 27

Partial Revelation Requires Faith

Jesus did many other miraculous signs in the presence
of his disciples, which are not recorded in this book.
JOHN 20:30

Why weren't all of Jesus' words and miracles recorded for me
to read? I'm more than curious about what I've missed. I
want to know it all and not miss one revelation. Oh, I can't wait to
someday hear the rest of the story.

I have to believe that God revealed just enough of his Son's life to
give me sufficient evidence regarding Jesus' divinity. I need no more to
convince me. Faith starts where evidence stops.

If the Bible had been conceived and written by people, most likely
it would have consisted of volumes rather than one book. People are
prone to tell all they know so others are convinced of their credibility.
They'd rather tell too much than not enough.

God need not do that. He inspired people to write his Word with
just enough information to convince those of us who are teachable.
He does not scramble to tell it all, for he is God and he writes with
confidence and security. He does not overstate his case with some
pathetic need to be right.

On a personal level I ache for more revelation. I wish God would
shed more light on my life. I feel there are too many situations in
which I have to walk by faith. I take heart. Though faith is an
uncomfortable exercise, it's not a misplaced one. Just as I choose to
trust that God inspired the right amount of Scripture to be written, I
choose to believe that he sheds enough light on my path for today. He
knows the way ahead, I don't.

*I can be confident and secure with you writing my future, Abba.
You reveal what I need as I need it. Amen.*

April 28

Empty-Handed

He called out to them, "Friends, haven't you any fish?"

"No," they answered.

JOHN 21:5

*T*he disciples, those closest to Jesus, went back to work after Jesus' death and resurrection. Perhaps they wondered what to do next, and it seemed natural to return to the trade they knew—fishing.

John tells a story of a day when they caught nothing. Their nets were limp. Their industry was temporarily unprofitable. Jesus appeared, commented on their lack of success, and told them where to drop their nets. When they followed his direction, the result was miraculous. Could it be that God allowed empty nets to prepare them for the joy of Jesus' provision?

I am encouraged. Many voices of our time promise that success will always be mine if I am God's child and I am willing to work hard. They assure me that God guarantees consistent, profitable results. "If you are in need," they say, "something is critically wrong." If I listen to their rhetoric, I will feel shamed. I'll conclude that poverty is a curse or punishment and that somehow I deserve the bleak outcome. Yet I must remember that Peter and the others experienced this dry spell in their business. When Jesus arrived, he wasn't appalled. He didn't scold them for a lack of faith. He took that opportunity to change deprivation to abundant supply—though I'm sure they would encounter a few days of empty nets in the future.

How big is your bank account? Is business booming? Ministry thriving? Does everything you put your hand to prosper? If not, you're in good company. We join hands with the saints of old who allowed God to deepen their faith through the changing seasons of their lives.

Your favor rests on me, Lord, whether or not I see prosperity. Amen.

April 29

Seeing What Others Miss

The disciple whom Jesus loved said to Peter, "It is the Lord!"

JOHN 21:7

After the Resurrection, Jesus appeared to his disciples but they failed to recognize him. Only John knew who it was. "It is the Lord!" John said to Peter. The one whom Jesus loved dearly was the one who recognized him first. John's love had always been radical. He had been known to lay his head against the shoulder of his Lord. The familiarity paid off.

As we invest in a personal relationship with God, intent to know him apart from intellectual study, there is a payoff. We will hear his voice, feel his presence, and see his fingerprints when others are yet blind to him. This sensitivity to the person of God increases as we become closer and closer heart mates of his.

Last weekend a woman asked, "I think God may have spoken to me, but I'm not sure. How do I know if it was really him?" I asked her to tell me what she thought she had heard. As soon as she related the message, I knew immediately that it was her heavenly Father who had spoken. The words were true to his character. The message brought peace to her soul. It encouraged her to trust him more and unwrap the gift of his great love for her. How could this not be of God? Yet she was a new Christian and simply not sure.

John, beloved of Jesus, had always valued time with his friend. Their relationship was one in which even the silences were comfortable. There was an intuitive knowing of each other that only intimacy can foster.

The more of God I know, the more of God I see. I have no greater desire than to know you, Lord. Amen.

April 30

No Need for Shyness

As soon as Simon Peter heard him say, "It is the Lord,"
he wrapped his outer garment around him ... and
jumped into the water.

JOHN 21:7

*P*eter was the most impetuous of all the disciples. He had a big
heart, expressed himself with passion, and was not afraid to act
impulsively. Once John told Peter that Jesus was on shore waiting,
Peter threw himself into the sea to get there first. This fits Peter's
personality profile. Yet I am amazed by his boldness. After all, it was
only a short while ago that he betrayed Jesus.

How did Peter know that the relationship was intact? How could
he be so sure that Jesus would be pleased to see him? Peter had never
read the New Testament passages on the nature of God's forgiveness.
The New Testament hadn't been written yet. He was flying by the seat
of his pants. He had no theological degree. He just knew Jesus. That
was all. That was enough.

Being forgiven with full restoration is a rare thing in this world. So
rare that we don't expect it. If we betray someone severely enough, we
never dare hope to gain their full trust again. We hang back, afraid to
approach with any sense of confidence the one we wronged. We're
constantly reading their facial expressions and body language to see
where we stand.

When Jesus declared us forgiven, he put our sins behind his back.
He will never bring them out again to accuse us. He won't remind us
of what we've done. We can approach him as Peter did. Whether we
throw ourselves into the sea or run across the threshold into his
embrace, we can be assured of a passionate and happy reunion.

*I always know where I stand with you, Lord. Thank you for such
extravagant forgiveness. Amen.*

May

May 1

Momentary Provision

Jesus said to them, "Come and have breakfast."

JOHN 21:12

*J*esus never ceases to surprise me. As soon as I think I have him pictured in my mind as divine rabbi, public teacher, compassionate minister, defender of truth, he appears in a new way. Today he is a culinary host.

Jesus is making breakfast for his disciples. They are famished after a night of fishing. Were it not for his guidance as to where they should drop their nets, they would have no food at all. It has been a long night. They are cold, wet, and weary. Can you imagine how wonderful it is for them to not only see Jesus alive and well but also smell the aroma of fish cooking over an open fire? His care for them is tender and practical.

The resurrected Jesus is still alive today. I know that in my head, but my heart is still surprised when he shows up and offers me a spiritual meal. This morning he called my name: "Christine, breakfast is ready." He prepared the right amount of nourishment for this day. As soon as I caught the aroma of his meal, then closed my eyes to inhale deeply, I found I was ravenous. Everything he created appealed to my senses.

Though today's banquet was more than satisfying, I have to admit that I will be hungry again tomorrow. Living here takes its toll. I'm easily depleted, needing daily infusions of wisdom, love, and grace. I can't generate what I need on my own. There's no need to panic, though. Jesus will still be tending the fire. I can smell the fragrance of his provision.

There is no friend like you, Jesus. You have anticipated my needs. You have already provided. I just need to sit down and eat. Amen.

May 2

Perfect Timing for a Tough Question

When they had finished eating, Jesus said to Simon
Peter, "Simon..., do you truly love me more than these?"
JOHN 21:15

I used to be afraid to spend time with God. I feared what he'd say
to me. I was convinced he was waiting to give many lectures about
the ways I had messed up my life. While I knew that he loved me on
some level, I was sure I wouldn't experience any of it until he got stuff
he held against me off his chest. I incorrectly assumed it would take
quite some time before he said his piece, felt better, and then turned
his tender side toward me. How wrong I was. Misunderstanding him
kept me away from the benefits of his love for decades.

Don't get me wrong. The Spirit of God may have a tough question
or two for me, but he asks them at the right time.

Jesus asked Peter three times if he loved him. The question seemed
so easy to answer at first, but like all spiritual truth, it was layered with
life-changing ramifications. Jesus posed it to Peter at the perfect time.
He had shown him where to fish to make his business profitable. He
had welcomed Peter to breakfast after a long night's work. His love and
tender care preceded talk. Jesus built a framework for new truth on
the foundations of love and security.

Like Peter, we are prodigals. Repentance unlocks the door for us
to go home. The Father's embrace awaits. We will be lavished with
love, bathed in mercy, and immersed in forgiveness. Within the
atmosphere of spiritual rest and restoration, God shows us how to live,
replacing our precarious thinking with his truth, setting us up to soar.

*I'll never be afraid to come home. Hold me, Lord, and then talk to
me. Amen.*

May 3

Prerequisite for Ministry

Jesus said to Simon Peter, "Simon son of John, do you truly love me more than these?"

"Yes, Lord," he said, "you know that I love you."

Jesus said, "Feed my lambs."

JOHN 21:15

*J*esus asks Peter this important question not once but three times consecutively: "Do you love me? Good. Feed my lambs." Jesus is so concerned about the welfare of his flock that he is very choosy about who he puts in charge of them. Only a sincere love for him will equip Peter to feed hungry lambs.

Jesus did not say, "Are you concerned about people? Feed my lambs." "Would you like a rewarding occupation? Feed my lambs." "Would you like to be appreciated and respected? Feed my lambs."

Feeding lambs is a difficult calling. Ask any pastor. Some lambs are hungry and want to be fed. Others want the food of their own choosing. They think they know what they need, not understanding that what tickles their tongues brings self-centeredness and instability. A small minority comes to evaluate the fare in order to make trouble. Only a love for Jesus will give shepherds the endurance and joy they need for the long haul. If they serve for any other reason, burnout and disillusionment are inevitable.

For far too many years I gave out spiritual food while my own spirit was shriveled from lack of nourishment. I had tried to feast on Christian education, but it was like eating sawdust after a while. It was dry and tasteless. Interesting facts failed to sustain my heart when hard times came. When I finally connected to the heart of my Father, I found the feast I had been looking for. Love constrains me to feed his daughters.

Keep my faith from becoming intellectual, Lord. Keep me connected to you so I can feed your lambs. Amen.

May 4

Only a Snapshot

Jesus did many other things as well. If every one of
them were written down, I suppose that even the
whole world would not have room for the books that
would be written.

JOHN 21:25

*G*od inspired people to write Scripture in such a way that we are
given only a snapshot of Jesus' life. The Bible paints a clear
though incomplete picture of who he is. John, the disciple, admits that
his account of Jesus' life is a partial revelation. He tells us that the
amount he shared is minuscule compared with what he could
have written.

We've been given only highlights. We have enough evidence to
bring us to saving faith and enough revelation to feed our souls for a
lifetime, but I wonder what I am missing. Who else did Jesus heal?
What else made him angry? Were there children he rocked to sleep?
What other debates did he engage in? What creative, tender gifts did
he give to those he loved?

Not only that, but John fails to tell us the endings to other
stories. How was Mary, the mother of Jesus, after the death of her Son?
She went to live with John but did her heart recover? What happened
to the Roman soldier who took part in the Crucifixion but said upon
Jesus' death, "Surely this was the Son of God!" Was he stripped of his
military position? Did he lose his life because of his identification with
Jesus?

We ache for a complete revelation. This will be one of the many
reasons we'll enjoy heaven. Nothing will be hidden from our eyes.
Stories will abound. We'll finally understand every spiritual mystery.

*My spiritual hunger is okay, Jesus. I long to be with you in heaven.
For now don't let me miss anything of you that can be mine in this
world. Amen.*

May 5

Arrogance

To fear the LORD is to hate evil; I hate pride and
arrogance, evil behavior and perverse speech.

PROVERBS 8:13

I'm confronted with the cobweb of arrogance most every day. I deal
with people who just can't admit they're wrong and who will go to
any length to defend themselves. They have an appetite for arguing.
They thrive on proving others wrong. When others capitulate out of
sheer exhaustion, they strut their stuff, presuming victory.

I know wives who pray for changes in their mates, but their
husbands aren't open to hearing about growth and change. Some men
even suggest that to disagree with them is to be unsubmissive according
to Scripture. Unity of opinion is not the same as submission.

Anyone, at any age, can exhibit arrogance. A small child can be
arrogant. Even while being disciplined, he can plead his innocence.
Parents, while sinning against a child, can be arrogant. They are in
essence convincing an impressionable young mind that grown-ups are
never wrong. It takes a lifetime to untangle the web.

The seed of arrogance is planted in each of us. We succumb to it
when we put ourselves on a pedestal to avoid being seen as we see ourselves. Perhaps we decided long ago to believe those who called us
worthless and unlovable. We perceive the power we derive from being
"right" as an attractive solution to our self-hatred.

Jesus can deliver us. He can touch our soul, make us whole
through the power of his love, and teach us that true spiritual power
begins by entering the doorway marked "spiritual poverty." We are
healed not with arrogant words but by the hushed embrace of a
perfect Father.

*Oh, Lord, I find my value by being the object of your love, not by
successfully wielding power and control. Amen.*

May 6

Empowerment of a Mission

The LORD will fulfill his purpose for me.

PSALM 138:8

When God chose to birth Daughters of Promise through me, I was sure he picked the wrong birth mother. He gave me a mission that exposed my sense of inadequacy. I was forced to admit that I was shortsighted. I knew I lacked the wisdom that the calling required.

I felt like Moses, who, after God gave him his orders, reminded God that he was not eloquent. He felt that this one fact alone disqualified him. In response God asked him one simple question: "Who made your mouth? I will be with you and teach you what you are to say." When Moses' objections ceased and it was evident that he would obey, I wonder if God sat on the edge of his seat, anxious for the show to begin. He knew what Moses would accomplish with heaven's power behind his efforts. God had already planned the future and written the last chapter of Moses' life.

I am continually comforted by the truth that God is not wringing his hands in despair over any of the things that rob me of peace. Why should I worry, then, since my life is in his hands? God's wisdom has already conceived a solution to everything that troubles or perplexes me today.

It is I who watch the parade of my life and see only what passes in front of me. From this vantage point it's easy to despair. God looks down, though, and views the beginning and the end of the procession. He not only knows tomorrow's challenges but also has already made provision for the answers. He is a King who rules with kindness.

My inadequacy is irrelevant. You will fulfill your purposes. I rest in anticipation of your provision, God. Amen.

May 7

The Power of Anointed Hands

Whatever you do, whether in word or deed, do it all
in the name of the Lord Jesus.

COLOSSIANS 3:17

I believe each of us knows intuitively about the anointing power of
God. Have you ever sat in a church service and listened to a
sermon or a song and not been moved? Chances are, apart from it
being a day when you were numbed to life, the anointing was missing.

Thankfully, our experience also includes the opposite. A simple
gesture, word of encouragement, or song sung with meaning and
passion can move us. We usually know when we have been part of an
anointed moment.

Anointing is a gift available to each of us. It's letting God have
complete control of our talents and spiritual gifts. It's asking him to
come and show how they are to be used. It's amazing that almost anything can be useful when God's power is behind it. Serving someone
a cup of tea in Jesus' name with a sincere prayer for his blessing, for
example, can become a spiritual act with eternal ramifications.

I remember a couple who lived nearby when I was first married.
They were retired missionaries, in the twilight years of their life, who
touched those God sent to them. They extended themselves on behalf
of God by offering love, prayer, and tea. Such simple gestures, but
powerful because God's anointing was present.

What is in your hand today? It might be love for children, or a
gift for making others feel welcome at your kitchen table. You might
be intuitive and know when to offer someone a simple hug. Let God
empower your gifts, for through them Jesus brings others to himself.

*Everything I have is yours, Lord. Use me in ways today that I
cannot even fathom. Amen.*

May 8

I Appreciate You

Your love has given me great joy and encouragement.
PHILEMON 1:7

*A*dvocating is tricky business. Often we find ourselves in a position to make appeals on behalf of others because there has been abuse, neglect, or wrongdoing. Our words are cries for the offending persons to seriously consider taking corrective measures. The book of Philemon subtly outlines the best way to motivate another to perform righteously.

Before he advocates for his friend Onesimus, Paul spends four verses telling Philemon why he loves and appreciates him: "I pray you would know God's gracious Spirit. . . . I am so thankful for you. . . . I hope you become more effective, because your gifting is strong. . . . I find deep joy and comfort in knowing you love me."

These kinds of statements are hard to make when we're frustrated. For someone to hear our words, however, they must be framed in the context of acceptance. "I have something difficult to say, but before I get to that, please let me tell you why I appreciate you so much!"

Perhaps your response is, "But the person I'm appealing to isn't a pastor like Philemon. In fact, I couldn't honestly say any of the things Paul said!" We may have to search long and hard for an accepting word to give such people, even looking back to help them recall their more godly selves. "You know what I appreciate about you? I remember when . . ."

This passage reminds us that the spirit of a human being is a fragile thing, easily wounded, and too quickly broken under the weight of criticism.

I need your wisdom and your gracious heart, God. Help me know how to confront evil behavior in a way that motivates others to change. Amen.

May 9

An Order or Request?

Although in Christ I could be bold and order you to
do what you ought to do, yet I appeal to you on the
basis of love.

PHILEMON I:8–9

*R*emember the last time you were pressured to do something? You
did what was asked of you but probably accomplished it without much enthusiasm. You might have even resented it.

Having learned in childhood that it was undesirable to say no, I
became the queen of performance. In twenty-plus years of ministry, I
was victim to the requests and demands of pastors, conference
coordinators, and record company executives who were all quite
willing to tell me how to live. Not aware of the validity of free choice,
I always complied, if possible. My face was unreadable as I carried out
the tasks, many of them ones for which I was not equipped. I privately
groaned until they were completed. I burned out when I turned forty.
Today I'm still learning to hear God's instructions apart from the
appeals of people.

Paul asks Philemon to take back a slave who has stolen from him.
The slave, a convert now, wishes to restore the relationship. Paul,
Philemon's pastor, has the authority to issue an order. He doesn't,
though. Paul knows that any action taken grudgingly will not bear the
sweet spiritual fruit of God's heart.

This models God's posture toward us, doesn't it? He has a longing
for us to be in vibrant relationship with him. He doesn't lack the power
to coerce us to comply! Yet he knows that we will enjoy him and the
benefit of our godly choices if we are allowed to choose freely.

*Show me the balance, Lord, between calling others to do the right
thing and giving them the freedom of choice. Remind me to bathe
these confrontations in prayer. Amen.*

May 10

Taking Up the Command to Advocate

I appeal to you on the basis of love.

PHILEMON 1:9

*S*hort and sweet" and "Less is more," the sayings go. Why is it that I often remember a short quote over a forty-five-minute sermon? Why did God put a tiny book like Philemon in the Bible? Might it have something significant to say to us, though it's not a heavyweight book like Hebrews or Isaiah?

Philemon has one chapter, composed of twenty-five verses. It is about Paul's advocacy for Onesimus, Philemon's former slave. Onesimus had stolen from his former master, run away, and now wanted to return to Philemon's household since becoming a Christian. Paul was successful.

Advocacy is a wonderful thing. I recall standing in lunch line in the third grade. A bully had his hands around my throat, choking me. I was not fighting back and was turning blue. My sister, three years older, happened to be walking down the hall. She decked the kid! Oh, her gift of intervention was wonderful.

Our society should not lack for advocates, because God calls every child of his to be one. He judged the nation of Israel because they neglected to represent the poor, intervene for the widows and abused, and protect and nurture the feeble in faith.

Who is the ultimate advocate? Jesus. When we were yet in Satan's family, we were hopelessly full of sin and forever separated from God, with no hope of connecting. But God sent someone fully qualified to intervene on our behalf. Look at the outcome. Jesus gave his life that we might be freed.

Lord, I am often too fearful to stick my neck out for others who need my help. Give me courage to help those who are too weak to help themselves. Amen.

May 11

Giving Undeserved Grace

Confident of your obedience, I write to you.
PHILEMON 1:21

*H*ave you ever received a compliment you knew you didn't deserve? A compliment that, though it seemed ludicrous, motivated you to live out your best?

This happened to me recently. A pastor turned to me in conversation and said, "When I'm in your presence, I sense such spiritual maturity." I wanted to laugh. It wasn't so many years ago that I burned out completely. I was disillusioned with God but asked him nonetheless to rebuild my life out of ashes. I still feel like such a hungry child. I take in his Word every morning for strength, knowing that if I miss my time with him, I will not live that day very well.

Paul ends his letter to Philemon by delivering a gracious comment that was perhaps undeserved. As he asks Philemon to take back into his household a slave who was once a thief, he ends his request by saying, "I have confidence you'll do the right thing."

Did he really think Philemon would? We'll never know, but this "gift of grace" might have been the very thing that moved Philemon to do what Paul was asking.

Today we have the opportunity to attribute to others character traits they have not yet earned. It's difficult to do, especially when we ache for justice. Will the one you're appealing to perform righteously? I don't know. Each person is free to choose and we can't always predict the outcome. However, God's principles are life-giving, and when we incorporate them into the structure of our interpersonal relationships, we set up the best-case scenario for success.

Help me see others through your eyes, Father. Just as you clothe us in grace rather than condemnation, may I gift another with a compliment he'll desire to live up to. Amen.

Abba, Father

You did not receive a spirit that makes you a slave
again to fear, but you received the Spirit of sonship.
And by him we cry, *"Abba,* Father."

ROMANS 8:15

*M*ost of the time we don't hear the approaching storm that will
eventually beat against our door. It takes us by surprise. The
winds howl. Deafened by it, we think there is no refuge. But there is.
Our Father is calling us home to rest, regroup, and restore.

> I can hear You calling gently, "Come and rest here
>   in My arms.
> Though the storms rage all around your head;
>   your soul is safe from earthly harm."
> I embrace your invitation. I've no need to walk
>   alone.
> My spirit knows Your Spirit's call.
> I'm coming home.
> It's not hard to recognize You; Your voice, sweet
>   to my ears,
> Calls me to a place so long ago, long before this
>   world of tears.
> Your arms were strong to hold me from before the
>   dawn of time.
> I've always known that You are my home.
> So I'm coming home.
> I say, "Abba, Father, renew me."
> I call, "Abba, Father, restore me."
> I cry, "Abba, Daddy, release me
> To live in Your Truth and walk in Your Light."[1]

*Thank you, Jesus, for making it possible to cry out to our Father and
call him Abba. I need a Daddy and I'll cherish him always. Amen.*

---

[1]Written by Christine Wyrtzen. Copyright © 1998 Eloise's Music Box.

May 13

Facing the Hurt

Though you have made me see troubles, many and bitter, you will restore my life again; from the depths of the earth you will again bring me up.

PSALM 71:20

While I live in a world where painful and confusing events occur, they need not cripple me. In God I have everything I need to face my grief and emerge with a teachable and tender spirit. It is possible for me to live resiliently.

However, unexpressed grief becomes a poison that hurts me. Driven inward, it cripples me emotionally and can manifest itself later in physical illness. It takes courage to face the extent of my losses and look grief in the eye. God knows the depth of my pain and will never turn away when I cry to him for help. If I pretend that I don't hurt as deeply as I do, I sabotage my own healing.

It's much easier, at least initially, to stuff the tears and postpone feeling the painful emotions. I can trick myself into thinking that the pain is manageable. "Look, everyone comes up against hard times. Everybody on the planet faces the death of a loved one. I can survive it, too."

I can also be tempted to excuse others' offenses against me by assuming that their behavior was somehow my fault. If I've been the family scapegoat, I'm used to taking blame. It feels normal.

God is truth and because I'm in a relationship with him, he asks me to live truthfully. If I trust him, I can dare to explore the truth of my own story, the good and the bad. The God of truth is my healer and refuge.

Hold me, Abba. This foreign land is full of minefields. I need you to help me face my injuries. Amen.

May 14

Weeds

"The worries of this life, the deceitfulness of wealth
and the desires for other things come in and choke
the word, making it unfruitful."

MARK 4:19

*O*nce desperate, I was driven to fill my soul with anything that
made me feel better. Every morning I wondered what I could do
to make the ache go away. The list of things that gave some measure
of relief was impressive:

Praise. For those of us who had it in sparse amounts growing up,
we never quite get enough as adults. However, it is still intoxicating.

Materialism. Accumulating treasures gives us notoriety. We stand
a little taller dressed in our finery. Others envy us and that feels good.

People. New relationships are exhilarating. We thrill to become
someone's soul mate. But oh, the emotional plunge downward when
they fail us! Never will we know such despair.

Attention. A crisis keeps us on center stage. We become addicted
to the highs and lows of a melodrama. We fear we "need to be in need"
or others will expect too much from us. Our identity is built on
appearing fragile.

Satan is cunning, and if what he offers didn't temporarily feel good,
we wouldn't settle for his counterfeits. Jesus warns that these are the
weeds that choke the seed of God's Word and keep it from growing.

Weeds make us double-minded. We can't grow a healthy plant and
a hearty weed in one space. They oppose each other. If I try to embrace
that I am God's cherished daughter but at the same time am not
willing to stop looking to others to make me feel loved, the seed of
God's love has no place to grow.

*Tragically, when I haven't given it the right soil to grow in, I've
concluded that your love isn't enough. Help me weed, Jesus. Amen.*

Gratitude-Driven Love

"He who has been forgiven little loves little."

LUKE 7:47

*E*ver feel washed up, as if you've made too many mistakes? Perhaps you are in mourning over wasted years. You believe that God only uses perfect people, and your past disqualifies you from any future blessing.

We often misjudge God. We project our own humanness onto his face. After all, we only give people so many chances. We have our limits. "If he does that one more time, I'm through!" we declare. We perceive that the heart of God is like ours. If I fail too many times, God is through with me! If I get my act together too late in life, it's just too late for me. If I commit too grave a sin, God disqualifies me.

Scripture showcases the relentless mercy of God. The Messiah, our Lord Jesus Christ, was born from the line of Abraham, Isaac, and Jacob. The four eldest sons of Jacob fell under great sin. Reuben and Judah committed incest. Simeon and Levi were murderers, yet they were patriarchs, and from Levi descended all the priests. The bottom-line issue with God is repentance. Because he has a heart that longs for intimacy, when we sincerely repent there is restoration.

God can use you in his kingdom, with all the scars, war stories, and places of shame. In fact, the more deeply you have been wounded, the more mercy you will show others. You can make a great imprint of grace in the kingdom. Bow your head and dare to receive the lavish mercy of our Father, the one who asks you to put your past behind you.

I have repented of my sin, Father. Give me the courage to look in your eyes and see the forgiveness that is mine. You hold nothing against me. Amen.

Soil Preparation

"A farmer went out to sow his seed. . . . Some fell on rock, and when it came up, the plants withered because they had no moisture."

LUKE 8:5–6

Ron and I planted rosebushes last weekend. They're beautiful. In fact, a vase of cut flowers sits nearby on a table. Their aroma is divine.

Planting them was easy; preparing the soil was backbreaking. Seeing everything at the nursery can be deceiving. What's the big deal? You buy some bushes, dig some holes, put them in, and throw some dirt over the roots. Voilà, they will bloom profusely, right? This naiveté yields a month of flowers at best. The bushes probably won't bloom for one full growing season, much less survive years. When they hit the soil, they'll begin to discolor and fade.

Still bearing sore muscles from digging, I woke up this morning thinking about today's Scripture. Working with the earth made me reflect on Jesus' words about seeds, roots, and bearing fruit.

If Scripture is powerful and transforming, why do we not see more life-change in others and ourselves? How can a believer study God's Word over a lifetime and remain emotionally crippled? How is it that a brilliant theologian can live void of a warm heart? How is it possible that a leader can pray every day for strength but have little?

And why do I often know so much but experience powerlessness? "Poor soil preparation," Jesus said this morning. Nothing can grow unless it is given a chance to mature in the right environment. God's Word planted in poor soil cannot develop a good root system. The enemy steals the seed of God's Word in broad daylight, right under my nose. I must plant his Word deeply enough that as it grows, it chokes out beliefs that are contrary to truth.

Examine my beliefs and expose bad roots, Father. Amen.

May 17

The Value of Roots

"Those on the rock are the ones who receive the word with joy when they hear it, but they have no root. They believe for a while, but in the time of testing they fall away."

LUKE 8:13

*R*oots are ugly compared with what grows above ground. Yet they get the job done. Try to uproot an old bush and you'll encounter just how stubborn roots can be, though. Ron and I worked last week to remove an old shrub to make way for new rosebushes. The shrub was not big yet we had to go deep to get to the bottom of its root system. It was backbreaking work. Both of us had to pull and yank to extract it from the ground. I suppose we could have cut the shrub off at ground level and planted roses around it. After we added mulch, it would have looked fine. But beneath the soil there would have been a war going on, one set of roots battling for domination of the other.

For decades I knew spiritual truth but I lived in conflict. My faith was sincere but my emotional life betrayed the very things I said I believed. Why? Conflicting root systems. I hadn't done the internal work necessary to make room for God's roots. When the storms came, my spiritual plant was endangered. Weak root systems yield weak plants. What are the root systems that need to be dismantled so God's growth can flourish? Lies that oppose his truth.

If you are discontented by the incongruities that rage internally, engage in the process. The end result will be stability, unshakable trust, and an emotional life that is consistent with being the much loved daughter of God.

Jesus, you came to give me abundant life. I'm going after it! Amen.

May 18

Embracing Tears

My soul thirsts for God, for the living God. When
can I go and meet with God?

PSALM 42:2

*G*etting close to Jesus teaches me that weakness is to be owned
and embraced. It is not something about which I should
be embarrassed. After all, I am not omnipotent. Only he is more
powerful than this world and the evil in it.

Many great men and women of God have paved the way for me
to embrace my needs. King David salted the pages of the Psalms with
his tears. No wonder I visit his writings so frequently. When I'm
hurting, I am drawn to David's poetry. I know that he has expressed
the things I often find difficult to verbalize for myself.

The apostle Paul, one whom I picture as a type A personality, said
that he "gloried in his weakness" because it caused him to discover the
power of Christ. And Peter shows me that tears are a proper response
to remorse. When he betrayed Jesus, Scripture says, he went out and
wept bitterly. Finally, I remember that Jesus wept on many occasions.
He expressed tears of grief at the tomb of his friend Lazarus. He cried
over a city because he felt sorry for the people who lived there. And
on the worst night of his life, he cried out to his Father with loud cries
and tears. His friends were nearby and heard him wail.

Many of the people in our world desire to dry tears too quickly.
Tears are often perceived as a sign of weakness rather than strength. I
choose to believe my Father, who says that "those who sow in tears will
reap with joy."

*If you cried, Jesus, I can too. Thank you for giving me permission.
Amen.*

A New Look at Faithfulness

Righteous are you, O LORD, and your laws are right.
The statutes you have laid down are righteous; they
are fully trustworthy.

PSALM 119:137–38

God has quite a reputation here. His hallmark—past, present, and future—is faithfulness.

Each of us has a reputation we've built over time. What do others say of us? "Her work is done in haste." "She's a perfectionist." "She takes the easy way out. Don't ask for her help!" However we choose to live leaves a legacy of remembrance. That is sobering, causing some of us to make different choices today.

God's legacy? "His work is done with faithfulness."

We are deeply moved by thoughts of faithful friends, a faithful husband of fifty years, even a faithful dog. How many times have I cried over a tender dog story? David says all God's work is motivated by faithfulness. He is incapable of ever letting us down. He can't forget us nor momentarily turn away. He is never sorry that he chose us to be his bride, and is never, ever tempted to stop loving us, despite our unfaithful love.

I find his faithfulness truly inspiring and humbling. If I am cold, his love stays warm. If I am apathetic, his passion never flickers. If I lapse into years of spiritual adultery with other gods, his voice beckons me home.

God's every word and loving act rests in his love and fidelity. This brings me such joy and inspires faith in him regardless of barriers that keep me from intimate love and unwavering obedience. With his help I'm dismantling them one by one.

Teach me to relax with you, heavenly Father, because your love for me is faithful. I want to turn my face toward yours with faithful love. Amen.

May 20

Which Harvest?

"The harvest is plentiful, but the workers are few."
LUKE 10:2

*M*any missionary conferences have been conducted under this banner. Surely there *is* a harvest and the workers *are* few. Jesus always speaks truth. But truth has many layers.

My concern is that churches pressure the ill-equipped to go to the front lines. Often missionaries are shamed into action. They hear the call for workers, and either guilt or an emotional plea prompts them to go to the altar. Many missionaries wipe out as a result because they didn't take the time to know themselves and their vulnerabilities before volunteering for service. Their habits and obsessions still lay buried deep within. Simply put, they did not grow up under God's parental care before leaving to live life on the edge.

The harvest must begin within! There are multitudes of internal thoughts and feelings to be held up against the truth of Scripture. There are dead branches to be pruned. There are roots that need the nourishing rains of God's Spirit.

Maturity is not gained overnight. Just as an adolescent spends years trying out his wings under careful supervision, so our faith needs time to mature under the watchful care of Abba. May we not volunteer for too much, too soon.

Those who embark in internal harvesting are few. May we not be fainthearted. Instead let's be diligent to allow God to transform us before he uses us to transform the world. We cannot give away what we do not first possess.

Father, there are things inside that need your touch. Reform me. I trust you with childlike trust, but don't let my service be childish. Mature me to feast on the meat of your Word. Amen.

May 21

Choosing the Right Mental Pathway

> Whatever is true, whatever is noble, whatever is right,
> whatever is pure, whatever is lovely, whatever is
> admirable—if anything is excellent or praiseworthy—
> think about such things.
>
> PHILIPPIANS 4:8

This passage of Scripture is misrepresented. It is used to shut down transparency before God and foster denial. It is often the scapegoat that prevents us from facing what is really true, which violates the very first command. We've been told that it implies this: "Don't embrace sad thoughts or acknowledge angry feelings. Think happy thoughts instead. Shut out anything negative or unpleasant for Jesus' sake, for he expects a positive attitude."

Is that what Paul, the author, is advocating? It can't be, for it contradicts God's primary agenda, that we deal with the state of our heart rather than just modify our behavior. God judged the children of Israel harshly because they served him with their lips but their hearts were far from him.

Above all else, God desires authenticity. We must allow his Spirit to bring the truthful things of our heart into the light of his presence. Whatever is painful needs his touch. Whatever is crippling needs a cast that will enable us to eventually walk limp-free.

When is the proper time for us to think of our Father, who is true, noble, pure, lovely, and admirable? After we have faced the truth within ourselves! For after we have confronted the darkness, we face a pivotal juncture. We will be tempted to travel down despairing pathways that lead to the pit of nothingness. God is offering us, through this divine prescription, another route. "Don't take the mental pathway that leads to futility. Think of me, for this road leads you to my presence."

Help me know my own heart, Father, but then may I think of you. Amen.

May 22

Violin Strings

God is faithful; he will not let you be tempted beyond
what you can bear.

1 CORINTHIANS 10:13

*O*ftentimes we fear we're going to break under the strains of life.
We feel like a piece of elastic after it has been stretched to the
limit. There's no more give. We're sure the next sound we hear will be
a snap as the elastic breaks. I've often asked my Father, "Do you see
where I am?"

Since I am a musician, he once gave me the picture of a master
violinist playing his instrument. With passion he performed
masterfully. His soul was expressed with his bow on the strings. I was
overwhelmed with the beauty of the phrases he played at a whisper as
well as the intense passages he delivered, pulling on the bow, straining
the strings to make them sing as they were created to do. He knew
how powerfully he could lean into them without breaking them. The
harder his bow pulled, the more powerfully the music communicated.

We are the instruments upon which the Master Musician desires
to play his original compositions. Our spirit, meant to be limp under
his control, can fully succumb to the Master's bow. At times he'll play
softly, at pianissimo, and the music heard is gentle and reserved. But
when he wants to display his power and glory, he delivers the dissonant
passages with the intensity they require. The resolution is all the more
satisfying after the tension of the plot. Will we break under his care?
Not with the Master in control of the bow.

*Make me a Stradivarius violin, an irreplaceable instrument upon
which you delight to play, Lord. I'll make my spirit pliable enough
to allow you to play with freedom. Amen.*

Pursuing the Intangible

Though you have not seen him, you love him; and even
though you do not see him now, you believe in him.
1 PETER 1:8

*D*aily I'm tempted to choose the easy way out. It's easier to pursue what I can see, feel, and experience now rather than choose someone who is invisible, someone whose reality and kingdom must be taken by faith. After all, my body is mortal and my senses are limited. I can't see the spiritual world around me, so I would often rather embrace what I can see rather than trust what I can't.

I realize again, even while writing this, that though exercising my spirit takes discipline and intentional hard work, the rewards are tangible. Peter reminds me that I will be blessed if I cultivate a spiritual life based on the person of Jesus, whom I cannot see!

Exercising my spirit by living according to kingdom principles is like exercising an atrophied muscle group, initially. But the more I exercise it, the stronger it becomes. At the beginning the exercise is painful and awkward, and I wonder if it's worth it. But slowly, over time, deep changes occur.

For the reality is that my spirit is already sitting with Jesus in heaven. My mind and emotions are playing catch-up. Today is just beginning and I'm faced with the same choices you are. Will I choose to live by the spiritual realities that nurture my spirit or according to worldly principles that only make me feel good temporarily?

Father, it would be so much easier to embrace your ways if we could talk face-to-face. My choices would be clearer. You know that, so give me the grace to love you through my decisions, though I can't see you. Amen.

May 24

No Longer Overlooked

Your right hand sustains me; you stoop down to make me great.

PSALM 18:35

*F*ailing to be noticed by someone who you thought cared can leave scars. I've experienced what is feels like to be overlooked. I've been excluded from private jokes. People who I thought knew me well forgot my name. On another occasion, when I reached out for a hug or a handshake, I realized the person didn't even recognize me. I ended up feeling pretty insignificant.

If the governor of Georgia asked me to dinner, I'd be surprised and flattered. If the president and first lady of the United States invited me to be their overnight guest, it would become the memory of a lifetime. Yet the God of heaven and earth has extended the invitation to me to become his intimate friend. He has removed all barriers that prevented free access to him. There are no guards at the door announcing he has far better things to do than meet with me.

I will experience profound joy today because I know that God notices me. I am not just one of his many creations. He calls me his very own "Christine" and picks me out from the crowd. He knows the state of my heart and the nature of my thoughts at any given moment in time. He stoops down to connect with me and alters my day every time.

This gentle affection changes my life. I can't stop talking about it. My fear of rejection is healed. The difficulties of yesterday are put into perspective because God touches me today. I have a future because he is planning it, even as I write.

I accept your favor with joy, Father. Though I know I don't deserve it, your love is healing me. Amen.

May 25

The God with a Green Thumb

The righteous will flourish like a palm tree, they will grow like a cedar of Lebanon; planted in the house of the LORD, they will flourish in the courts of our God.

PSALM 92:12–13

*I*t's summertime, the season for working outside. Planting, mulching, weeding, and feeding shrubs become part of my routine. As I worked in the yard this morning, I remembered this verse. It came to mind because I was heartsick that I'm losing a prized gardenia bush. I have tried in vain to keep it alive but failed. Admittedly, the soil, as well as my care perhaps, is not conducive for growing healthy gardenias.

Everything thrives and blooms when planted in God's garden. Can you imagine how green, how fragrant, heaven is? I close my eyes and envision the blooms from his greenhouse. Rare orchids abound. Gardenias, which can be so finicky here, are lush and fragrant.

God is never stumped over a particular plant. There's no guesswork. He doesn't have to wonder if it is acid-loving or not. He knows because he made the plant.

He's as intuitive with human beings as he is with plants. What is it like for us to be planted in the courts of our Lord? Regardless of our age, we are given a new beginning. We are nurtured in his presence, destined to yield fruit, even though people tell us we've used up all of our second chances. It's never too late for us in God's garden. Even at midlife and beyond, we are poised on the mere brink of eternity. The best of life is ahead if we are being nourished and fed by the living waters of the Holy Spirit.

You never give up on me, Father. I can't help but thrive with you as my Gardener. Amen.

May 26

Confusing Saying of Jesus

"If anyone comes to me and does not hate his father and
mother, his wife and children, his brothers and sisters—
yes, even his own life—he cannot be my disciple."

LUKE 14:26

Jesus' comment can be very confusing. He told us throughout the
Gospels to love our neighbors, friends, and family as ourselves.
Then, out of the blue, he said that if we don't hate our family, we
couldn't be his disciples. Doesn't that seem contradictory?

Family traits, both visible and invisible, are passed down from
generation to generation. We say, "I have my mother's eyes. I have
Uncle Charlie's chin. I inherited my father's Irish temper." The
generational legacies, holy and unholy, have a way of defining us,
unless there is great commitment on our part to be defined by
something or someone else.

When we are adopted into God's family, we become his
daughters, yet we spend a lifetime becoming daughters (pertaining to
how we see ourselves). We learn to look to him as the one who defines
and leads us. We replace our intuitive modeling of our earthly parents
with an intentional commitment to model our new Father. Unless we
leave our family in this regard, we are not true disciples. Jesus'
comment about hatred is intended to make us identify, and hate, the
carnal inheritances of our family. He's asking us to be daughters of his
new order.

Just as parents pencil in marks on a doorway to measure the
growth of their child, so God measures our growth as he compares us
with his Son. It doesn't matter how tall we are. All that counts is our
good-faith effort and our sincere intention to be his devoted daughter.

*I am your daughter, Lord. I want to be more like you than like
anyone else. Amen.*

Perfect Empathy

In all their distress he too was distressed.

ISAIAH 63:9

We seldom recall those who laugh with us, but those who cry with us are remembered tenderly. Friends who respond emotionally to the pain in our eyes give us permission to hurt and then heal.

Most of the time this isn't our experience. Consider with me others' less-than-ideal reactions:

- We receive a look that says, "You're upset about that? What's the matter with you?" The result? Shame is added to our pain. We might never dare speak about it again for fear of another rejection.

- We hear, "You poor thing!" and receive a patronizing pat on the shoulder. The result? Isolation. There might be validation for the pain but there's no offer to enter into it emotionally.

- We experience an awkward silence and the subject is changed. The result? We feel we are out of order and our pain is unacceptable. We feel pressure to get it together!

- The other person stays analytical, manufacturing a platform from which to preach to us. The result? Our story is cheapened by a lack of emotional response, and we sense we are considered fixable with a tidbit of advice.

Jesus wept when Mary expressed the pain of her brother's death. Jesus was the consummate friend! He didn't quote verses. He didn't say, "I know you're upset, Mary, but I'm going to perform a miracle. Dry your tears!" He didn't pat her on the shoulder or wag his head in pity. He didn't tell her that her tears were out of line. Scripture says that when he heard her weeping, he groaned! This merciful man showed us how to weep with others. Jesus embalmed the memory of his friend Lazarus with his tears.

Jesus, you are not afraid of my emotions, nor do you condemn them. As I weep at the tomb of my losses, your tears blend with mine. Amen.

May 28

The Need for Self-Disclosure

Surely you desire truth in the inner parts; you teach
me wisdom in the inmost place.

PSALM 51:6

God is truth. There is no error in his thinking, no lapse in
his judgment. His truth is the basis for his wisdom. His precepts
are pure, and a life structured according to them brings fulfillment
and peace.

David knew the heart of God. He knew that God valued truth,
and therefore David purposed to know truth. David was also in touch
with his own divided being. He realized he was capable of saying one
thing while in his heart believing something entirely different.

Wisdom rarely exists in every corner of the soul. To protect ourselves from pain, we play pretend. We choose to believe that things are
better than they are, so we can avoid the ache of this imperfect world.
But God wants us to face the truth, good and bad, because the truth
will set us free.

Spiritual maturity involves knowing the truth about ourselves,
knowing the truth about God, and letting the truth about God impact
the truth about us! This enables God to accomplish his ongoing
redemptive work in the world. Lies are exchanged for truth. Hidden
wounds are laid open, treated, and healed. Distorted perspectives are
realigned. Confusion yields to clarity. Apathy turns into longing, and
longing can then be satisfied in the embrace of our Creator.

Self-disclosure is successful only when the process is placed in the
hands of the Great Physician. He who created our minds longs to
restore us to perfection. We are promised the mind of Christ, but such
an end is possible only as God makes truth available to us.

*My passion is to know you, Lord. You are the truth, so shine your
light in every part of my mind and heart. Amen.*

May 29

Learning from Children

"I tell you the truth, unless you change and become like little children, you will never enter the kingdom of heaven."

MATTHEW 18:3

*J*esus' statement is loaded with implications! It must have been shocking for the educated, religious crowd to hear that they must come to heaven by way of a child's heart. Jesus told them that they couldn't assimilate spiritual principles thoroughly unless they processed them with a childlike spirit.

Throughout the ages, God refers to his creation as children. However, as a result of living in a fallen world, we've ceased trusting, dreaming, and playing as children. We've chosen to live behind pretenses and defenses. God invites us to enjoy him as our Father. We can be spontaneous, impulsively honest, and playful. We can admit our limits and be bold to ask for help.

Being childlike also means we believe what our Father tells us. If you told a child God was about to divide the Atlantic Ocean as he did the Red Sea, the kid would be the first one with his toe in the water!

Can you imagine what life would be like if we allowed God to recover our childlikeness? We would look at the world with an undivided heart, speak the truth in love, and stand by our convictions with no apologies or hesitations. We would admit when we needed help and ask for prayer without apology. Without a doubt we would shake up the patterns of isolation experienced in church. We would be fully alive, free to hurt and free to celebrate.

Show me where I lost my childlike spirit. Whatever that event, walk me through it again so I may take your hand, Lord. You are my perfect Father. I can enjoy being a child in your kingdom. Amen.

May 30

Comforting Whispers

He will cover you with his feathers, and under his
wings you will find refuge.

PSALM 91:4

Some of our spiritual ancestors were inspired to write portions of
Scripture that revealed God as their shelter, a place where they
could hide. Were they telling us the secret to living triumphantly and
securely? I believe so. They were showing us how to avoid being blown
apart by the winds of change and adversity.

If these men and women of God were here with us today, they
would want us to know that these metaphors are more than just words
on paper. They wrote them not because these words possessed a poetic
flair but because they chronicled their experiences.

When I think of someone powerful providing refuge, I think of a
father holding a small child in his arms. If his little one were in
danger, he might whisper words like these to drown out the cacoph-
ony of noises: "You'll be all right. I'm keeping you safe. Shhh, we'll get
through this. I'll be with you."

The longer we live, the more aware we become of dangers and
temptations that could cause us to shipwreck and fracture
emotionally. Today we can begin nurturing our internal world, where
we can know and feel that we are wrapped securely in our Father's arms.

Let's allow his Spirit to repeat the words he spoke so often in
Scripture. May that be the audiotape that plays while the cruelties of
life attempt to undo us. God may not cover our eyes to the trouble, but
he will whisper in our ears, "I'll be with you. We'll get through this. I
can mend your broken heart. . . ."

*Father, may I hear you above the storm and feel you amid the chaos
of pain. Amen.*

May 31

Proactive Empathy

Cast all your anxiety on him because he cares for you.
1 PETER 5:7

*E*mpathy is a valuable gift. We often feel the lack of it. How heartbreaking it is to ask for help and have our cries fall on deaf ears. Our distress may be evident, our tears plentiful, the damage visible, but there is no caring response. Many times we restate our case, try again on another day, and fall in disbelief when we are not heard. There are few things more despairing. We just cannot believe the other person is unmoved. It's unthinkable!

In the presence of Jesus empathy is plentiful. He sees every scratch, wipes every tear, and cares about every detail of our story. He will never turn a deaf ear toward us, no matter how many times we ask for his attention. In fact, his empathy motivated him to spend thirty-three years on this earth with us. He walked in our shoes, felt our pain, and struggled with temptations similar to ours.

If Calvary had been God's only agenda, Jesus could have come to earth as an adult on Good Friday, died, rose again three days later, and then gone back to heaven. But his extended stay on earth gave us time to know him. His heart for us was revealed. His expressed love gained credibility by the investment of his life.

Whatever we need today, he hears and he cares. Do not shy from him or from the magnitude of your weakness. Be bold to ask for what you need. And know that in your pain, his tears blend with yours.

Isaiah described you prophetically as a "man of sorrows." While I ache to know that you had to experience the pain of this world, Jesus, today it is comforting. Meet me where I need you. Amen.

June

June 1

Strong and Courageous

"No one will be able to stand up against you all the days of your life. As I was with Moses, so I will be with you; I will never leave you nor forsake you."

JOSHUA 1:5

God gave Joshua the monumental task of taking the children of Israel into the Promised Land. Moses, his mentor, was dead. He was on his own and was feeling intimidated about his calling. God spoke to him, and his words resound through the ages to reach our ears today.

Do you doubt yourself? Have you been given an assignment for which you have no confidence? Are you in a marriage that seems impossible to navigate? Are you raising children who are simply not receptive to what you're trying to teach? Are you in a job that seems God-sized, not woman-sized, and giving it your best doesn't seem to be working?

God's words to Joshua are for you. "Moses my servant is dead; now therefore arise. Just as I have been with Moses, I will be with you. I will not fail you nor forsake you. Be strong and courageous. Don't tremble or be dismayed, for the Lord your God is with you wherever you go."

Don't disqualify his words by saying, "This is for Joshua, not me!" The God of Joshua is ours today! The God of Moses is by your side, saying, "I will never, never, never leave you or forsake you" (did you know that in the Greek, *never* is repeated three times?).

So stand up tall. Take a deep breath. Just as Moses and Joshua looked to God for moment-by-moment direction, so must we. This is the time for courage and faith.

I am anxious, Lord. You are not. I am limited. You are powerful. You will help me do the work you called me to do. Amen.

June 2

The Swollen Jordan

Joshua told the people, "Consecrate yourselves, for tomorrow the LORD will do amazing things among you."

JOSHUA 3:5

*M*en and women of faith have walked this road before us. They want to tell us that we are never trapped if God is on our side, for he is never out of options.

The children of Israel, with Joshua as their leader, faced the Jordan River. It was all that stood between them and Canaan, but it seemed impossible to cross. It might as well have been the Red Sea. God spoke to Joshua about this and told him to tell the people, "Consecrate yourselves, for tomorrow the LORD will do wonders among you." They listened, repented of sin, and then refocused their attention on the power and glory of God. They made sure they were poised to receive the miracle God had planned for them.

I don't know what your "Jordan River" is today. It could be a fragile emotional state, a difficult relationship with a long history of dysfunction, or a child so rebellious that it seems there is simply a heart of stone. When we see no options, in essence we stand at the mouth of a swollen Jordan River. There is no way across. God delights in the impossible. It is his opportunity to show us that he is our God, our ark of the covenant, and he has already gone before us into the water.

So put on your best clothes, so to speak. Rise from your bed of disbelief. Your tenacity and your faith chart the course that will provide God's intervention.

I am never trapped as long as you are my Father. Every obstacle is an opportunity for faith. I turn from my fear and await your next move. Amen.

June 3

Doom or Deliverance?

As soon as the priests who carry the ark of the
LORD — the Lord of all the earth — set foot in the Jor-
dan, its waters flowing downstream will be cut off.
JOSHUA 3:13

Oftentimes I'm not able to appreciate a miracle, because I don't
understand the history behind it. Such is the case with the
miracle of the Israelites crossing the Jordan.

I'm sheepish to admit that I always pictured a dried-up riverbed to
begin with. Not much was required of God to drain it completely so
his people could walk across it. A little history reveals that at the time
the Israelites confronted the river, the Jordan was at its highest. The
waters were raging because the snow of the mountains of Lebanon had
melted, run down, and emptied into the Jordan. It was the beginning
of spring and the river was simply impassable.

Is it a mistake that God led them there at that particular time?
They might have thought so. And so do we when God opens a door,
we walk through, and we come face-to-face with an obstacle so big
that it seems we're trapped. We cry out, "God, where are you? Why
would you lead me to certain doom!"

Yet from God's perspective nothing is too difficult for him to
manipulate. If he's going to perform a miracle, why not get the most
mileage out of it? Smiling, he plans to do it when the obstacle is the
most menacing.

His people were told to prepare themselves for a miracle. The
priests carried the ark into the river first, and when their feet touched
water, instantly the river parted and the bottom of the riverbed was dry.

*Help. I'm poised on the edge of raging waters. Make a way, Lord.
Amen.*

June 4

Meaningful Memorial

These stones are to be a memorial to the people of
Israel forever.

JOSHUA 4:7

*T*he children of Israel are safely on the other side of the Jordan
River. They doubted they would ever make it. Their crossing was
a miracle, for the river was swollen and raging. It seemed impassable.
Yet women, children, and cattle navigated the riverbed, due to God's
miraculous hand.

Now the only ones left in the water are the priests carrying the ark
of the covenant. God tells Joshua to build a memorial. He says, "Gather
twelve leaders together, have them go back into the riverbed, and have
each of them collect twelve stones. In Canaan, at a place called Gilgal,
have them build a memorial of my power. When their descendants ask,
'What do the stones mean?' they will answer, 'God was faithful and
parted the waters of the Jordan, just as he did the Red Sea.'"

Memorials are important markers in our own stories as well. God
had the Israelites collect stones from the middle of the Jordan, from the
lowest place on their journey, from their place of deepest doubt. What
would God have you remember today? Did you record your journey?
Did you note your despair? Did you chronicle your deliverance? Have
you told your children and loved ones the story?

Build a memorial. Put it on display. When others see it and ask,
"Oh, what is this? What does it mean?" you will be released to speak
of it. There is power in remembering, power in the telling, and power
in passing on a heritage of faith to those around us. Relive, remember,
celebrate, and be strengthened.

*I have stories to tell, Father. You can be glorified. Show me how to
build a proper memorial that captures your miraculous work in my
life. Amen.*

June 5

Outrageous Orders

"On the seventh day, march around the city seven times, with the priests blowing the trumpets."

JOSHUA 6:4

*D*o God's ways ever seem silly to you? Because they appear to make no sense, do you ever question whether it's best for you to walk in them? Do you often think that his precepts cramp your style? You would rather make your own choices. You feel you know yourself. You know what you need. Right?

God told Joshua how he could capture the formidable city of Jericho. He revealed no war plans, however. The soldiers had only to walk around the perimeter in silence. They were told to follow the priests, who would carry the ark of the covenant, parade-style. This march was to take place once a day for six days and then seven times on the seventh day. At the appropriate moment they would all shout and the city walls would collapse. How preposterous it must have seemed!

It makes me think of poor Naaman, a well-respected military leader, who came to God's prophet to be healed of leprosy. Sure he wanted a cure, but don't tell a diplomat to go to the dirty Jordan River and dunk himself seven times! How demeaning.

Yet we know the end of both stories. The city of Jericho fell and Namaan was healed.

Do we obey God's commands when they make no sense to us? Do we have such respect for who God is that we'll do anything he asks, just because he is God? The answer needs to be yes. When we finally get to heaven and review our lives from God's perspective, I'm sure the word *silly* will cease to be in our vocabulary.

Whatever you want me to do, Lord, I'll obey. Amen.

June 6

Enough Repentance

Joshua tore his clothes and fell facedown to the
ground before the ark of the LORD, remaining there
till evening. . . . The LORD said to Joshua, "Stand up!
What are you doing down on your face?"

JOSHUA 7:6, 10

Joshua, the great leader, is on his face. He has covered himself in
ashes, bearing the guilt of a nation under God's displeasure. He
repents on their behalf for an extended time, and then God delivers
this message: "What are you doing? Time to rise up!"

How much time was appropriate for Joshua to weep in
repentance? How much time is adequate for us? These are good
questions because we often wallow too long in guilt. Many of us never
get off our knees. We are so destroyed by the revelation of our own
depravity that we struggle to recover. We cannot believe that forgiveness
is instantaneous (even though we bear ongoing consequences). Somehow
we think it's more spiritual to walk around saying, "Woe is me."

God endeavors to change our mind today as we review his message
to Joshua. God didn't want to see any more melancholy postures! God
did not, and does not, delight in a grief that exceeds his peace and
forgiveness. Our weeping must not hinder proactive change and the
sowing of a different seed.

I've made my share of mistakes. I've spent too much time living
with a defeated spirit. There was joy when I finally understood
forgiveness. I allowed it to wash over my soul. I decided to get up the
next day with the intention of living differently. I found joy in the
reality that I served a God not only of second chances but also of many
chances.

Transform my countenance, Lord! Today I finish my weeping and,
by your grace, write a new chapter. Amen.

June 7

Everybody Pays

Joshua said to Achan, "My son, . . . tell me what you have done; do not hide it from me."

JOSHUA 7:19

*H*ave you ever suffered because of the sins of a partner, a spouse, or a parent? You know well that one person's sin affects more than himself. God desired, from the beginning of time, that we live in community rather than independence. Consequently, when people walk in his ways, a community flourishes. But as soon as one sins, everyone is affected.

After the Israelites crossed the Jordan River, God told Joshua that the spoils of the city were to be used only for his house. But imagine you were an Israelite. As you wandered around Jericho and investigated vacant homes, churches, and places of business, you encountered great wealth, such as gold artifacts, jewelry, and beautiful tapestries. Would you have been tempted to tuck away just one piece for yourself? Out of all the Israelites, only one person stole something. That's pretty amazing. But it only took one man's sin to infect the whole nation. God's blessing was removed until the theft was dealt with.

When a husband or wife is irresponsible with money, the whole family suffers. When an employer puts a dishonest person in charge of accounting, the entire company suffers. It seems unfair at first glance. Yet perhaps the sting of this injustice will also breed accountability. The innocent who suffer the consequences will also be intent to bring justice to the wrongdoer.

Each of us who has felt the effects of another's mistake is comforted that we're not alone. May we also be motivated to live in holiness so we might bring prosperity to our brothers and sisters.

Give me grace to handle the sins of others, Lord, and the courage to make changes when I can. Amen.

The Loneliness of Leadership

"Do not be afraid. . . . Take the whole army with you,
and go up and attack Ai."

JOSHUA 8:1

*P*ower is a coveted thing. Without double-checking our conscience, we'll try to climb our way to the top. We want the prestige that accompanies leadership.

Most every leader tells of great loneliness. Such was the story of Joshua, the leader of Israel. He crossed the Jordan River by a miracle. He was told to conquer the kingdoms on the other side. He made an attack against Ai, yet because there was unknown sin in Israel, his presumed victory became a defeat instead. Men of Israel were killed. The sin that caused their demise, Achan's theft, had to be dealt with.

Afterward God told Joshua to go up against Ai again. He already did this once and lost. How would you like to command this exercise? What did Joshua do? Before he made a move, he went to a valley outside the city walls of Ai and met with God alone. Can you picture him? It was four o'clock in the morning and one lone man was stretched out on his face in a field, hoping to hear God impart battle plans. Have you been there, metaphorically? I have.

Yes, God came through. Joshua's sword became his spiritual weapon, just as Moses' rod had been his token of leadership. But when we seek God in the night while everyone else sleeps, we don't know the outcome yet. We only know that we are alone, that it's up to us, that if God's mind is to be explored and victories are to be won, it will be done by our solitary gesture. Spiritual power is cultivated in a closet, achieved with discipline and hard work.

You have given me a place of influence, Lord. I feel lonely. Meet me. Amen.

June 9

Easily Tricked

Joshua asked, "Who are you and where do you come from?"

JOSHUA 9:8

No one likes to be tricked. Yet trickery is part of our world. People can pose as one thing but in reality be quite another.

The nation of Gibeon saw Israel approaching their land. They feared Israel's strength, so they set up an elaborate scheme to escape the sword. They sent an envoy to Joshua and pretended to be from a far-off country. They dressed in old, tattered clothes and attached cracked wineskins to their mules. They wore shoes that looked worse than those the Israelites had worn for forty years! When Joshua noted their attire and heard their claim, he had an intuitive flash and asked, "Where are you really from?" But again the visitors declared it was "from a far country." Scripture says that Joshua and the leaders did not consult with God about this matter. God would have given insight and truth, but sadly, Israel was deceived and bore the consequences.

Here are the lessons for us. First, we should pray about everything. Second, it might be disastrous to make a decision in haste. God promises wisdom to his children but tells us that we must ask for it. Our gut instinct is not always reliable, for we are subject to cunning people who are empowered by the Prince of Darkness.

Is someone at your door today needing something, wanting something, proposing an alliance of friendship or a business partnership, perhaps even marriage? Stop. Pray. Don't answer till you know the mind of God. His desire is that you live under his protection, for you are his much loved daughter.

You are the only one who knows the hearts and plans of people, Lord. I need your wisdom today. Amen.

June 10

The Longest Day

The sun stood still, and the moon stopped.

JOSHUA 10:13

o you need to be reminded of God's power? Do you think him to be a bit impotent? Does he fail to act when you think he should?

God has called me to bear the message of his tender and extravagant love. It is my privilege to encourage women to come close to him, to deliver the news that he has not forgotten them and that he aches for their love. However, describing only the gentleness of God could be misleading if I didn't also purposefully talk about his power.

If you are one who believes that his love is anemic, let me defend the truth that God is mighty. His love is rooted in his power and he does not shy from using it to intervene for his children.

Joshua dared to call upon the power of God. Five kings and their greatest warriors attacked Joshua and the Israelites. They were formidable yet God assured Joshua that Israel would win. Though the Israelites killed many, God intervened to help. He rained stones from heaven, stones so large that they killed more men than were killed by the Israelites' swords.

That's not all. Dusk was approaching. Israel was winning and didn't want to lose momentum. Joshua thought, *If only we had eight more hours of daylight, we'd finish the job!* So by faith he commanded the sun and moon to stand still. They did, and for an additional twenty-four hours it gave the Israelites more than enough daylight to achieve total victory.

The nations who worshiped the sun and the moon met God that day. The Israelites witnessed the power of God when their faith was on the line.

Wow, you're my tender Father and you are also a powerful warrior. Amen.

June 11

Ripened Faith

Joshua took the entire land, just as the LORD had directed Moses.

JOSHUA 11:23

The Israelites had come so far. As spiritual infants they were delivered out of Egypt. They had little faith and no toned spiritual muscles. God knew their frailty, so he performed miracles. He parted the Red Sea, provided daily manna, even made crossing the Jordan River possible. But as their faith in him grew, the nature of his contributions changed. He asked them to get to work, uniting their labor with his empowerment.

Now as they continued their conquest of Canaan, the Israelites faced their most formidable enemies yet, the kingdoms of the South. God saved the hardest till last. This battle took seven years. Forty years earlier the spies of Israel had predicted that these kingdoms were too powerful for them. Yet here the Israelites were, four decades later, waging war with Jehovah as their commander. The giants of the land were dwarfed by God's omnipotence!

Are you engaged in battles that you have previously lost? Are you facing challenges that once seemed too formidable? God is gracious to allow us to grow up a bit before we tackle them a second time. He deepens our faith and sharpens our spiritual skills before we again confront the "giants of the land." This time the outcome can be victorious, because our spiritual muscles are fully developed.

Perhaps he has saved your greatest battle till now. If you do your part with everything you've got, God will do his. It's a cooperative effort and God uses all the lessons of our past to make us wise and strong.

Thank you for all the skirmishes you have helped me win, Lord. They have prepared me for what is ahead. I trust you to help me face the giants. Amen.

June 12

Pauper or Heiress?

"How long will you wait before you begin to take possession of the land that the LORD, the God of your fathers, has given you?"

JOSHUA 18:3

*T*housands of people have inherited a fortune and have never claimed their riches. Many live in poverty, not having any idea that their deprivation is needless. Such is the story of certain Israelites who were unaware of their spiritual inheritance.

Joshua and the people of God entered the Promised Land. They were ordered by God to drive out their enemies to make the land theirs. They did! Finally it was ready to be occupied. Joshua divided up the land into nine portions, commanding the people to disperse and "dwell in the land of promise." Many did. Many did not! He calls the latter together and asks (perhaps incredulously), "Why are you still standing here with me? Why haven't you gone out to take your land? It's waiting for you!"

Instead of sending them out with a scolding, he offers to go with each tribe into their land to show them about their inheritance. He wanted to walk the property with them, describe its potential, and bring them into an awareness of the beauty of their gift.

Are you aware of your rich inheritance in Christ? I ache for you if your answer is no. Dear one, claim your inheritance! Explore the riches and learn to live in the joy of God's provision. Discern the spiritual boundaries of your promised land. It is fat with potential and flowing with milk and honey. It's time to dig in and enjoy the feast. May Deprivation no longer be your middle name.

Lord, I don't want to live as a pauper. You have given me riches beyond my comprehension. Give me the eyes to recognize them, and the heart to value them. Amen.

June 13

A Gift with Responsibility

"Now then," said Joshua, "throw away the foreign gods that are among you and yield your hearts to the LORD, the God of Israel."

JOSHUA 24:23

After forty years of wandering in a wilderness, the Israelites have entered the Promised Land. They must be joyful and relieved to finally have a home. At this point God gives them some instruction about this new land and how they are to handle it.

He says, "I have not brought you out of Egypt for nothing. It is so I could be your God and you could be my people. Please don't commit the sin of putting other gods before me. Remember where you came from and honor all I am giving you."

That's quite a speech. It reminds me that gifts from God aren't cheap. I think of how many times I made an idol out of a gift rather than focusing on the one who gave it to me. What he intended for my pleasure became a wedge that stood between my Father and me. Poor God! He must have felt like the parent who indulged an ungrateful child.

Without intention to do otherwise, I'll use his gifts as a means of gratifying myself. I'll sing for applause and write books for rave reviews. Without taking time to savor God, I'll forget that it's all about him. He birthed his gifts in me. Just as a newly engaged woman exclaims, "Look at the ring he gave me!" so it should be with me as I display my Father's gifts that adorn my life. Others will be able to see them as they truly are: love gifts.

I live to be your child. I find such joy in showing others what you've given me. It makes them want you as their Father, too. Amen.

June 14

Develop Childlikeness

Both high and low among men find refuge in the shadow of your wings. They feast on the abundance of your house; you give them drink from your river of delights. For with you is the fountain of life.

PSALM 36:7–9

Throughout Scripture God refers to us as children. He invites us to enjoy a perpetual childlike relationship with him regardless of our age. He knows we need that. When tragedies occur and we are reminded how powerless we are, we long to know that we have a person to run to for safety. How comforting to know that God gathers his children under his wings even while the storm rages.

Every day, I must remind myself that because God sees me as his child, it's okay for me to be one. It's only natural for me to foster childlikeness and come to him as my Father. After all, my insight is flawed. My stamina is limited. My body is mortal. My ability to trust others completely has been injured. I can't see what's around the corner; therefore I'm forced to admit that life is out of my control. I need to turn my affairs over to a Parent who is more powerful than the tragedies that cross my path and the events that could easily crush me. He is in control. He is redeeming my past and writing my future. His plans for me are driven by loving-kindness. Who better to trust than my Father?

Our society praises self-sufficiency. Bookstore shelves are crowded with books about self-management. Independence is exalted. But in the privacy of my prayer closet, I'm free to come as a child to the heart of God to renew and restore.

I am your daughter. I don't have to manage my life, Lord. You're in charge. What a relief. Amen.

June 15

Your Search Is Over

Because you are sons, God sent the Spirit of his Son
into our hearts, the Spirit who calls out, *"Abba,* Father."
GALATIANS 4:6

*I*f you could construct your own perfect father, what would he be
like? Because so many in our society today are fatherless, I'm told
that there is a place on the Internet where you can build your dream
dad. If someone had a bad father, it must feel good to create the ideal
one, even though he is fictitious.

Many are pining for a better father, often marrying someone much
older, when all the time God wants us to know that he is the Father
we seek. It is possible to connect with him and finally experience
unconditional love.

As I looked through the Bible for an exemplary father, I came up
short. Proverbs thirty-one is the text most often used to describe the
perfect mom, but it seems there's not a similar chapter for dads. I
thought of King David as a father, but then remembered that his kids
tried to kill him. I considered King Solomon's track record, but he had
problems with women. I jumped forward in time to perhaps remember the apostle Paul, but he was single.

Maybe God is doing something far greater in his omission than we
can imagine. He's trying to teach us that he is our Father. In the Sermon on the Mount, Jesus referred to God as "Father " seventeen times.
He called him "Abba," which means "Daddy," "tender and dear." This
way of addressing deity is unheard of in the realm of all other religions
of humankind.

If you are looking and longing for a Father's heart, I know where
you can find him. He's wondering where you've been all this time, for
he's been calling you.

*Is it possible my search is ended? Show me who you are, Father.
Amen.*

June 16

Giving Away What You Don't Have

They are always generous and lend freely; their children will be blessed.

PSALM 37:26

There's a kingdom principle that teaches that if you need love, give love away. If you need money, give money away in Jesus' name. If you need compassion, give mercy away generously and your wounds will be healed. Let me tell you a real-life story of when I saw this principle at work.

A church in Cincinnati had long outgrown its facilities and had planned to build a larger complex in a new location. Funds had come in dribbles. Then the pastor felt that God told him to give his present church building away to a struggling church across town. What seemed difficult to him about God's directive was that his church had to pay off a mortgage on the old building before assuming a loan for the new auditorium.

The people joined together in faith. In eight weeks they paid off the old mortgage, and on an Easter Sunday they gave away the church building to a new African-American congregation and their new pastor from South Africa. Guess what? The funds poured in for the new building. This Cincinnati congregation is currently worshiping in their new facility.

When Joseph was in prison, he passed the cell of two men and noticed that they were downcast. He stopped and asked them the reason for their sadness. He handled them with tenderness. He gave away what I'm sure he needed himself. We know how the story ended for him.

Need a friend, a listening ear, or food on the table? Try giving something away. Share your last pot of soup. Receive the tears of a friend though you feel your own grief. Your gift of faith may heal you.

I'm glad I live in your kingdom, Father. I value your principles. Amen.

June 17

Love-Driven Power

I will sing of your strength, in the morning I will sing
of your love.

PSALM 59:16

*W*hat is the distinguishing characteristic of a powerful person?
It is usually their charisma, their intellect, their financial
status, or even their physical strength. They can be powerful in our
eyes, often without making any contribution to another person. Jesus
is powerful; none of us would argue that. But what drives his power?

Miracles can't be accomplished without it. Raw power is not what
drives his miraculous acts. Jesus never gave a smoke-and-lights show
simply to flaunt his might. His power is derived from a love for people.
Love drives the healings, deliverances, and the supernatural acts. It is
human need and suffering which causes God to stretch out his hand
of mercy in miraculous interventions.

I remember when I was a kid. Whenever I learned some new skill,
I tried to catch the attention of the nearest adult. "Look, Mommy!
Look what I can do!" I loved the praise. Jesus never said, "See what I
can do? Aren't I great?" That was not the purpose of his visit to earth.
His power was restrained in wisdom, released when the purposes of
his love could be showcased.

I often think of my neediness as a bad thing, yet it connects me to
the heart of God. The things I tend to most despise—powerlessness,
depravity, and brokenness—are the gifts that ignite the power of
heaven to come to my aid. "See what I can do, Jesus?" is replaced by
"I'm nothing. Let me see what you can do!"

*Almighty God, your power is unfathomable. I marvel that your
power is cradled in your hands, hands that hold exquisite love for
me. Amen.*

Spiritual Safety

You have been my refuge, a strong tower against the foe. I long to dwell in your tent forever and take refuge in the shelter of your wings.

PSALM 61:3–4

King David knew what it was like to be hunted. His reign was marked with political unrest. His story was laced with words like spies and betrayal. We can identify with him in these days of uncertainty and political unrest.

September 11, 2001, will forever be etched in my mind. I remember the days following the tragedy. I simply could not watch one more replay of the jetliners penetrating the World Trade Center. I imagined the passengers on the planes, braced during the steep turns that marked the end of their terrifying flights.

Since then we've asked, "Are we physically safe?" The answer is no. The answer has always been no. None of us knows what the next moment may bring. We might have a heart attack, be struck by a drunk driver, or become the victim of a tragedy like the one that befell New York City. Bad news is ever present in this world. We were rendered hopeless in many respects the moment we were born. If we presume safety, we only play pretend.

The real question is, "Are we spiritually safe?" The answer is yes if we are God's children. My body may be in mortal danger but my soul lives forever.

If I am God's child, I am held securely in the arms of a loving Father. Nothing can threaten my future. My spirit resides safely with God. Daily I can nurture the reality that I am a child under my Father's protective wings.

You never wring your hands in despair, Father. I take refuge in you. You are my rock, unchanging and faithful. Amen.

June 19

Running from the Answer

Trust in him at all times, O people; pour out your
hearts to him, for God is our refuge.

PSALM 62:8

"Hey, Dad?" a little boy cried out one Saturday morning. "Let's play darts. I'll throw the darts and you just stand there and say, 'Good shot!'" Leave it to kids to be that vulnerable and honest about their needs. This little guy needed lots of attention that day and wasn't afraid to ask for it. And he knew who to go to.

Knowing where to go to get our needs met is critical. The trouble is, we often go to the wrong places. "I am your refuge and strength," God says, "a very present help in trouble." Yet when we want refuge, we go to empty sources.

We approach yet again that parent who has rarely given approval. We contrive and manipulate, thinking we'll finally get what we need, but we come away empty. Or we often look for the closest anesthetic in the form of distractions. Staying busy allows us to run away from the presence of the One who says, "I am your refuge." Does that make any sense? Not really. God knows we need him, and he reminds us over and over again that he's the answer.

Oh, daughter of promise, God is wooing you, wants to embrace you, and in the environment of his love calls you to freedom and fulfillment. Take that first step. Believe him and walk toward him. Bow your head and see yourself accepting his invitation. His arms are waiting. Finally you have a refuge, a place of safety.

I've been silly, Father. I've run from you for so long when I've needed you so badly. Forgive me. Thank you for not giving up on me and for welcoming me home. Amen.

June 20

A Morning at Wal-Mart

May your unfailing love be my comfort.

PSALM 119:76

I went to Wal-Mart this morning. As I picked up my cart, I noticed an old woman fumbling through her wallet. She was sorting through bits of paper, distressed and disoriented. I touched her and said, "You look very upset. Can I help you?"

"I can't find my list," she said. "In fact, I can't seem to do anything today. I'm so upset because I just found out my cat has to be put to sleep. She's my only companion. I can't imagine life without her. I don't know how I'm going to say good-bye." Her eyes were brimming with tears.

I listened. I talked about my own cats and how they are like children to me. I asked if she would like my company when she took her cat to the vet. She was touched but declined. Then, taking a deep breath, I said, "Can I tell you something special?" She nodded, seeming stronger now.

"This morning I asked God to send someone into my life who needs to know that he loves them, that he sees their life and cares deeply. You are that person!" At that point her eyes lit up. Hope crossed her face. I've seen the look many times. It says, "You mean, God has not forgotten me?"

Think of what this woman would have missed had she not known that God empowered our conversation. My gift of kindness extended far beyond me; it became supernaturally charged. Instead of remembering me as a nice lady at Wal-Mart, she will be able to recall that someone sent her home with God.

How many opportunities have I missed, Father? Talk to me as I live my life. Make sure I don't overlook a chance to tell of your love. Amen.

June 21

Free to Be Me

I run in the path of your commands, for you have set
my heart free.

PSALM 119:32

Think of the person who loves you most. When you're together, you undoubtedly revel in the freedom you feel to be yourself, right? You might even say, "I'm not like this with anyone else. Others would be shocked to see me now! I'm carefree, so unguarded, so playful."

When I began to heal in the presence of perfect love, within the embrace of my Creator, I was shocked to discover who I really was. My talk didn't sound like me. I thought outside of the box. I dreamed of doing things I had stopped dreaming of long ago. "Who is this woman?" I asked Abba one morning. "One who is being freed by love," he answered. I perceived that he sighed in deep satisfaction.

The radical changes that I experienced in his presence served to expose the many masks I had worn in other relationships. I thought I had been pragmatic in my attempt to disguise myself. I had changed clothes by the hour, making myself presentable for the next set of expectations. I got so used to donning others' wardrobe choices that I failed to discover the outfit Abba had tailor-made for me. If you had asked me my favorite color, I couldn't have told you. If you had questioned me about my dreams for the future, I would have frozen. Foolishly I lived for others because I didn't know I could live freely in God.

Now I know. I can be me finally. If someone doesn't like the real Christine, it's okay. The stakes aren't high anymore, because Abba loves me and I know where to go to get my broken heart mended.

Help me continue to recover the me you created, Father. Amen.

June 22

The Art of Meditation

He makes me lie down in green pastures, he leads me
beside quiet waters.

Psalm 23:2

I love Psalm 23. I'm not alone. It is the most quoted portion of
Scripture. In it David speaks of God leading him to green
pastures and still waters. Is this just exquisite poetry or an actual place
our souls can visit? I have learned it's the latter.

God gives this privileged excursion to each of his children. He
encourages us to meditate on Scripture because he knows we need safe
havens for our souls. God desires to help us develop the art of
meditation. He intended it for our pleasure and as provision for the
security of our souls. I believe our emotional stability depends on it.

Today I can close my eyes and experience the joy of running in a
carpet of tender green grass. Nothing cuts my bare feet. This mental
image is sumptuous and stretches as far as I can see. Beyond the
pasture lies a small lake. The waters are calm and crystal clear, and I can
see all the way to the bottom. As I cup my hands and take a drink, I
realize how thirsty I am. Water never tasted this good!

Meditation has become a buzzword in the New Age movement.
Without thinking, many Christians have come to view meditation as
an evil practice. Satan's agenda is to steal and corrupt the best of God's
gifts. Like meditation, for example. Wouldn't you agree that it's time
to reclaim one of God's most valuable gifts?

*Jesus, you led a life of prayer. The inner life of your soul was highly
developed and rich enough to sustain you through excruciating times.
Help me discover all that you enjoyed. All that was yours can be
mine. Amen.*

A Father of Comfort

I will fear no evil, for you are with me.

PSALM 23:4

Our family has a black and white cat named Marcia. She's fifteen, a little eccentric, but a much loved member of our family. A few weeks ago we discovered she had an abscessed eye.

Antibiotic ointments worked to no avail. The veterinarian told us her eye could not be saved, so we set a date for him to surgically remove it.

My heart was heavy that morning as I drove her to surgery. Animals are intuitive. She was edgy and upset, so I put my fingers through the bars of her carrier so she could curl up against them. I sang to her all the way, fighting tears for what lay ahead.

On the way home I heard God say to my spirit, "Remember the verse, 'I will never leave you nor forsake you'?"

I said, "Yes, Father."

"Well, what you did for your cat this morning is the very least of what I do for you! I stretch out my hand, as you extended your fingers through the cage, so you can curl up next to me. Think of this scene the next time you are frightened by your circumstances. I too want you to draw comfort from my presence."

In loving others, you and I can powerfully reflect how our Father loves us, even in the ways we reach out to our pets. Just as we remind those who are dear to us that we have not abandoned them, our heavenly Father wants us to know he is just a whisper away.

Thank you for coming to me when I am most afraid, Father. Help me be that merciful to others in their distress. Amen.

Ever Accessible Feast

You prepare a table before me in the presence of
my enemies.

PSALM 23:5

King David made this statement in the well-known Twenty-third
Psalm. This has long been the theme of God's provision for his
people, provided that they walk in obedience. Have you ever feasted
in the midst of enemy territory? Joshua and the children of Israel had
that experience.

God miraculously brought them across the Jordan River. Perhaps
they thought their battles were over and this would be a time for rest.
But once across, they found themselves in enemy territory. However,
word about them and their God had spread swiftly, for when they
advanced into the land surrounding Jericho, they found that the
natives had fled for their lives. Why? The rumors were, "A formidable
people are coming. Their God delivered them from the Egyptians; he
parted the Red Sea for their crossing and dried up the Jordan River so
they could pass through. They are too powerful for us." Having been
uprooted, these natives left their barns full to overflowing with corn
and other crops.

The daily provision of manna ceased, for God provided the
bounty of the land for his people. Israel celebrated a Passover that day.
It was a feast in the presence of their enemies.

God tells us that he is our daily bread. And no matter what our
circumstances look like today, there is a feast waiting if we come near
to the person of God and feast on his love and mercy. In loving him
our deepest needs are met. We are able to say with David, "My
cup overflows."

*Lord, though my circumstances vary and though I sojourn in
foreign territory, you restore my soul with the feast of your heart.
Though my body is deprived, my soul can thrive. Amen.*

June 25

New Clothes

As God's chosen people, holy and dearly loved, clothe yourselves with compassion, kindness, humility, gentleness and patience.

COLOSSIANS 3:12

*I*f I were asked to think of someone kind, my friend Christina would get my vote. Someone humble? A man's face enters my mind. Patient? Definitely my friend LeAnn. The exercise would become far more difficult, though, if I were asked to think of one person who exhibited all the character traits in today's Scripture. The field would narrow immediately. Even more humbling is wondering whether or not anyone would say that any or some of these things are true of me.

Why is it rare for all these traits to be present? Paul reveals that the key to putting on the clothing of compassion, kindness, humility, gentleness, and patience is knowing that I'm dearly loved. Until I experience Jesus' love daily, I will only be able to pretend that I'm like him. Jesus is selfless and others-centered. Unless I know that I'm loved, I can't forget myself and serve others altruistically. I'll be inclined to be gentle to receive love, to be kind to impress others, and to be compassionate so when I'm hurting down the road, the favor will be returned.

Living as a loved daughter gives me new lifestyle options. I will wear the attributes of Christ as effortlessly as I would a sweater. I'll live life out of the overflow of his love rather than mimicking the nature of it through gritted teeth. I have lived far too many years trying to conjure up the energy to be Christlike, when all the grunting and straining should have been a wake-up call to the reality of spiritual disease. His love cures all self-centeredness.

I can't wear your clothes, Lord, until I allow you to love me fully. Amen.

You're Not Alone

Resist him, standing firm in the faith, because you know that your brothers throughout the world are undergoing the same kind of sufferings.

1 PETER 5:9

We are engaged in a battle with the enemy of our souls. Temptations abound. Condemning thoughts threaten our peace. Doubts erode our confidence in Abba. Fear cripples our faith. Anger undermines our belief in God's justice.

This is a global war, not a solitary one. Forgetting that, I can fail to disclose my struggles to my spiritual sisters. I can begin to think that something is wrong with me if I battle temptation, fear, anger, and doubt. I can easily view myself as someone who disappoints God. I can assume others are more advanced spiritually. I can be inclined to feel a sense of shame over the things that plague me.

This perception is untrue. We are all in the same predicament. Spiritual power to resist our enemy and achieve victory is collectively ours if we bare our burdens to one another. We're family. The same royal blood courses through our spiritual veins. War has been declared on us simply because of Who we belong to. We need to be vulnerable with each other. We can stand firm as long as we stand together.

You will come against arrows of opposition today. They may be numerous, causing you to believe that the power behind them is formidable. But you do not fight alone. I link my arm with yours. We sing a song of deliverance. The song is contagious, for as our voices are heard, more daughters begin to learn this song of hope. There is strength in numbers. The battle is transformed from a senseless massacre to an overwhelming victory.

Together with my sisters, Lord, we create a daunting line of defense. Amen.

June 27

A Warrior, a Woman

When he rose from prayer and went back to the
disciples, he found them asleep, exhausted from sorrow.
LUKE 22:45

I am encouraged. Women are beginning to internalize the truth of
their God-given identity. As a result, they are praying more.
Indignant that Satan would steal their inheritance, they are getting on
their knees to engage in spiritual battle.

This is a strategic hour for us. Satan is rejoicing over his
anticipated victories, but we can thwart his efforts by accessing the
power of God. How? By utilizing the spiritual tools he gave us for our
victory. We live by faith, daughter. Therefore sing songs of praise by
faith. Read Scripture out loud by faith, passages that tell of God's
power and faithfulness. Anticipate victory in advance!

Do troops go into battle without preparation, ample ammunition,
and intensive training? Never! We are not to meet our adversary
unequipped, unarmed, or undisciplined. We are not to live impotently,
merely ducking the arrows of Satan's kingdom. We are not to live
defensively. God invites us to move ahead offensively! Let's go after the
ground Satan intends to steal from us.

We are not contending with flesh and blood and matching wits
with people. The very enemy of our souls, Satan himself, is
ambushing us. He is not out to torment; he's out to destroy. He doesn't
plan to inflict a scratch; he intends to wound mortally. Learn to reign,
for God has made us to become kings and priests, starting now. One
day when we reign with Christ in his new kingdom, it will be an
extension of our reign here.

*I am weak, but with you I am strong. I am willing to be a warrior,
Lord. I take hold of the spiritual weapons you have provided for me.
Amen.*

June 28

What He Really Wants

What does the LORD require of you? To act justly and
to love mercy and to walk humbly with your God.

MICAH 6:8

I've often wondered in the past what it was exactly that God wanted
from me. The messages I'd received were varied and conflicting.
"Be joyful." "Witness every chance you get." "Leave a gospel tract at
every toll booth." "Use your gifts whenever you're asked." "Be holy."
I could add to the list and so could you, most likely. Each had
something in common, however. Pressure to perform, the code of
conduct extensive.

I'm glad that Micah took the time to record God's thoughts for
me. God wants three things: a holy life, a heart that loves mercy, and
companionship marked with humility.

I can be good at imitating the behavior of Jesus. I'm trained to do
what's right, whether I feel like it or not. Rarely am I confused about
what's just and righteous. Committing myself to do it with the right
heart is the key.

Loving mercy is a bigger challenge. I'd often rather see fairness
extended than mercy. I have tons of sympathy for those I think deserve
it, but that's not the essence of mercy. Mercy is born when the one
who asks for it is entirely unworthy. Mercy isn't mercy when offered
through gritted teeth. As I allow God to be merciful to me, mercy for
others will be born in my heart.

Walking with God is a revolutionary thought. Taking God by the
hand, humbled by the reality that he stoops to take mine, is a
different definition of "living the Christian life" than is memorizing
Christian dogma and aligning my life accordingly. How refreshing to
have it clarified finally.

*I remember the day you graced my life, Lord. You are changing me.
Amen.*

June 29

Waiting

As for me, I watch in hope for the LORD, I wait for
God my Savior; my God will hear me. Do not gloat
over me, my enemy! Though I have fallen, I will rise.
Though I sit in darkness, the LORD will be my light.
MICAH 7:7–8

We relish the thought of deliverance but we despise the reality
that causes us to need it. We hate the imprisonment. We love
the release.

However, there can be no healing without sickness. There can be
no appreciation of freedom without having tasted of bondage. There
can be no dancing in the light without having experienced the terror
of darkness. Joy is made sweeter by our acquaintance with grief.
Spiritual rest is more valuable following a season of striving. But oh,
how difficult while we wait for God to say, "Enough!"

I sat at the red light of pain for years. It seemed interminable. The
discomfort was severe. My undeveloped faith was nearly driven to the
edge of apostasy. In desperation I cried out for relief. When God didn't
answer as quickly as I thought he should, I was tempted to step back
from my relationship with him. Oh, I'm glad I didn't. I pressed in
closer to his heart, dared to believe that his intentions were kind, and
then waited.

I couldn't see the coming redemption. I couldn't see who I was to
become through the testing. Now I know. The arduous task of
walking by faith resulted in ecstasy when God finally granted supernatural sight to my eyes. I am now one who reaches out with passion
and confidence to others who falter.

*Though I may fall in the future, I will rise. Though I may sit in
darkness, you are my light. I give the enemy no cause to rejoice, Lord.
Amen.*

June 30

Too Good to Be True

The LORD your God is with you, he is mighty to save.
He will take great delight in you, he will quiet you
with his love, he will rejoice over you with singing.
ZEPHANIAH 3:17

*T*his is by far my favorite Scripture verse. God inspired Zephaniah to write this message down so his heart for us would be revealed.

I'm amazed that God delights in me. As the quality of that kind of love registers, I find the leading edge of restoration. It's as if living water trickles down into my spirit, bringing with it energy, light-heartedness, and a confidence that shores up the very foundation of who I am. He doesn't just like me; he delights in me. I've never known such contentment.

I'm even more awed by the truth that God is taking the time to quiet my heart. Tired but happy, I can collapse into the safe arms of the one who wants to change my reality with his endearing ways. A deep reservoir I was unaware of is being filled to the brim with joy, a joy that emanates from having found my way home and discovered that God is everything I ever needed.

It is then that the sounds of music are heard. Joyful singing erupts from my Father's lips. Nothing breathes life into the words on an old prophet's page like the picture of the Master Musician singing and dancing over me. It is the expression of the fullness of his love. He is overcome. It is a celebration for no formal occasion, a celebration just for my being his daughter. The best part is, he invites me to come home to experience it all again whenever I need it.

Thank you for such sweet love, Abba. You are my home. Amen.

July

July 1

Sharing the Loss

Carry each other's burdens, and in this way you will fulfill the law of Christ.

GALATIANS 6:2

Losses are meant to be shared. None of us was designed to live isolated from other people. We were created to live interdependently. When God created Adam, the first man and the only human being on earth at that time, he was moved by Adam's sense of aloneness. "This is not good," God commented. So he created Eve.

When we fail to relate to each other as God intended, we can end up feeling as isolated as Adam did. Unfortunately, this is quite common in the church. I receive dozens of letters each week from women who tell me of the loneliness they feel while sitting in church. They feel their world has fallen apart, yet they dare not speak of it. They sit in silent pain.

My mother was diagnosed with inoperable cancer in 1982. The day after I heard this shattering news, a good friend walked into my kitchen, wrapped her arms around me, and cried. I can't tell you how much that meant to me. Over the course of the next two years, few were willing to make that kind of emotional investment, but the ones who did changed the solitary nature of my journey.

Ironically, my friend who cried felt she had shown weakness, that she had not been strong for me. I wish I could have convinced her that her willingness to weep with me was as therapeutic as anything anyone else said or did for me during that painful time. It was a moment I will never forget. Her tears said more than any words could ever say.

Jesus, you share your tears with me. I never grieve alone. Help me to be generous with my heart. Amen.

July 2

Deathbed Conversation

To Timothy, my dear son: Grace, mercy and peace
from God the Father and Christ Jesus our Lord.

2 TIMOTHY 1:2

When someone speaks from their deathbed, their words have our full attention. Paul's last words to Timothy are written from prison. He is about to be martyred. His last wish is that Timothy might know grace, mercy, and peace. If Timothy had been in Paul's presence, I can picture Paul's hand on Timothy's head as he prays out loud.

I think of others' last words to their children: "Work hard for God, my son!" "Give life your best." "Be the best you can be!" Why Paul's prayer for grace, mercy, and peace?

Perhaps we fail to know the gracious heart of God and the various ways he longs to demonstrate it by giving gifts we don't deserve. They are meant to be received with open arms, not with one eye cocked in skepticism. If we do not say to Jesus, "I am so overwhelmed that you did all that for me. Your love is so great," then we do not fully understand grace.

Perhaps God's merciful heart is foreign to us. On days when I see the havoc of my own making and the repercussions of my choices over the years, I pray, "Lord, have mercy on me and this house." I know he answers, for he has broken through my dread with hope and promise.

Peace—the inner calm we have because we know to whom we are connected—can also escape us. God is King of our kingdom and he rules well. Though he allows people to make their own choices today, and we may experience pain because of them, he is always the ultimate Redeemer. If he is our shelter, we are at peace.

I pray that I would know grace, mercy, and peace. They are characteristics of your heart, Lord. Amen.

July 3

Sharing Versus Preaching

The goal of this command is love, which comes from
a pure heart and a good conscience and a sincere faith.
1 TIMOTHY 1:5

Isn't it nice when people who write us a letter state their intention
up front? Thirty years after the death and resurrection of Jesus, the
wear and tear of ministry has taken its toll on Paul. These are rough
political times. Paul has just survived two years of house arrest in Rome
and has had a lot of time to pray. He is concerned about his spiritual
children, the ones with whom he has shared his love for Jesus, because
they have embraced the Messiah at great personal cost.

He writes to Timothy, his spiritual son, who pastors a church at
Ephesus. He states his intention for writing in his first few lines. He
wants Timothy to know that love motivates his words, that he didn't
become a teacher to make a name for himself. He doesn't instruct
others for the joy of appearing right and wise. I do well to remember
that today. For, like you, I have sat under the teaching of many who
condescend, making those who listen feel they are beneath them. The
listeners leave the worship service with a sense of inadequacy.

If others ever sense that my ministry has made an unwelcome
transition from sharing to preaching, making others feel less than
significant, I hope they'll tell me. Like Paul, my intention is to bring
Christ to you from a pure heart, a good conscience, and a sincere faith.
How tragic if ungodly agendas ever creep in and destroy that.

*Help me never communicate your pure heart with mixed messages,
Lord. Keep my motives clean. Amen.*

July 4

Consider the Audience

Some have wandered away from these and turned to meaningless talk.

*T*he highest percentages of those attending church are not the rebellious but rather God's sons and daughters. Yet in many churches people are bombarded with messages of the Law that are not intended for their ears. Paul calls it "fruitless discussion." It has no other function than beating down Christians, heaping a huge sense of inadequacy on their shoulders. Those sitting under years of this kind of teaching feel a vague sense of discouragement without understanding why.

Let me ask a question. Do you dread going to church? When you leave, do you feel more in love with Jesus or more discouraged about your performance?

If Paul were installed as our pastor this weekend, we would hear the ring of his letters to the churches. Each is filled with passion, calling to remembrance the beauty and power of the gift of Jesus, lighting the fire of love and devotion to him who gave his last breath for us. The themes of Paul's writings are grace, mercy, and peace. If that is not the prevalent theme of our church gatherings, it may be time to take stock.

If "I can't wait to worship this weekend" or "I can't wait to dig into God's Word with our pastor" isn't our heart's cry for what should be spiritual refreshment and restoration for the week, take Paul's warning to heart. God is to be panted for (Psalm 42:1). Leaders who have truly found profound joy in his presence will lead us there easily. Time with them will be contagious, not draining. Let's go feast where the food is. I'm hungry.

I need to sit under the teaching of one who has your heart, Jesus. Show me where to go. Amen.

The Divine Go-Between

There is one God and one mediator between God
and men, the man Christ Jesus.

1 TIMOTHY 2:5

When companies hire managers, part of their job is to
mediate for others. They must be selfless, able to see others'
needs and put them before their own. They must be respected and
trusted by those working under them. Only then will mediation
be successful.

Mediation becomes necessary when there has been a conflict or
standoff. Why would Paul refer to Jesus as a mediator? Do we need
one? What is the conflict?

Our sin put us under the condemnation of God. Intimacy with
God, whom our soul craves, is out of reach, and there is no way to
settle this matter without a mediator. So Jesus was chosen. His Father
saw that our sin, separating us from him for eternity, created a standoff that was hopeless without loving intervention. How did Jesus
mediate? By living thirty-three years on earth, walking in our shoes,
and living our stories. He became acquainted with disgrace and rejection.

Then he gave his life as a ransom for all. Talk about credibility!
Talk about being selfless and trustworthy! He earned the right to plead
on our behalf.

My response is, "Wow, I can't believe what you've done for me,
Lord Jesus. Owing me nothing, you chose to give me everything!"

Today he stands in mediation for each of us. When Satan is
disgruntled and accuses us before our Father, Jesus is the mediator who
says, "Forgiven. She's mine. No condemnation!"

He sweeps in as our defense attorney, puts his robe around our
shoulders, and pronounces us innocent!

*Jesus, your Father and I had no way of connecting without you. You
bridged the gap to make my journey to him possible. I owe you my
life. Amen.*

July 6

Pressure for Nothing

I also want women to dress modestly, with decency and propriety, not with braided hair or gold or pearls or expensive clothes, but with good deeds, appropriate for women who profess to worship God.

1 TIMOTHY 2:9–10

*P*aul outlines some distinguishing characteristics of the Christian woman, someone who chooses appropriate clothing and doesn't get carried away with adornments such as jewelry. If I don't read the rest of the verse carefully, though, there's pressure to perform. The standard of excellence has just been raised, choking the life out of my faith. I don't need one more expectation placed on me today, and I certainly don't want to approach obedience with gritted teeth. "I must dress exactly this way. That's what Jesus wants!" This would be a tragedy. I know. I lived this way for decades.

We must not miss the critical phrase "appropriate for women who profess to worship." Our lifestyle choices are to be an extension of our worship, the adornment of our praise. As we experience connection to our Father, our relationship with him is expressed through something as mundane as what we choose to wear. If there's no relationship with Abba, only head knowledge, sooner or later there is anger against a God who expects so much. His intentions for us are the opposite of joyless servitude.

I used to grind out good works like trophies on the mantel for others to admire, but my spirit felt brittle and unbecomingly arrogant. I'm learning to spend more time worshiping. As I emerge from God's company, I can't help but respond as a woman of 1 Timothy. I am like a new bride whose face radiates with the love of her life.

I worship you, Father. Make your face to shine upon me in all my choices today. Amen.

July 7

God's Real Agenda

... which is the church of the living God, the pillar and foundation of the truth.

1 TIMOTHY 3:15

*P*aul reminded Timothy that the church in Ephesus was not the truth but a pillar and support of the truth—a classic distinction. Too many times church leaders forget that they serve truth rather than generate it. When that happens, isolation results.

God grieves deeply over the fragmentation of his church. In a small city in Georgia there are over one hundred Baptist churches. Some are in existence because of quarrels that broke out in their former congregations. Each is isolated, not associating with the others. The disputes usually had nothing to do with tenets of the faith. These churches have deviated from God's plan.

I have been a part of such churches. The telltale signs were obvious. People worked feverishly. Fatigue lined their faces, and their eyes revealed emptiness. There was an unhealthy fear of leadership. People tiptoed around the pastor. I remember living in fear that people would discover I was not perfect. I would become an outcast, unfit to worship with the others.

We're the first to acknowledge that we came to Jesus out of our sinfulness. But we spend the rest of our lives denying that we are sinners! Let's come clean. We're all basket cases without God's daily intervention. Only time with Jesus gives us a faint resemblance of his character. Godliness cannot be generated by peer pressure and fear of disclosure.

Are you anxious to meet the eyes of your spiritual leaders? Do you know that you will find warmth and acceptance there? Is your leader teachable? A healthy church is one that serves people the truth in love.

Help my church family be a congregation of grace, Lord, teaching your truth with humility and authenticity. Amen.

July 8

Hope of Vindication

He appeared in a body, was vindicated by the Spirit.
1 TIMOTHY 3:16

I'm taken by this verse. It reviews Jesus' history on earth. I know that "he was revealed in the flesh," but hadn't considered that he was "vindicated by the Spirit."

He has not yet been vindicated on earth, only in the spiritual realm where his kingdom exists. How do we know he has not been acquitted here? Because he is not recognized as King! Not every person calls Jesus the Son of God; not all worship him as the Messiah. "One day every knee will bow"! But for now we wait in a world where we are not vindicated, either. We're misunderstood visitors on our way to our real home.

We were born wanting life to be fair. When we've been falsely accused or when we've been victimized and the perpetrators go free, we ache for vindication and exposure of evil. But that may not happen in this world. I've had my share of betrayals. Those who caused years of pain continue to go free and even prosper. What do I do with my soul's cry for justice?

This verse gives me the key. I must remember that my King, who rules fairly, is overseer of the spiritual realm. In that realm he sees all. In that realm I am made clean and whole and am clearly vindicated. Any of us suffering unjustly have the joy of knowing deep in our heart that the truth is known in his kingdom. One day all will know. All will understand.

Abba, allow the eyes of my heart to see you on the throne today. I worship you for your just and holy ways. I abdicate my right to judge others and I put justice in your hands. You rule perfectly. Amen.

July 9

Effective Teaching

If you point these things out to the brothers, you will
be a good minister of Christ Jesus, brought up in the
truths of the faith and of the good teaching that you
have followed.

1 TIMOTHY 4:6

Ever sit under lifeless teaching? Good teachers make or break our ability to absorb the material. Some just deliver mountains of information, while others share with passion, making learning easy and enjoyable.

If we're interacting with people, we're teachers. Others learn from us. They can tell by our passion, or lack thereof, what is important to us. When we communicate with them about our relationship with God, are they hit with a barrage of facts or are they impressed with heartfelt words?

Paul writes to Timothy in today's Scripture. He encourages him to share with others what has nourished him from childhood. Take a look around you on Sunday morning. When your pastor shares from his heart and becomes transparent with the text, there's a connection with the listeners. Usually you can hear a pin drop. If, however, he's on an intellectual trip of his own making, there won't be much bonding happening. Just napping, doodling, and a game of hangman being played on the back of a bulletin!

These devotions are meant to share how God is impacting my heart. I want to share with you what moves me and why. Consequently, I pray that you sense passion between the lines. May the Holy Spirit say to you as you read, "Yes, this is for you. This is living truth. Be encouraged." When that occurs, chances are you'll share this message with others, joining me in my desire to teach in a contagious way.

I take your Word to my heart, Lord. Nourish me and make me a powerful communicator. Amen.

July 10

Holding Things with an Open Hand

Command those who are rich in this present world not to be arrogant nor to put their hope in wealth, which is so uncertain, but to put their hope in God, who richly provides us with everything for our enjoyment.

1 TIMOTHY 6:17

I have meditated on this verse for days, waking in the middle of the night to think about it. God's plan is to wean me from this world so I can be firmly connected to a better one. When God asks me to give up something that's difficult to let go of, it is only to give me something better. Because his nature has been so misrepresented to me, though, I have failed to know that important distinction until recently!

For many years I thought God to be the ultimate killjoy, asking me to sacrifice everything I loved, to prove something. When I was finished relinquishing, I would feel sad and empty. God, the ogre, would be satisfied with my state of deprivation.

I had to build a truthful foundation of God's character. He is not one who loves to withhold. He is a Father who delights to give good and perfect gifts. And he does! He has in his hands the riches of Christ for us to enjoy. If we are asked to turn away, give up, or abstain from anything, it is only to direct us toward something perfect for us.

Today our being can vibrate with an enjoyment of God. We are also free to enjoy things! Holding things of this world loosely, we delight in them more, because they are gifts from a loving Father.

I am a sojourner. Nothing here reflects my true status in your kingdom, Father. So whatever I have is a gift for me to enjoy. Thank you! Amen.

July 11

Discovering Our Real Gift

God did not give us a spirit of timidity, but a spirit of
power, of love and of self-discipline.

2 TIMOTHY 1:7

*T*his verse is often offered as a general cure-all for fear. However,
Paul addresses timidity as it relates to spiritual gifts. Those he was
writing to were fearful to exercise their God-given gifts. Why? Why
are we often afraid?

In a perfect world children are mentored, applauded, and
encouraged to be creative. Their uniqueness is accepted. They become
confident adults. In a fallen world uniqueness is marred by the neglect
of imperfect parents, teasing from childhood friends, and tainted
advice from authority figures.

Satan is orchestrating this destruction behind the scenes. If you
and I swapped stories, we would most likely discover that we suffered
our greatest criticisms in the area of our spiritual giftedness. Therefore
the very thing we were good at made us feel the most insecure.

My spiritual gift of mercy was evident early on. Kids with broken
hearts would tell me their stories and cry on my shoulder. A few close
by watched this and, without malicious intent, labeled these friends as
"scarves." (Perhaps they saw these kids as somehow draped across my
shoulders.) I began to think something was wrong with me. Why did
I have scarves when others didn't? What should have been honored
was ridiculed. It took many years for me to discover that I could
embrace my gift. Presently when I speak or sing, I always wear a scarf
to honor mercy!

Has criticism crippled you? Probe the possibility that what you
were devalued for just may be God's gifting. We must grieve the
comments but then in spiritual newness rise up as daughters of a
new order.

*This opens new doors for me, Lord. I can be the person you created,
with joy. Amen.*

Faith and Love

What you heard from me, keep as the pattern of
sound teaching, with faith and love in Christ Jesus.
2 TIMOTHY 1:13

*I*t's easy for me to hear an inspirational sermon, read a book, grab a verse, and feel the poignancy of the moment. I feel strong enough to conquer the world. But when life kicks in hours later, that experience is often lost. I need to learn how to hold fast to God's truths.

Holding on to words with faith means that we love the truth and believe it to such an extent that we're willing to act upon it. Faith and love go together. It's easy to believe words on a page, but do we love their essence?

I'm continually struck by the theme throughout Scripture that head faith is never enough. While God loves Christian education, he is concerned with our heart first. May the result of our education be informed love.

Today if I see that my head is working but my heart feels disconnected, what do I do? Before reading Scripture, I ask God to reawaken my heart to his truth. I ask him to allow his truth to seep into my system. I watch for slow transformation over time. I will see the callused places grow tender because of the power of his words. I will say, "Wow, I didn't think like this five years ago! His words really are changing me." One woman, at the end of a Daughters of Promise event, said, "Today I feel like Sleeping Beauty just waking up from a deep sleep. I died slowly after taking one bite after another of a poisonous apple. Today, though, I will start spitting it out one bite at a time!"

Whatever I love I'll invest in. May it be you and every word that you speak, Lord. Amen.

I Don't Want to Be a Soldier!

No one serving as a soldier gets involved in civilian
affairs—he wants to please his commanding officer.
2 TIMOTHY 2:4

*G*rowing up in a stoic environment can color the spiritual
concept of being a soldier for God. God assumes the role of a
rigid general with little regard for the welfare of those in service. He
browbeats them into submission, demanding grueling obedience,
without preparing them or regarding their well-being.

To support our distortion is our experience of working for some
Christian organizations. People make up a nameless rank that simply
serves the institution. "All for the sake of the gospel," they are told.
There is little personal encouragement. "Onward Christian Soldiers"
is a popular theme among the leaders, who administrate God's work
in an environment where the program demands the ultimate sacrifice.

God is asking us to put on a new pair of glasses today. We must
not allow our eyes to be tainted by our homes of origin or past
ministry experiences. They must not be colored by our view of our
present military models throughout the world, where there is the
cruelty of boot camp to initiate newcomers.

What kind of commander in chief is our heavenly Father? He does
not require anything of me that he has not already done. He leads
crusades that promote his work of setting captives free. As a recruit, I
understand my mission and share the passion of my Leader. I am given
assignments with respect to my maturation level and abilities.

We are not sent to the front lines defenseless. Everyone is equipped
to enjoy ultimate victory.

*I should have known, Lord. You can be the captain of your army
and not compromise any of your character traits. I trust you to lead
me. Amen.*

July 14

Surprising Source of Power

This is my gospel, for which I am suffering even to
the point of being chained like a criminal. But God's
word is not chained.

2 TIMOTHY 2:8–9

*T*hings of the Spirit are not bound by earthly suffering. Paul's
captors sought to extinguish his ministry by chaining him in
prison. Despite Paul's physical confinement, his ministry to others
nevertheless continued, because God's Word cannot be chained. His
Word, ignited by the Holy Spirit, travels by way of people's spirits.

We all have things that hold us back. Limitations in relationships.
Financial restraints. Illnesses that keep us from being fully functional.
Public stigmas that limit our influence. We pound our fists against the
walls of our cells in frustration, thinking that we are hemmed in. But
Paul's words are for us. We can become free and empowered if we allow
God's Spirit to show us the meaning and power of his Word.

Pray Scripture out loud and your spiritual enemies will flee. Pray
it on behalf of a loved one and their very nature may be altered. Pray
it over yourself and oppression will lift. Pray it out loud over your
home and people will exclaim, "It's so peaceful here!" Pray it silently
to yourself the next time an angry person criticizes you, and you may
see anger dissipate. Pray it over someone who is so depressed that
they cannot speak, and watch for God's Spirit to bring about
healing conversation.

There is no prison of the spirit. Though it might appear that the
flesh has rendered us powerless, may we not forget the greatest power
of all: God's Spirit at work in people, brought about by our bold use
of God's Word and the belief that our prayers matter.

*My Bible has gathered dust, and the cobwebs in my life prove it.
Help me maximize its potential, Lord. Amen.*

July 15

"I Need to Be Right!"

Warn them before God against quarreling about words;
it is of no value, and only ruins those who listen.

2 TIMOTHY 2:14

My friend Steve Brown said, "God didn't save me to make me right; he saved me to make me his." Yet in the nature of every human being is the carnal need to be right. I certainly enjoy the feeling, finding it intoxicating when others agree with me!

Steve's quote is liberating. It gives me the freedom to say, "This is what I believe today. But in five years I may amend it."

Paul has strong language about this issue. To challenge people in such a way as to "warn them before God" sounds formal and official. Apparently, this is how strongly God feels about his children who are marked with a reputation for being argumentative! Yet we know many, don't we?

My purpose here is *not* to throw stones at the argumentative. As soon as I do, I become as guilty as they. These words from Paul cause me to look inside. Seeds of insecurity and insignificance become dangerous if not acknowledged. They are watered by an addiction to the praise of others. When I argue over preferences and peripheral Christian beliefs, it not only destroys my own faith but ruins others' as well. Sin is always a contagious spiritual disease.

What is the cure for the need to be right? Allowing God to embrace me. In the environment of such extravagant love, there is no insecurity. Truth is taught in the context of love. Poignant silences and gracious words constitute the language.

Lord, thank you for giving me all I need to live securely. I do not need the validation of people to feel significant. You love me. That is enough. Amen.

July 16

Rediscovering Meekness

The Lord's servant must not quarrel; instead, he must
be kind to everyone, able to teach, not resentful.

2 TIMOTHY 2:24

*T*ruth must always be expressed through love. Those who have a
reputation for being argumentative are out of line with the
character of godly teaching. Not only must teachers refrain from
arguments and the wrangling of words, but also they are to correct
those in error with a spirit of meekness.

Truth is lost to the listener if presented any other way! When truth
is framed with an ego, a need to be right, or a spirit of harshness, the
character of God's heart is assassinated! Truth taught without love has
tragic outcomes. Those who hear it feel shamed, make changes out of
fear, and turn away from the truth in anger.

Church pews are full of those who wear the face of shame and
anger. They feel wrong but are unable to pinpoint the sin they
committed that makes them perpetually bad.

Perhaps our greatest prayer today is, "Lord, work in me to make
me meek." Meekness is an awareness that all I know and all I am are
only because of God's gracious work in me. I do not stand on my own
deserved platform; I stand on one that has been gifted to me out of
mercy. Meekness is being in touch with my own frailty. I know that I
could at any time be deceived, stumble, and fall. I must extend my
arms of grace to bring others back to the fold, just as I would want to
be enfolded.

*Am I arrogant or haughty, Father? Perhaps it's because I have been
unjustly criticized. You know my story. Help me to never destroy
another's spirit. I want to speak the truth, but only with your heart
of love. Amen.*

July 17

Dead-End Pursuits

There will be terrible times in the last days.

2 TIMOTHY 3:1

I've heard many sermons preached from this passage. We've been told that God is warning of coming threats against the church from outside forces. Guess what? Like me, you may be surprised that Paul is talking about threats from within. Perilous times refer to carnality within God's house. Let's face it: two traitors in our midst are far more dangerous than an army outside!

Paul lists those who are dangerous:

- "Lovers of selves"—those who look out for themselves
- "Lovers of money"—those who bow to the rich and dishonor the poor
- "The boastful"—those preoccupied with their accomplishments
- "The ungrateful"—those who look at the half-empty cup and feel resentment or entitlement
- "The irreconcilable"—those who hold sinners at arm's length, not allowing them to gain solid footing
- "The reckless"—those who give unsolicited feedback without regard for its outcome
- "Those who hold to a form of godliness although they have denied its power"—people who can exhibit all the trappings of the Christian faith but who lack God's presence

Paul says these people are always learning but never arrive at truth. I fear that many Christians love only the intellectual study of Scripture. It's easy for them to value their knowledge and enjoy their edge. Sadly, there is no realization that they've done it all without experiencing God! Studying his Word forensically to further an intellectual pursuit does not birth true spiritual power. Time in God's presence is what transforms the heart of a person.

Your Word is not a textbook but a living revelation that is intended to change me into the image of Jesus. Father, may my education be an outgrowth of our love relationship. Amen.

July 18

The Metastasis of Sin

Evil men and impostors will go from bad to worse,
deceiving and being deceived.

2 TIMOTHY 3:13

None of us stands still in our development. If we nurture
spiritual things, we will grow spiritually. If we water carnal
elements, we will grow carnally. No one stays the same.

God instituted a world of sowing and reaping. If I water seeds of
fear with out-of-control thoughts, fear will grow. If I water seeds of
lust with forbidden fantasies, lust will grow. If I water seeds of shame
with self-destructive thoughts, shame will grow. As a seed grows, it
becomes a mature plant with well-developed roots. The longer growth
is left unchecked, the harder it will be to completely dismantle the
plant's root system.

I'm old enough to have seen friends, family members, and
acquaintances grow older. Whatever was a stumbling block to them
when they were thirty is now crippling them at sixty! Most of them
had opportunities to see the truth about themselves, call on God for
help, and make the necessary changes. But they chose to ignore it—
probably for many of the same reasons we procrastinate over our own
unhealthy sinful patterns. Left alone, a sinful seed becomes a slow-
growing cancer, capable of even metastasis!

The message for us here is to make changes when a problem is still
a seed. If I water the seeds of God's character in my heart, those seeds
will sprout, grow, and develop his root system. In time I can become
a "tree firmly planted by streams of water which yields its fruit in
its season."

*I want to become more fully alive to you as I grow older, Lord. I'll
do whatever it takes to water the right seeds and weed out the wrong
ones. Amen.*

July 19

Preparing for Confrontation

Correct, rebuke and encourage — with great patience
and careful instruction.

2 TIMOTHY 4:2

How do I adequately prepare myself for a confrontation?
I must allow my passions to decline until there is rationality.
My goal must be to hear God's voice above my pain. I must wait for
God's green light. People will change only when their heart is receptive to truth. No amount of brilliant rationales on my part will cause
others to see the light. It is a work of God, so I must bathe the potential confrontation in prayer, waiting on him to reveal whether I am to
move immediately, wait, or bring the matter up at all.

I must also take time to engage in spiritual warfare. Satan is the
master of deception. He hates truth and will have his nose in every
encounter where truth is presented. I must ask God to bind Satan's
work so the other person can hear the truth without interference.

I must not speak until love frames the message. Teachable hearts
are the only ones that receive course corrections, and men and women
are only teachable when they know they're loved! No matter how
difficult the message we have for others, it must hang on the
extravagance of love.

Outcomes are varied. Even with God's guidelines, at times there will
be less-than-ideal results. We still reside in a fallen world where pride,
fear, and insecurity rule others' reactions of anger and defensiveness.

However, I want God's smile of approval more than I desire the
positive reception of those around me.

*Heal my fear of rejection, Father. Help me love you more than I love
my own comfort. I will prepare to speak when and where you nudge
me. Amen.*

July 20

Fairy-Tale Love

They will gather around them a great number of
teachers to say what their itching ears want to hear.

2 TIMOTHY 4:3

I like to hear things that make me feel good. I like to know that
I'm important and that someone loves me deeply. I like to know
that my opinions and insights count. It's what fairy tales are made of.
Born with a need for love and significance yet also with a sinful nature,
we learned early to try to get our needs met away from God.

Last Sunday morning while dressing for church, I could hear the
preacher from the television in the living room. His sermon title was
"God Will Make Your Dreams Come True!" He told his viewers how
to get God behind them, get their dreams funded, etc. It sounded so
good but it was a myth, leading listeners to disaster. Tragically, they
would then perceive God as the one who let them down! Who's in
charge of this plan?

Let's talk about dreams. If our dream is to be loved extravagantly,
then yes, God will fulfill it. If our dream is to know joy, then yes, God
will fulfill it. If our dream is to know God and glorify him, then yes,
God will fulfill it. But any dream that does not begin with the desire
to love God and enjoy him is idolatry. Idols eventually break our heart,
leading us to spend wasted years waiting for their payoff.

Let's go where the gold is. Let's run to where love begins and holy
dreams are born.

*What I need is you, Lord. You are the very center of my dreams.
Amen.*

July 21

Beneath the Turbulence

Do your best to come to me quickly, for Demas,
because he loved this world, has deserted me.

2 TIMOTHY 4:9 – 10

*P*aul asks Timothy to come to him. He lists those who were once
friends, true to the faith, but are now deserters. Isn't this where
we live? We cry out to a true friend, "Please come and see me. I'm
lonely. I've been betrayed by someone close to me." Paul doesn't wear
a self-sufficient facade.

He adds, "Oh, please bring my coat." He is in prison, below
ground, shivering perhaps. He reviews those who failed to stand by
him when the heat from his arrest scared them off. Amazingly, there's
no bitterness in his writing. "The Lord will deliver me from every evil
deed and bring me safely to his kingdom." Paul's perspective is
gracious. If he were sitting in the comfort of an inn, his words would
not be as striking as they are coming from these stark surroundings.

What is my response when I'm tired and raw from the fresh
wounds of a once trusted friend? In the midst of stinging tears, are
there whispers of faith?

Each of us could write a book about how we've suffered measures
of deprivation, embarrassment, and betrayal by those we least
suspected. How would our novel read? Would others see a life of
tragedy and little redemption? Would they sense futility and senseless
suffering? Would they see someone who trusted once, twice, but then
turned cynical and distant? Just as one must go deeply beneath the
surface of the sea to escape the turbulence of surface waves, we must
nestle in deeply with God when storms rage.

*Lord, it is in this safe place where Paul's perspective was born and
where I too will be saved from my own fears and irrational thinking.
Amen.*

July 22

New Shoes

You broaden the path beneath me, so that my ankles do not turn.

PSALM 18:36

A friend made the comment that she is walking in shoes that are too big for her. She's miserable.

Remember playing dress-up when you were a kid? You put on mom's jewelry, her long dress, and then her shoes. Mobility was immediately restricted. You were reduced to a shuffle.

Some people have shuffled along for the duration of their lives. A turtle's pace is all they know. They were given another's shoes at birth, but because they've never known shoes that fit, burdensome seems normal. Most people will live and die never knowing how to really walk, much less run, with freedom. They'll never get to wear their own shoes.

It's so unfair to be squeezed into another's mold, like the pressure many feel to walk in father's footsteps or to be more like a sibling. Churches hand out ill-fitting shoes when they hold up super-spiritual role models to emulate. Oftentimes the select few who appear to have picture-perfect lives are on display, always in service, always appropriate, always resourceful and self-sufficient. Oh, the pain of shuffling around in their shoes! Where have we gotten the idea that plastic is perfect?

God applauds authenticity. He fashions spiritual shoes that are perfectly molded to our feet. After all, he created us. Every arch and curve. He would have us be no other way than authentically complete in him.

Let's invite God to unveil our own, uniquely designed pair of sandals, sandals that can accommodate large steps without slipping. We might even take up dancing, like King David.

The shoes you've designed for me are a perfect fit, Lord. I disown all others and anticipate the joy of being who you created me to be. Amen.

Lesson from an Eagle

"You yourselves have seen what I did to Egypt, and how I carried you on eagles' wings and brought you to myself."

EXODUS 19:4

God uses metaphors and parables to bring truth in the back door of our heart, where it can spring to life. Unless the gospel moves us, our Christian life is passionless. To reawaken our senses, God chose to speak through nature. He knew we would discover rich spiritual lessons in the way things grow, bloom, die, and resurrect. He knew we'd find wisdom in the instincts and habits of animals. He uses metaphors from the animal kingdom to describe spiritual truths.

In today's verse he compares his role in the deliverance of Israel to that of an eagle. Most birds carry their young by their talons. The young birds hang beneath the belly of the parent bird. In predatory situations the young are exposed. But eagles are different. They carry their young ones on top of their wings. Why? So if an archer shoots, it must kill the adult first.

We know the theological truth that Christ died to bring us to God. We have heard it, sung about it, and rehearsed it far too intellectually. It used to reside in me as a mere, sterile fact.

This morning I'm more aware than ever that I have been brought out of Egypt, a place of bondage, slavery, and tears. I have been borne out on the wings of Jesus, whose mission it was to bring me to Abba. On the journey he was wounded and murdered unjustly. Because of my position on his wings, my life was spared. Jesus literally died to bring me to God.

Thank you for speaking to me in such creative ways, Father. You'll do anything to help me understand your love better. Amen.

July 24

Sacrifice of Family

After David had finished talking with Saul, Jonathan became one in spirit with David, and he loved him as himself.

1 SAMUEL 18:1

We're familiar with the legendary friendship of David and Jonathan. David loved Jonathan "as himself," and they "became one in spirit" together. But it is a miracle that they had a relationship at all. Jonathan's family ties threatened his loyalty to David. Is blood thicker than water? Usually. But in this case Jonathan made the unlikely but godly choice. It was one made against family, for God, and for God's plans for David's advancement.

Saul was Jonathan's father, the king who ended up hating David. What began as a mild jealousy was ignited through the years by Saul's appetite for power. He plotted to murder David. Can you imagine how Jonathan felt, straddling the fence between his father and his intimate friend?

To add to the intrigue, Jonathan by birthright should have been next in line to be king. But Jonathan recognized David's anointing. When Jonathan's father tried to prevent his friend from ever inheriting the throne, Jonathan stayed true to the purposes of God. In fact, he gave David his own kingly garments to wear, honoring him prematurely as the next king. He went against his family and sacrificed his own self-interest.

Each of us will be called upon to take a stand for God. Perhaps it will require us to stand up to parents or other authority figures. Spiritual brothers like Jonathan see our dilemma. Can you hear their cheers? Jonathan is part of the great cloud of witnesses praying that we will exhibit the courage of our ancestors.

I have a spiritual family, Lord. Jonathan is my brother and I am standing tall to follow in his footsteps. Amen.

July 25

Let's Stop Pretending

We all stumble in many ways.

JAMES 3:2

I'm a daughter of promise. You are, too, if you have been adopted into God's family. We're both being reparented by our perfect heavenly Father. While he achieves perfection status, we do not.

I've put pressure on myself in the past to appear perfect. The mask of piety was put firmly in place. I was anything but what I appeared. I would have been the first to say that I adhered to the tenets of the Christian faith, espousing that Christ came to save sinners. So why did I try to pretend throughout much of my Christian experience that I was above sin? Did that make sense?

Let me say that I'm far from perfect! I get angry when I'm wronged, and I want to get even. I'm basically selfish unless I work on it continually. I like my own way and can be a poor loser. I have to labor to take every thought captive, because there are many of them that need to go under the blood of Christ. Sound familiar?

I have an idea. Let's admit what we are! Let's be a part of a Christian community that allows us to show each other our imperfections. Let's confess our sins and pray for one another. I want friends around who will motivate me to love God and who will inspire my obedience. I want to spend time in the company of believers who won't stumble when they discover that there is carnality left in me. That's how God planned it. We can love fellow sinners unconditionally while provoking one another to kingdom thinking and living. Let's dare to be authentic by walking in honesty, humility, and forgiveness.

Lord, help me stop pretending with you so I can begin to be real with others. Amen.

July 26

Dethroning Myself

To him be glory both now and forever.

2 PETER 3:18

We think we need praise and attention, right? Many of us spend our entire lives setting up a kingdom to feed our appetite for personal glory. Seeing our name in lights feels good, lulling us into believing that we were right about needing it in the first place.

Jesus asks us to die to what we think we must have, revealing how we are wired and what we need for freedom and contentment. It's the opposite of personal glory.

We're presented with a dilemma. We can believe him or continue living for ourselves (which feels pretty good). Most choose the latter and live out their lives in spiritual conflict.

Jesus brought his friend Lazarus back to life. How wonderful! Yet the religious leaders called a meeting, expressing their fears. "If we let him go on like this, everyone will believe in him, and then the Romans will come and take away both our place and our nation" (John 11:48).

In other words, he'll be worshiped, we won't.

They were ignorant of what they really needed. They set themselves up as gods, expecting the world to feed their insatiable appetite for power and prestige. Jesus threatened their whole value system.

If we allow God to become the center of our lives, living becomes an act of worship. We live prostrate, bowing and deferring to the one we serve. "Is this living?" we ask. "Does this honestly feel better than serving myself?"

Absolutely. Created for the purpose of worshiping God, we can be confident that choosing to bring glory to God connects us to our highest joy and calling.

Though what you ask of me sounds like painful self-sacrifice, I dare follow your prescription for profound joy, Father. Amen.

Manna You Can Count On

Do not worry about tomorrow, for tomorrow will
worry about itself.

MATTHEW 6:34

*M*any of us face things today that are quite simply
overwhelming. We can't foresee how we'll cope. Navigating
our way through the challenges seems improbable. The resources we
need, whether financial, physical, or emotional, are out of reach.
Putting on a brave face seems self-betraying, yet curling up in fear
betrays our faith. What do we do?

God is asking us to trust him. He has a track record. He tells his
children to walk by faith, one step at a time. We must not allow visions
of tomorrow to dominate our mind. We must harness our thoughts,
taking every one of them captive, and stand in faith that a Father who
loves us will provide when the time comes.

Faith's house is built with the timbers of uncertainty. It allows us
to trust when it makes no sense. Tomorrow morning, God says, there
will be manna. We must go out to gather it, and when we sit down to
dine, we will eat until we are full. It won't arrive early and it never
comes too late. If God gave us ample resources ahead of time, we might
become self-satisfied and forget that he is the giver. His kingdom is
built on the principle of childlike dependence. We live, breathe, and
move by the power of his hand.

So don't despair. Your need does not go unnoticed. Each time God
moves his hand, he sees your imprint on his palm. You are
unforgettable. He holds himself responsible to meet your needs.

*I don't have some blind faith that things will work out. My faith
rests in you, Lord. Your love upholds me. Your care is dependable.
Thank you. Amen.*

July 28

Certainties and Uncertainties

The LORD will guide you always; he will satisfy your needs in a sun-scorched land.

ISAIAH 58:11

I don't like uncertainty. I'd rather live my life with some degree of predictability. I'd like to know my future. After all, I have dreams and I think it would be helpful to understand whether or not they will be realized.

Uncertainty can make me feel powerless, but that's only because I fail to embrace the certainties that are offered. Of what can I be sure today? God. His love for me. His pure character qualities. The precepts of Scripture that outline his life-giving ways. My heart and mind can be so firmly rooted in these that I experience peace when everything around me is shifting.

Yes, friends fail, marriages disintegrate, children die, and events turn out unexpectedly. But consider this: Faith says that I can be secure in uncertainty. When the winds of change howl at my door and I feel as if my entire world is about to splinter with irreparable damage, there's an anchor for my soul.

You and I do not know what today will be like. We can either cringe in fear or be breathless with expectation over how God will reveal himself to us. Whatever comes, he will be there to experience it with us. God can keep the depth of our heart quiet, though circumstantially, the storm rages. He will be our anchor in the chaos.

Let's not give in to fear. We're firmly in his grip. He whom we trust in life and death is unchanging. God never sleeps and he is the Lord of the deep.

I only have to look inside to find you, Lord. Your Spirit resides in the core of my soul. When I look for you in the deep, you'll be there. You are my security. Amen.

July 29

It Doesn't Take Much

What he trusts in is fragile; what he relies on is a
spider's web.

JOB 8:14

When was the last time you felt on top of the world? You woke up with energy. It was a Saturday, your day off. The sun was shining and it was the perfect temperature. Everyone in the household was relatively happy. You felt at peace. The thought crossed your mind, *Life's not so bad. I can handle this. Everything's under control.*

I had a day like that last week. I was taking a long walk, assessing my world. God whispered to me, "Your sense of balance is a delicate thing. It wouldn't take much for you to crumble. Keep putting your trust in me." I thought about that and had to agree. A car accident, a frightening medical diagnosis, even an unexpected large bill would alter my equilibrium.

It's easy for me to think that my well-being is directly related to my circumstances. If all is well around me, I am well. If something is badly amiss, I will flounder unless I am anchored to someone strong.

My spiritual barometer needs to change. I need a new set of criteria that determine my well-being. Perfect days are hard to come by. Each day usually presents one set of challenges after another. Putting my trust in a beautiful spring day or whether or not my mortal body feels well is so foolish. I can certainly enjoy both, but contentment and mood can't be dependent on them. May I say every day, "I'm on top of the world today because God loves me and holds my hand tightly."

You want me to live my life from the shadow of your wings, Father.
In that place all is well. You are my anchor and hope. Amen.

July 30

Live Cherished

He predestined us to be adopted as his sons through Jesus Christ, in accordance with his pleasure and will—to the praise of his glorious grace, which he has freely given us in the One he loves.

EPHESIANS 1:5−6

God is love yet we often feel that God loves everyone but us. We are dressed in the shame of others' labels, the shame of our sins and failures, or both. God's arms are open wide and he invites us to make him our home. Not because we deserve it but because the nature and character of his heart is loving. It takes courage to stretch out our arms and embrace God's gift of love, received in Jesus Christ. How life-changing when we do! We can live with the warmth of his smile on our shoulder and the light of his countenance on our face.

When our son, Ryan, was seven years old, he came bounding into the family room, where the rest of our family was sitting, and said, "Ta-da! Here I am, your bundle of joy!" We burst out laughing yet we knew that he was serious. He was absolutely convinced that he was a source of joy for us, so much so that words streamed from his subconscious.

God is love—all the time—no matter what I do. If I sin, I do not lessen his love for me. If I perform flawlessly, I cannot increase it. He loves because that is the nature and character of his heart. Tomorrow morning I can roll out of bed, look in the mirror, and declare as his much loved daughter, "Ta-da! Here I am, your bundle of joy."

Wow, you don't just love me, Father. You cherish me. Help my heart understand that. Amen.

July 31

A God Who Cannot Lie

Do not withhold your mercy from me, O LORD; may
your love and your truth always protect me.

PSALM 40:11

*G*od's character is flawless. He cannot lie because he also loves.
Truth and love are linked together many times in Scripture
because God wants us to understand that they are wedded in his very
nature. They are the two foundational characteristics of Yahweh.

He tells the complete truth, all the time, about everything and
everyone. Consequently, Scripture provides wisdom I can trust
regarding matters of business, ministry, marriage, parenthood, and
friendships. When I go to God and seek answers with a sincere
intention, I know I will receive a perfect reply, because he loves me.

When I sin, he is truthful about that too. He doesn't tell me what
I want to hear. He has no other agenda than helping me become more
like his Son. He is straightforward in his approach. If I am teachable,
his way with me is tender. If I am stiff-necked, he'll need to be firmer
to get my attention. He'll do whatever it takes to prevent me from
heartache down the road. He hates sin, mostly because it hurts me! He
let his own Son pay with his life to provide a way for me to eradicate
the effects of it in my life.

While other authority figures often withhold information and let
me find things out the hard way, God is kind and gives me truthful
instruction ahead of time. He doesn't manipulate me in an effort to
control me. He gives me choices, cheers me on to make the right ones,
and rewards me for my obedience with security, peace, confidence,
and joy.

*There is none like you, God. I am completely at ease following your
type of leadership. Amen.*

August

August 1

Review and Remember

With Bethel on the west,… he built an altar to the LORD.
GENESIS 12:8

Our faith is strengthened when we remember the strategic places on our spiritual journey. Do you face a scenario today for which you have no wisdom, a battle for which you have no strength, or an obstacle that seems immovable? God wants us to discover how we, as women, can harness the faith that will help us navigate challenging times.

Jacob, the blessed son of Isaac, was chosen to be the father of a great nation. This he only knew intellectually until God showed up at Bethel and confirmed it in his experience. God spoke powerfully to him there. It was a personal encounter and it bookmarked a place in his life that he would never forget. When Jacob faced impossible hurdles in the future, God appeared and identified himself as "the God of Bethel."

Can you recall a time when God met you personally? There was no mistaking his presence, his message, and his intention? For me it was a place in Ohio, on Finch Lane, where we lived. When despair knocks at my door, God whispers to me, "It is I, Christine, the God of Finch Lane." Ah, then I remember. It was there that Daughters of Promise was conceived and mountains were moved for its birth. I learned firsthand that God is not passive. The God of Finch Lane marches again when called upon.

Take a walk down memory lane today. Perhaps God wants you to remember afresh that he is the God of your Bethel. He is still in covenant with his people. He has not forgotten you nor does he waver in his commitment to provide for your spiritual well-being.

I can't trace your hand right now, Lord, but I remember yesterday. Strengthen me. Amen.

A Strong Resemblance

Jacob said to him, "My lord knows that the children are tender."

GENESIS 33:13

*J*acob stole his brother Esau's birthright. He paid dearly for it, too. (Our sin has consequences, even though we repent of it.) He had to flee his own country, labor in a foreign land for over twenty years, and fear of ever returning home because of his angry brother.

When at last God directs him to return to Canaan, to his promised land of blessing, Jacob knows he needs to go through Esau's country. This is of great concern. He wrestles with God, proclaims his terror, and then lays it to rest in God's hands. Jacob has learned that it is God who turns people's hearts in whatever ways he chooses.

When at last Jacob and Esau meet, Jacob bows in humility. Both brothers weep, for Esau has had a heart change brought about by almighty God. Esau offers Jacob protection on his travels, and Jacob pleads for the sake of his wives, his children, and his flocks. He asks that they not be driven hard. "My lord Esau knows that the children are frail and that the flocks and herds which are nursing are a concern to me. If they are driven hard, some of them might die."

Jacob is a tender caretaker, a reminder that Christ, who is our shepherd, knows our frailties and does not require so much of us that we might break. He is a compassionate leader. Jacob and Jesus at this moment in time resemble one another. They provide two identical types of leadership as the tender face of God is exhibited in humankind.

I have been as manipulative as Jacob. I have also been angry like Esau. Anything in me that resembles you, Lord, is a miraculous work of your mercy. Amen.

August 3

Imperfect Children

"Get rid of the foreign gods you have with you, and purify yourselves and change your clothes."

GENESIS 35:2

*I*f we have a child who walks away from God, we can easily slip into guilt, feeling failure as a parent. We are embarrassed to tell others how he is really doing, thinking that his lifestyle reflects badly on us. Let's go back and review the story of Jacob. There's rich encouragement for us.

Jacob was the man God chose to carry on the promise of Abraham. Yet God tells him to take a trip to Bethel and instructs him to prepare for the journey by going through his family's camp and putting away all idols. When I first read that, I thought, *Jacob's family worshiped other gods? How can that be? He's a patriarch!* But then, I know better. Even in families where there is a face of Christianity, much can be amiss. Each child has a free will and makes his own choices.

Jacob did as he was told. He gathered up all the graven images and buried them. Then God told him to have his sons change their garments. Changing garments before a sacrifice signified purification. But God didn't take any chances on them misunderstanding. He said, "Purify your hearts and change your clothes." The command implied, "What good are clean clothes without a clean heart?"

Godly parents can have wayward children. God, who is the perfect Father, has rebellious children, does he not? So we labor in prayer for our wandering children. We repent of any responsibility we potentially hold in their rebellion. Then we remember that they are God's children. He will be faithful to work in them to accomplish his purposes.

My family isn't perfect, Lord. Deal with us according to your mercy and grace. Amen.

Timely Deliverance

"Mention me to Pharaoh and get me out of this prison."
GENESIS 40:14

*I*s there any part of your life in which you feel trapped? Perhaps you have prayed for God's deliverance, but it seems as if God has forgotten you. I know what it's like to be in a situation in which you cry for release. I knew such a situation for over twenty years.

Joseph's story showcases important spiritual lessons. Through the betrayal of his brothers, through slavery and unfair imprisonment, there were moments when he experienced a crisis of faith. For instance, when he was in prison, he had an opportunity to interpret the dreams of a fellow inmate. This man happened to be a former servant of Pharaoh, and Joseph prophesied that he would serve in Pharaoh's palace again. "And when that happens," Joseph said, "will you remember me and plead my case?" The man forgot, though he was reinstated to his former post. Did Joseph's hope die? Perhaps.

Two years later the man finally told Pharaoh about Joseph, and even then in nonpreferential terms. Pharaoh was anxious, having just had some bad dreams, and this man told him there was a lowly prisoner who could interpret them.

If this man had pleaded Joseph's case two years earlier, Pharaoh might have pardoned Joseph and sent him home. But because God ordained Joseph to appear before Pharaoh as the dream interpreter, he found favor with Pharaoh and was named prime minister of Egypt.

There is a time set for the deliverance of God's people, and when that time comes, though it always appears elusive, we end up saying, "Yes, this was the best time after all."

My despair is only because my view is limited, Lord. I am not trapped if you are God. I trust you with my future. Amen.

August 5

Secret Keeper

Pharaoh gave Joseph the name Zaphenath-Paneah.
GENESIS 41:45

*J*oseph was given a new name after Pharaoh appointed him prime minister of Egypt. I love the meaning of the name and in fact wish I could tack it on as another middle name for myself. It was Zaphenath-Paneah. Quite cumbersome to the tongue but here's the value: it means "revealer of secrets." I'm sure this was given to him primarily because he had, through divine revelation, interpreted Pharaoh's troubling dreams. He shed light on what was elusive and allegorical.

This morning I went on a long walk around the lake near our house, and I was thinking about the meaning of Zaphenath-Paneah. I love secrets, don't you? The secret of being healthy, the secret of staying young, and the secret of beautiful skin. Can you imagine being so in tune with God, his heart, and his ways that you become a kind of spokesperson for him? Your reputation earns you the name "revealer of secrets."

That title is available to any of us today who love God's ways better than our own, to any of us who realize that godly wisdom is certainly something foreign to our way of thinking. We understand that God's secrets must be sought after through prayer and the study of Scripture. The Spirit of God reveals them. They are plentiful and we are meant to delight in their truth. And they are meant to be shared. Are you one of his messengers, and when you speak, do others say, "Yes, she speaks for God. What wisdom!" If so, you know the joy of being a Joseph.

I love your thoughts, Lord. I hunger for them more than anything else. Bathe me in the riches of your mind and heart. Amen.

Unexpected Mercy

Joseph said to his brothers, "Come close to me."

GENESIS 45:4

I'm moved by Joseph's revelation to his brothers. They had sold him into slavery decades earlier, yet when he reveals himself (and they expect condemnation), he says, "It is I, brothers. Come closer to me. Don't be afraid."

Can you feel the grace as you picture the story? The brothers had acted abominably. They had done the unthinkable to their own flesh and blood, but now they are forgiven and told, "Be at peace. All is well. Come and embrace me."

Joseph is a type of Christ in the Old Testament. We are like the brothers, for we sinned against Jesus. It was our betrayal and sin that sent him to the horrible death of crucifixion. Yet when we are repentant, we hear him call to us, "It is I. Don't be afraid. Come closer. Embrace me!" When we expect condemnation, radical forgiveness is offered instead.

Joseph invited his brothers to move to Egypt to be near him. He said, "Go back to Canaan, but don't be concerned about your goods. All of Egypt is yours!" Sound familiar? Jesus likewise is preparing all of heaven for us. And we are told, "Don't be wrapped up in the stuff of this world. After all, heaven is yours!"

Celebrate the love story between you and your Savior. The very one who could have pronounced judgment against you was the one who offered you his love. He put your sins behind his back, never to remind you of them again. He thinks of you as a friend, not an enemy. Can any mercy compare with his?

I have been afraid to really trust your forgiveness, Jesus. But today I come close to embrace you. May your love melt away my fears. Amen.

August 7

Wisdom out of Folly

"God sent me ahead of you to preserve for you a remnant
on earth and to save your lives by a great deliverance."

GENESIS 45:7

braham Lincoln was quoted as saying that he learned the most
from failure. Each of us would probably agree. Our errors in
judgment, the ones that cost us dearly, yielded valuable lessons that
went deep into our hearts. We are not likely to make the same
mistakes twice.

Such was the case with Joseph's brothers. In their youth and folly
they were quite willing to betray their brother. They threw Joseph in
a pit and sold him into slavery, all because they wanted their father's
favor, blessing, and advancement. Now, years later, when the life of
another brother, Benjamin, is on the line, they remember the sins of
their youth and finally make a godly choice. They stick by him and
reveal the sins of their past to Joseph (not knowing it is him), and God
is finally able to redeem the past. Joseph was the wise one who brought
this principle to light. He said to his brothers, "Don't be grieved or
angry with yourselves. God sent me before you to Egypt to preserve
your lives."

You and I often grieve over our sins, to the point of sabotaging
our future. After repentance God wants to make good out of evil.
When wisdom is born out of folly, our grief can turn to great joy. God
is celebrated. His glory and power are evident to all who watch him
rebuild our lives. I trust your heart is dancing today over the
redemption of just one of your past mistakes.

*You are a merciful God. You have compassion for your children. Jesus
made a way for me to start fresh today with nothing held against
me. Thank you. Amen.*

August 8

God First

Israel set out with all that was his, and when he reached Beersheba, he offered sacrifices to the God of his father Isaac.

GENESIS 46:1

*T*he story of Joseph and his brothers and father is one of the most dramatic in all of Scripture. As you read it, you can feel the betrayal, the losses, the grief, and the injustice of many of the principal figures of the saga. Joseph was torn away from his father at a young age, only to be sold into slavery. He spent time unjustly in prison and mourned that he might never see his father again, but we know the end of the story. Joseph, crowned as the prime minister of Egypt, reveals himself to his brothers and sends them home with a message: "Tell Father to come to Egypt, he and all his descendants, and I will provide for him." Can you imagine what news this was to his father, Jacob? To find out that his favorite son was alive, not dead?

I marvel that he didn't pick up everything right then and leave for Egypt. But the story, told in Genesis, says that he didn't. Instead he went to Beersheba, where his father, Isaac, had often met God to pray. Jacob waited for God to give him permission to go.

I am struck by this devotion. Jacob's experience of God was so profound that his desire to obey Yahweh eclipsed the story of his long-lost son. Yes, he loved Joseph dearly, but not enough to forego the blessing of a God who had remained in covenant with him and his family over the course of generations.

I look at all my desires today, Lord. If any of them are more important than your blessing, I ask for forgiveness. Amen.

August 9

Jacob and I Are One

When Jacob had finished giving instructions to his
sons, he drew his feet up into the bed, breathed his
last and was gathered to his people.

GENESIS 49:33

*J*acob's life was much like mine. If I review the highlights of his
time on earth, there would be surprising parallels to my own existence.

Jacob was the younger of two children. He was the one with a
gentle, quiet nature. Yet he tricked his father into giving him his
brother's inheritance. He paid dearly for his clever manipulation. He
had to flee home to escape Esau's wrath.

He met his soul mate, Rachel, in the land of his exile. Yet even
love wasn't easy. Her father tricked him into marrying Rachel's older
sister. Trickery was to be a theme in Jacob's life.

Decades passed before he ventured back to Canaan. He had twelve
sons. One of them was Joseph. Jacob was tricked again when his sons
announced Joseph's death. Actually, they had sold Joseph into slavery.
Years of grief followed, which included grave disappointment in the
lack of godliness in his children! Had God's divine promise been
nullified?

The God of his father, Isaac, and grandfather, Abraham, was all
he had. His faith deepened. We know the wonderful end to his story.
Joseph was really alive and brought his entire family to live in Egypt.
Jacob's last days were the sweetest of his life.

And so may it be with us. We've suffered rough starts, imperfect
marriages, wayward children, even unexpected betrayals that tricked
us into believing our lives were over. Just as Jesus was born through
the line of Jacob, we bear the divine seed of promise.

*My wounds do not disqualify me, Father. I bring them to you for
healing and redemption. Amen.*

August 10

An Irony

When the Canaanites who lived there saw the mourning..., they said, "The Egyptians are holding a solemn ceremony of mourning."

GENESIS 50:11

I can be so fickle, feeling strongly about something this minute but six months later feeling differently. A nation can be fickle, too. It gives support to a cause today but retracts it later. We have the advantage of looking back at history and viewing others' mistakes. We see where they were unstable.

There's an interesting story told at the end of Genesis. Jacob died and Joseph asked Pharaoh if he could take a leave of absence from his post as prime minister and take his father back to Canaan to be buried. Pharaoh told Joseph to take high-level Egyptian officials, military protection, wagons, chariots, whatever he needed to make the trip. It was quite an entourage that carried the body of Jacob hundreds of miles. We're told that the Egyptians, out of respect for Jacob, mourned his death as one of their own for seven days, then for another twenty-one days at the burial place. In fact, natives of Canaan talked for hundreds of years about how the Egyptians mourned the death of a godly patriarch. Jacob was buried with high honors.

Isn't it ironic how far Egypt fell? Years later they would enslave and beat the descendants of Jacob. How quickly they forgot the affections of their forefathers.

Do you value your godly heritage? No legacy is perfect, and ungodly inheritances should be prayed over and cleansed, but what about the godly legacies? Let's embrace the work of God in our ancestors. May we not provide spiritual ironies years later to those who would have loved instead to find us faithful!

Bless every work of yours in my ancestral line, Lord. Help me walk in the footsteps of my godly ancestors. Amen.

An Unlikely Teacher

It is God who arms me with strength and makes my
way perfect.

PSALM 18:32

Joseph wore a multicolored coat that had sentimental value. His
father gave it to him because Joseph was his favorite child.
Jealous of Joseph's preferment, his brothers betrayed him. They took
his coat and sold him into slavery. Was this a tragic plot with no
redeeming purpose?

His bondage was providential. Joseph was sold to Pharaoh's
officer, enabling him to become acquainted with public personalities
and government policies. His unprecedented success as ruler of Egypt
was enhanced by his experience with matters of state. His
imprisonment was his tutelage.

Has God permitted you to live for a period of time in an
oppressive environment? Perhaps your childhood home was less than
ideal and you feel it destroyed your chances for a different life. Maybe
you work in an environment that is demeaning. No one notices or
appreciates you. Possibly, like Joseph, you were stripped of your
inheritance by a betrayal of some kind.

This is leading you somewhere of value if you're committed to
look to God with the eyes of faith. He is the Master Carpenter who
shapes all things for the good of those who love him.

If we climb a mountain and keep our eyes on each stony or
difficult place of ascent, how profitless it all seems. But if we think that
each step leads to the summit of God's perfect plan, we will be
introduced to glories and beauties never before seen with our eyes.

*All I see is where I am. It seems futile. You are all powerful, Lord,
and I believe you are working all things for my good. Help me stay
faithful to your calling. Amen.*

August 12

Joy Explained

"Now is your time of grief, but I will see you again and you will rejoice, and no one will take away your joy."

JOHN 16:22

We often equate joy with good circumstances. A promotion, a breakthrough in a marriage, the trip of a lifetime—these can trick us into thinking we have joy. This is not the kind of joy that Jesus speaks of. He says that in the midst of sorrow we can know joy. Not the plastic kind Christians often paste on their face to look spiritual but a joy reflected in the secret places of our hearts.

References to joy in the New Testament are sorely misrepresented. Yes, we're told that we can be joyful and thankful, but often we are taught verses like these to run from pain. Tears are deemed inappropriate, a sign of weakness. A "joyful" face is praised. If a woman's heart is breaking, no one must know, for she would be seen as a spiritual failure.

This does not represent the teaching of Jesus. He wept openly, was often troubled in spirit, and taught us that life in this world brings sorrow. If our joy is dependent on whether our day goes well or not, it is fragile and shallow.

What kind of joy can't be taken away from us, no matter what? The joy of spiritual truth. No matter what happens to me today, nothing can separate me from Abba's love. No one can take his presence from my soul. No one can steal my spiritual inheritance. No one can break in and pillage my eternal home. Eternal things are secure. Though my face may weep, my joy is my strength.

I renounce false teaching. I can fully express my sorrow while my heart knows a joy over my spiritual riches in you, Lord. Amen.

Learning to Laugh at Ourselves

"The LORD does not look at the things man looks at.
Man looks at the outward appearance, but the LORD
looks at the heart."

1 SAMUEL 16:7

Sometimes we do the best we can at the time with the information that's available to us, but because we lack a critical piece of knowledge, we end up falling flat on our face. On a lighter note, allow me to illustrate.

I took a trip a long time ago that resulted in one of the most comical nights of my life. Right after Ron and I married, we traveled with a musical group. Six of us toured the country in an eight-passenger van. One night we were to drive all night, heading south from northern New Jersey via the New Jersey Parkway. Every ten miles or so we had to stop to pay a toll.

At each booth our group leader, a guy named Bob, paid the fare and then gave the toll booth attendant a tract and said, "Here, I'd like to give you this. The message in it changed my life."

It wasn't until the early daylight hours that one of us pointed out to him that what he had been passing out was not tracts but instead a stack of *Riddle Diddle Fiddle* booklets from Burger King. Can you imagine what the people thought as they glanced through the booklets a little later on their break? "This changed someone's life?"

A mother who receives burned toast on a tray, made with love by her four-year-old, eats it with a warm heart because motive is everything.

I may not do it all right, Lord, but thank you for not holding that against me. You reward a heart that is bent toward you. Amen.

August 14

No Credibility, Yet!

"Then I will send rain on your land in its season . . . so
that you may gather in your grain, new wine and oil."
DEUTERONOMY 11:14

Is God birthing a new work in you? Most likely, you have a difficult
time verbalizing the nature of it to other people. The words are new.
The concepts are foreign. The outcome is uncertain although glorious.

You sense you're being changed at the very core of who you are.
These changes appear subtle to others, but you feel the cataclysmic
shifting inside you. Intuitively you know that life will never be the
same again. Your future is being rewritten. You are becoming the
carefree daughter God created.

When God raises up something new out of ashes, rebirth happens
over time. The gentle winds of the Holy Spirit kick up the dead leaves,
and they swirl upward to make a new form. The shape, merely a
shadow, does not yet appear concrete to spectators. They will poke at
it and discount it, all because they do not have the eyes of faith to see
it yet for what it is.

Don't be discouraged. God will provide a few who will confirm
his work in you. They will note it with joy. They will perceive God's
creativity as a glorious thing. Their applause will sustain you during
this time of waiting.

Daughters of Promise was born out of ashes. At the beginning the
ministry was all about me. God was remaking me, preparing me to
lead this ministry. So allow me to lift you to your feet. If your new
work lacks credibility, this is normal. God is preparing you and your
audience for what's ahead.

*Father, I know you will grant me favor with others according to your
perfect timeline. I trust you and love what you're creating. Amen.*

August 15

Crippled by Fear

"Be strong and courageous. Do not be afraid or terrified
because of them, for the LORD your God goes with you."
DEUTERONOMY 31:6

I was victimized by fear for many years. The fear produced panic.
The panic crippled me and stripped me of functionality. I simply
didn't have the spiritual skills to be an overcomer. Over time, though,
God has taken me backstage, behind the drama of panic, to examine
the thought processes that created such a crisis. He wanted me to
understand what led me to abdicate my God-given privilege, as his
child, to know peace.

Fear is what results when we allow lies to take our mind on a
journey of their own. We are afraid because we forget that God is more
powerful than whatever threatens us. He is faithful to deliver us. He is
not wringing his hands in despair. Having forgotten these core truths,
we cup our hands around lies like, *I'm alone. This is going to destroy me.
I can't face this.* These thoughts take us down the pathway of fear.
Tormented, we look frantically for someone powerful enough to trust.
Given a big enough crisis, we feel there is no one to deliver us.
Rehearsing the absence of someone trustworthy and powerful, we
embark on the journey of panic.

How do we find peace? The next time we're afraid, let's stop and
examine our thoughts. Let's verbalize them. "I've concluded things are
hopeless because _____." What we'll hear are lies. It's necessary to
confess them and renounce them. We must harness our thought life.
Peace can be the hallmark of our testimony. It starts when we embrace
the powerful words of our Father and then stand on them no matter
how fierce the storm that beats on our door.

Father, my trust in you is well founded. Amen.

Never Abandoned

"The LORD your God goes with you; he will never leave you nor forsake you."

DEUTERONOMY 31:6

*M*any know the pain of abandonment firsthand. Their father or mother died when they were young, or worse yet, one or both parents chose to leave with little regard for the long-term consequences. This tragic occurrence introduces a series of lies that is difficult to dismantle later in life, lies such as, "I must take care of myself." "I can trust no one." "Sooner or later everybody leaves." "I'm not worth much; that's why I was abandoned."

This intrinsic distrust causes most to back away from even God. After all, he's a father and fathers can't be trusted. Those who have made a profession of faith in Christ but still have little faith in the very nature of God's love fill many a church pew. Their heart is closed off from him by their own choice, but God is still nearby. He watches, waits, whispers their name, and hopes they'll flex their faith muscles to discover that he offers them a new reality. To believe that God is different is a challenge, but we must choose to believe that he is!

Abba never leaves his children, not even for a moment. We are being reparented by a perfect Father. He's there for every major event—promotions, the birth of our children, the purchase of our first home, every occasion in which there's good news to celebrate. He's also around on the saddest day of our lives. His tears blend with ours. Not one sigh goes unnoticed. He's not turned off by our weakness but rather sees our need as an opportunity to show us how deeply we are loved.

I am deciding to trust you, Father. Meet me at the door of my heart. Amen.

Cool Your Jets!

In your anger do not sin; when you are on your beds,
search your hearts and be silent.

PSALM 4:4

The psalmist understands anxiety. He says, "Tremble and do not sin." We know what he means. A harsh comment is made or rude behavior is exhibited against us, and we're shaken to the core. We feel ready to fly off the handle and give the offending party a piece of our mind. But the psalmist says, "Stop!" He advises us to freeze when we're first aware of our anger, so we do not sin. I recall the old adage "When the heart is hot, the tongue should be silent."

I'm relieved that the psalmist doesn't leave us trembling and holding our breath. He's practical enough to give us the next step to self-control. Meditate. Be still. Offer sacrifices of righteousness.

I'm taking his words to heart. The next time I'm angry and given to trembling, I'm going to get away to regroup. I'll find a quiet place to think and talk things out with God. I won't have to edit thoughts or feelings. My heavenly Father values authenticity. He is intimately acquainted with the one who offended me. He created that person and might offer insights that are critical for my understanding of that person.

At this point God might ask me to be merciful, as he is merciful, even though the person really doesn't deserve it. He could suggest that I extend some kindness while being firm. What if I don't feel like doing the righteous thing? I'll make a sacrificial gift to God, whom I worship. It's the least I can do.

You didn't deal with me in anger, Father. You reached out in love through Jesus. Make me like you. Amen.

Misplaced Trust

Some trust in chariots and some in horses, but we
trust in the name of the LORD our God.

PSALM 20:7

I have a sense of dread this morning. I'm to fly across the country
later today, from Atlanta to Los Angeles. There is severe weather
from Atlanta westward. I slept fitfully last night, envisioning the worst
possible plane ride. While I'll tell others that what worries them most
will probably never happen, I was still seized with enough fear
throughout the night that I had trouble resting.

The least favorite part of my occupation is flying. I've been
through some pretty nasty weather, and one might think that, having
lived through the worst, I could relax about what will probably be
better than that. But I still struggle.

As I prayed about what to write this morning, God nudged me
and said, "Be transparent. Show them how faith works. Demonstrate
how, in spite of the fear, you anticipate my faithful comfort." So I offer
myself to you as a friend and wounded healer. Many of you write to
me to say that you value these devotions for several reasons. First,
Scripture is presented as the living revelation of God rather than an
abstract textbook. Second, the Bible is personalized through my
willingness to be transparent.

How is God reaching out to me even now? He brought today's
verse to mind. As soon as I recalled it, I paraphrased it. "Some trust in
pilots, worthy aircraft, and good weather, but I trust in God." This
will be my mantra. Once the plane takes off, I'll be in my seat, eyes
closed, seeing myself in the safe embrace of my Father.

*I am carved on the palm of your hand, God. Your presence is my
refuge. Your words are my lifeline. Amen.*

August 19

Unseen Wounds

Above all else, guard your heart, for it is the well-spring of life.

PROVERBS 4:23

*M*any of us were raised in homes in which the rule was, "No crying unless you're bleeding!" We grew up believing that if we couldn't see any wounds, maybe they weren't real. Friends and clergy made comments like, "Spending time in pain is just a cop-out for justified self-centeredness. People can snap out of it with God's help." Statements like these make me cringe.

What do we do about the tears we're afraid to cry? As Christians, we often think we should be above having inner wounds. We might believe any of the following lies: "If I were a stronger Christian, this wouldn't bother me" or "My parents always told me I was too sensitive" or "My pastor said I should have more faith." If we think about these statements, what they really mean is, "No matter how severe the injury, I should not be wounded."

The next time we start to believe this myth, we should review the life of Jesus. He expressed grief, compassion, and anger. He modeled the truth that those who live in this world will suffer. He demonstrated that he is primarily interested in our unseen lives and therefore cares deeply about the places where we have been wounded.

Today we have a high priest who is able to understand our pain. He knew we'd need healing to live free of what has crippled us. He said, "No matter what you've done, no matter what has happened, you can confidently approach me for grace and mercy."

As my divine physician, examine me, Lord. You see my broken heart and you know what I need to heal. I hide nothing from you and place all my hurts in your tender hands. Amen.

Tigers Are God's Handiwork

Since the creation of the world God's invisible
qualities—his eternal power and divine nature—have
been clearly seen.

ROMANS 1:20

I love cats, specifically gray tiger cats with the perfect marking of the
black W on their forehead. I am convinced that they are the most
magnificent of God's creations. I delight in them, from the subtleties
of their markings to the individual eccentricities of their personalities.

I currently have two tigers. Charles Dickens (a cat I acquired at
Christmastime) and Herman Ebenezer. Dickens is my all-time favorite
pet, though. If I talk to him from across the room, he'll knead the air.
We are uniquely connected. In fact, he has been on my lap through
most of the writing of this book. He has dozed through its creation;
I've even written to the sound of gentle snoring.

Most of the time he was patient as I reached over his head to peck
the computer keys. Once in a while, though, when he'd had enough
of my jerking movements, he reached out and bit my wrist. That's
okay. There's nothing about him I don't find charming.

Dickens reminds me of God's love for me. He was created for my
enjoyment. Sometimes while petting him, I'll exclaim, "You are so
incredible. I'm crazy about you!" For any of you who aren't fond of
cats, this may sound absurd and sappy. That's okay.

The point is this: Much of what we will enjoy today has been given
to us by a God who loves to bring us pleasure. Whether it's the flora
in your backyard or the bond you share with your pets, God's fingerprints are seen. Let's take the time to smell the roses.

Signs of your love are all around me, Lord. Thank you. Amen.

August 21

Mind Transplant

The mind of sinful man is death, but the mind controlled by the Spirit is life and peace.

ROMANS 8:6

*C*hristianity is set apart from all other religions because it is built on a living Savior who beckons us into an intimate relationship with him. If we've not come to Jesus from outside the boundaries of the Christian faith, we can be so familiar with the language of the gospel that we lose the wonder of it.

Jesus' bride is undergoing more than just renovation. We're under total reconstruction. Through the process of love, we're being remade into the image of our Lover. We will have Jesus' heart. Our mind is undergoing a metamorphosis to become more like the mind of Christ. What is the reward? Peace.

If we allow anyone other than Jesus to do our thinking for us, we'll be distressed. If we try to think for ourselves, we will be guided by error, limited knowledge, and misinformation. If Paul could sit and talk with us today, he'd say, "Let Jesus' thinking displace and supersede your mind and the thoughts and reasoning of others. Do this and you will be kept in peace and order. You will know precisely what is true, what is prudent, and what is the proper course of action at any given moment."

Jesus offers us a transplant of the mind. This daily, spiritual, surgical procedure will bring astounding results. We'll be directed by divine intelligence. God will freely give to us out of the resources of his intellectual powers. I finally understand that Solomon asked for the best gift. His mind and mine, directed by God's thoughts, yield a life rich in abundance.

Solomon leads by the power of example. Like him, Lord, I ask for your wisdom. Amen.

August 22

Advantages of a Turbulent Past

> We know that in all things God works for the good of
> those who love him, who have been called according to
> his purpose.
>
> ROMANS 8:28

an a turbulent past produce positive outcomes in adult life?
Absolutely. Many of us were born on the train tracks of pain,
and we need to hear that our traumatic life experiences can work to our
advantage. We need not be doomed to a life of deprivation, for we are
empowered with a choice today about what we can become.

The death of Jesus is the best illustration that good can come out
of evil. No wonder he is so skilled at taking our tragedies and
transforming them. It doesn't happen overnight, though, and it didn't
happen quickly for Jesus either. He waited thirty-three years on
earth alone!

He was born into a bloodline that rejected him. He was misunderstood throughout adolescence and adulthood. He was misjudged
and hated to the point of being crucified as a criminal. But his
seemingly fatal end yielded redemption and resurrection.

All things can work together for good for all who love God and
those who are called according to his purpose. No mistake is too great.
No trauma is too severe for healing. No betrayal is so injurious that
God cannot create a new beginning. No financial failure is so
extensive that God's providential hand is crippled.

Trust your Father today. Give him your deepest hurt. He will be
faithful to transform the darkest part, the place you labeled "untouchable,"
and bring it into the light of his grace for healing. Taste and see that the
Lord is good.

*I had lost hope for my future, Lord. I thought my past condemned
me for life. I open my heart to the truth that you can make all things
new. Amen.*

August 23

Favoritism

He who did not spare his own Son, but gave him up
for us all . . .

ROMANS 8:32

The Bible has much to say about playing favorites. Challenging us
to look at our exclusive behavior toward others, it also addresses
our hurts when we have been discriminated against.

We've committed discriminatory acts against others, have we not?
In subtle ways we have preferred a certain race or person of similar
religious beliefs. We've been preferential to someone of means and
reputation rather than the poorly dressed, uneducated person
requesting our attention. The economy of heaven is hard for us to own,
going against our fleshly instincts. The work of Jesus transforming our
heart can enable us to love everyone.

Jacob's favorite son was Joseph and we know what happened. His
brothers hated him, plotted to kill him, and sold him into slavery.
Whenever a parent plays favorites, there's trouble. The ones deprived
of affection take out their revenge on the fair-haired child.

We also know what life is like on the other side of the fence. We
know how painful it is to not be picked for a team, to be overlooked
for a promotion, or to be discarded by a boyfriend while he chooses
another. We are often discriminated against because of our looks,
abilities, lack of talent, or even because we possess extreme talent.

The heart of Jesus has unconditional love for all at the foot of the
cross. When we look up into his blood-streaked, agonizing face, we
heal from the abuses of this world. Then we will be in a position to
share his love with others.

*Jesus, forgive me for not loving everyone equally. Help me see your
heart reaching out to all people on Calvary's hill. Amen.*

August 24

The New You

Be transformed by the renewing of your mind.

ROMANS 12:2

*T*ransformation doesn't mean putting a new face on something old. That's remodeling! Transformation is the total re-creation of something from the inside out.

God desires to transform the inner being of each of his children. But many of us have opted for self-imposed behavior modification. Instead of giving Jesus free reign to indwell and change our hearts at our real place of need, we take matters into our own hands and do a makeover of our outward behavior. We become like the chronically angry person who uses his energy to sit on his anger rather than to explore why he's angry in the first place. Often spiritual maturity is equated with having achieved self-control rather than Spirit control, which is obtained only through regeneration.

My maiden name is Hewitt. I have often thought, *My problem is Hewitt-ism!* because I was indoctrinated (as we all are) with our family's dysfunctions, fears, and insecurities. The transformation I have needed is a slow and gradual one, at the heart level, generated by time spent with the One who loves me unconditionally. As I receive his love, I am changed. Often I don't even notice it's happening at first. But others do.

Join me in this exciting metamorphosis. May we not be on good behavior to impress others, like kids in church! Pressure to behave only makes us resentful and rebellious. The Bible is not a rule book for Christian living. It is a love letter beckoning us to the heart of the One who changes us through his love.

I've tried hard to change on my own. When I've succeeded, I've become proud. But all I've accomplished is a new paint job, Lord. Pick me up, peel off the layers of paint, and change me through your love. Amen.

August 25

Elusive Tears and Joy

Rejoice with those who rejoice; mourn with those
who mourn.

ROMANS 12:15

Today's Scripture sounds fairly simple, doesn't it? Yet human nature
interferes most every time.

When I am hurting, it is hard to rejoice with others who are
experiencing great blessing. If my children were going through stages
of spiritual coldness while my friend's children responded to God's call,
ventured out on mission trips, and came home with glowing stories,
it would be hard to rejoice with them.

It's equally difficult to enter into another person's pain when our
lives are going well.

Tears are hard to access and, selfishly, we want to enjoy our good
times without interruption. They're rare and we've worked hard for
them. We may have just come through a painful period, and we're
relieved to put the tears behind us. Isn't God asking a lot?

The truth is, we are self-focused and we will battle with our flesh
for a lifetime. How do we turn the corner toward obedience? We can
certainly ask for grace, but it is also helpful to remember the friends
who danced with us in our successes and held us in our grief.
Remember how it felt? Instinctively we knew their gift was rare. We
have the power in us to give such a gift.

*Lord, I need you to expand my view of the world and see others'
needs. Give me tears for their pain. And when they experience good
fortune, help me remember that you are the God of blessing. If I
withhold my joy from them, I am really angry with you for giving
it. Do your work in my heart to make these spiritual principles part
of my outreach. I confess my sin of jealousy and indifference. I need
more of your heart. Amen.*

Winning the War from a Resting Position

> "The LORD will fight for you; you need only to be still."
> EXODUS 14:14

I used to have a difficult time believing that God loved me enough to fight for me. I thought he was passive. I believed he was unmoved by my plight. To think of him intervening in any way seemed preposterous. If you'd reminded me that he died for me—and that certainly counts as an act of intervention—I would have brushed you off with, "He died for the world and I'm a measly part of it."

Now I know differently. I've met God. I've experienced him apart from just reading his words on a printed page. He and I have established a track record. How did this happen? I was in a crucible and could do nothing but pray. My life would have been over if God hadn't intervened. The outcome was glorious as the ministry of Daughters of Promise was born. God moved mountains and left his fingerprints all over the place. I prayed, rested, and waited. He did the rest.

Are you fighting a war that's not yours to fight? Are you trying to change a spouse, sibling, or parent? Have you been accused of something you didn't do? Are you seriously ill? Have you seen something to which you've given your life crumble in front of your eyes? While God would certainly have us be proactive regarding things we *can* change, there are times when he tells us to rest. He is the one who rearranges circumstances behind the scenes while we take our place in the shelter of his wings. He takes the heat while we repose in the shade. He takes the brunt of the wind while we doze in the sanctuary of his embrace.

I give up the fight, Lord. I rest in your arms. Amen.

August 27

Open to Correction

The LORD has a charge to bring against you who live in the land: "There is no faithfulness, no love, no acknowledgment of God in the land."

HOSEA 4:1

I remember trying to teach my children to be kind to each other. Ryan was four and Jaime was seven. They had been squabbling all day. Out of patience, I made them sit in a chair with their arms around each other for thirty minutes. Not only did it break the contentious mood, but it has also become one of the most humorous memories of our family. In hindsight, I guess I should have tried it again when they were teenagers. I'd have even more of a story to tell!

Just as parents place a high premium on teaching character qualities to their children (and are grieved when important virtues are ignored), God is also a parent who longs to see his children model godly character. If he sees us engage in continued patterns of unfaithfulness and unkindness, he takes issue with us.

How receptive am I to his correction? It is far easier to receive God when I know he wants to speak tenderly to me than when he wants to contend with me. However, I can rest in the security of his correction. If I stay close to his heart today, I'll be able to hear the first stirrings of disapproval when I sin. He'll make my heart uneasy, urging me to see my error, apologize, and correct my ways. But I must also know that if I walk away from friendship with God and "do my own thing" over a long period of time, his contention with me will be far deeper and the consequences more severe.

He is a parent, after all. The more serious the misbehavior, the more serious the discipline. Those boundaries remind me of his love and kindness, though. He is so intent on blessing my life that he'll do whatever it takes for me to come home so I can experience his love and favor.

I want to hear your voice all of the time. You are a perfect father, perfect even in your discipline. Amen.

August 28

Wanted: Peace

He promises peace to his people.

PSALM 85:8

I love the old prophets. I read their work voraciously and because of that I'm beginning to understand at what great cost they wrote down God's messages for us. Some were martyred. Many others were ostracized and sorely misunderstood. Jeremiah was called the Weeping Prophet but I feel certain that others wept as well. They were the ones chosen to communicate God's grief over his children who strayed from the perfect ways of his kingdom. Perhaps they wept not only on behalf of God but to reveal their own sorrow. After all, their calling was most difficult.

Jeremiah was commissioned to tell Israel that they had gone too far, that hard times were coming. This prophet, though he was a peace-loving man, lived with intense rejection and ridicule. That's the way it often is. The quiet, nonassertive types are thrust into a lifestyle of confrontation and upheaval. Jeremiah was certainly one of those. How did he cope? Scripture says that God told him how to sustain himself. He was instructed to live contemplatively and spend much time in quiet to glean inner strength from God's words.

Jeremiah's secret is invaluable and provides the method for each of us who needs to know how to find inner peace in the middle of a turbulent atmosphere. True peace of mind must come from the inside. Lasting peace is not something you and I can generate on our own. It comes from spending time with the person who is called the Prince of Peace.

I thrive on peace. Others I know love the challenge of conflict. But each of us comes to the end of ourselves and needs the inner peace of knowing you, Lord. Grant us that peace as we spend time in your presence. Amen.

August 29

A Well-Seasoned Guide

Send forth your light and your truth, let them guide me.
PSALM 43:3

If I need a guide to take me up Mount Everest, I make sure I hire someone personally acquainted with the terrain. The most qualified may be a Sherpa who lives at base camp altitude and has spent his life on the mountain. He knows the hidden dangers, the unpredictable weather, and the other hazards that catch novices unawares.

A guide must be more than a know-it-all and must not have gained his knowledge just from books. While reading can initiate a good education, the best education is gained by experience.

Credibility is a wonderful thing. While it's easy to hand out advice, the one receiving it can usually tell whether or not the giver has lived out what he's so readily dispensing. You know how the trend goes: the ones most vocal about child rearing can be those who have not yet had children. Do we trust them?

The Spirit is a guide like none other. Internally he provides a map through the confusing pathways of our soul. Because in God he was our Creator, he casts light on our thoughts. He leads us into truth about who we are: loved but broken, in need of truth that heals and frees.

Externally he guides us safely through the elements that could cause us to shipwreck without his navigational expertise. He who is truth is the lighthouse guiding us through the fog, stormy weather, and hidden rocks that would surely sink our ship. If we take our eyes off him, we'll lose our perspective and reference point.

Oh, Spirit, you are a guide with credibility. Your face fills my horizon. Amen.

August 30

Our Powerful Subconscious

"A kingdom ... divided against itself ... cannot stand."
MARK 3:24

A teacher I know uses the illustration of an iceberg to show how strong our subconscious is in dictating our beliefs and feelings. She explains that the part of the iceberg we see, the part exposed above the water line, is minuscule compared with the massive formation beneath the water's surface. She stresses that the part we see is completely controlled by what transpires beneath.

We operate in much the same way. What we know and believe intellectually, on the surface, is not what controls us.

Tragically, I said for years, "God is loving and God is gracious," but I felt unloved and swore I bore his punishment rather than his grace. I was a student of Scripture but it didn't stick because lies, hurts, resentments, and disappointments festered beneath the surface. My unresolved issues controlled my feelings, just as the part of the iceberg that is underwater controls everything that happens above the water's surface.

I fear that our churches are full of those who sing hymns and say the right words, but behind the postured smiles they wonder why they still feel profoundly empty. Even brilliant theologians can know it all but have a cold heart.

We must do rugged introspective work. It is our subconscious that dictates what we really believe to be truth. Our feelings emanate from there. Our addictions begin there. Our insomnia or recurring nightmares originate there. This diseased structure, the part others never see, is the place that needs God's light. Unless God's words reach that level, there will be no life change.

Lord, you never intended for me to live at war internally. I want my feelings, beliefs, and behaviors to be congruent. I want my subconscious rooted in you. I want to think like you and live in the joy of your truth. Amen.

August 31

The Waiting Game

Guide me in your truth and teach me, for . . . my hope
is in you all day long.

PSALM 25:5

*H*ow good are you at waiting? Today I'm waiting for potentially
bad news that will require God-sized faith. I'm on edge and in
prayer. It's hard to wait, even for good news. Waiting can bring out
the worst in us. We may pace the floor and become short-tempered.
In our less-than-sterling moments we can get angry and rail at God.

Much of King David's life was spent waiting. Interestingly, he
didn't see waiting as being stuck. He articulated that he waited on God,
not on people or circumstances. He recognized that God was the all-
powerful force in his life by whom all things moved! If doors were shut
and opportunities blocked, it was God who directed the affairs of the
earth. For David, waiting was a spiritual issue, not a temporal one.

What a perspective. When David, although an anointed king, fled
as a fugitive, he saw that God was the one who instituted the timing
of kingdoms. For he said, "My hope is in you all day long."

David also allowed God to teach him. He believed that if there
was a waiting period, he must not yet know all he would need to know
for what lay ahead. He used waiting as an opportunity to be instructed
by the Author of wisdom and insight.

A period of waiting is what a loving Father gives us when we are
not yet equipped for future tasks. How kind of him to hold everything
up while he gives us tools we will need to navigate the future successfully.

*I trust your timetable, Father. Teach me, strengthen me, and infuse
me with all I need to face what lies ahead. Amen.*

September

September 1

Preach, Teach, or Cry?

"Go to the great city of Nineveh and preach against it."
JONAH 1:2

God told Jonah to go to Nineveh not only to preach but to "cry" against it (NASV). God knew that crying is what brings revival. A cry is what our pastors need today. Preachers are a dime a dozen. Teachers are plentiful. But those who are willing to cry over a city, as Jesus did over Jerusalem, are rare. In fact, they are so rare that we might be prone to send our pastor for counseling if we beheld him wailing over the lost!

What does crying represent? The broken heart of God. His primary agenda is never judgment and annihilation. Rather he aches to fellowship with his creation. His heart of longing is expressed through his cries of pain. They reverberate throughout the pages of Scripture. "Come back. Repent. Come near. I love you." Jonah's tears would give the people of Nineveh a picture of the love and mercy of the Holy One of Israel.

Oh, friend, may it be the love of God that constrains us to share, teach, declare, and most of all cry. After a rebellious detour Jonah finally went and cried, and the resulting revival was evidence of the power of love. God's heart was so effectively communicated that the king of Nineveh took off his robe and dressed in sackcloth. He ordered every Ninevite to cry out to God for mercy. The people repented because of God's tears shown on the face of his servant Jonah.

How often have I communicated spiritual truths without the heart of the message? Forgive me, Lord. Do whatever it takes to connect me with your passion and heartbeat. Amen.

September 2

Just Whom Is God Blessing?

Jonah ran away from the LORD and headed for Tarshish.
JONAH 1:3

I was seven when I gave my heart to Jesus. Perhaps you've walked with God for a lifetime, too. There's a danger for us, though. Because we have a history with God, we might feel we have earned his blessing. After all, we've been diligent, and while we would not trade our surrendered lives, we are quick to admit that it's not been easy. We might think God's blessing is a direct result of our hard work.

Jonah, a prophet with godly legacies, was commanded to go to Nineveh. But he ran the opposite way. Perhaps Jonah ran not because he feared for his life but because he feared that the Ninevites would repent and come to God! It didn't seem fair that God should extend his mercy to such wicked people. Why should Nineveh share in the same blessings as Israel, who had enjoyed a long relationship with God?

We understand, don't we? Those who commit heinous crimes in our society are often considered so evil that they don't deserve forgiveness. We place them in a special category and set them apart as "special cases."

It's hard to submit to the precepts of God's kingdom. "It's not fair," we cry. We feel like the brother in the prodigal son story who stayed home, worked hard, remained loyal, and was angry when his wayward brother's return launched a celebration.

God is not willing that anyone should perish; reconciliation is still God's foremost agenda. Only his work of grace in our hearts can dismantle any indignation stemming from our carnal nature.

I want revenge, not mercy, for those who have hurt me. My heart is not like yours, Father. Help me. Change me. Amen.

September 3

Bringing About Peace

"Pick me up and throw me into the sea, . . . and it will become calm."

JONAH 1:12

Jonah runs from God and a ship is available to aid him in his running. When the ship is out to sea, God sends a severe storm. The crew onboard is made up of seasoned sailors used to tempestuous weather. However, they are aware of the uniqueness of this storm. They conclude that it must be a message from the gods, that one person on board has brought this calamity to them.

They go to the bottom of the ship. What is the prophet of God doing? Sleeping! This astounds me. He who should be praying is sleeping while the rest of the men cry out to their false gods.

I am moved by the compassion of the godless sailors toward Jonah. Once they find out he is the culprit, you would think they would be angry enough to throw him overboard. But instead Jonah has to ask them repeatedly to throw him into the sea, while they try everything to save his life, even rowing harder to get to shore so they can leave him there.

Jonah's conscience has been awakened from its deep sleep. He knows there will be no calm for the sailors until they part with the sinner who caused the disturbance, and no calm for him until he parts with the sin. Jonah, like his sin, is cast into the water. No wonder God, again, made reference of the importance of "hurling our iniquities into the depths of the sea" through the prophet Micah (Micah 7:19).

Repentance and forgiveness are the only paths to true calm, true peace. When our own sin nearly drowns us, we must be intentional to drown it before it brings about our demise.

Are others suffering because of my choices, Lord? Show me. I'm ready to make things right. Give me a repentant heart. I need your forgiveness and restoration. Amen.

September 4

The Miraculous Prayer of Faith

"You brought my life up from the pit."

JONAH 2:6

I'm familiar with prayers for deliverance, cries for discernment, and even prayers of thanksgiving following a victory. But prayers of faith are something I need to know more about. Today is the time for faith, not despair. We are never hopeless or helpless with God. "The king's heart is in the hand of the LORD; he directs it like a watercourse wherever he pleases" (Proverbs 21:1).

Jonah is in the belly of a big fish. His story is one-of-a-kind. He may be the only human being we know who survived being swallowed by a fish. It is from the fish's cavernous and dark belly that Jonah makes a prayer of faith: "You brought my life up from the pit." Notice the tense of the verb. He didn't say, "You will bring my life up from this pit." Rather he said, "You have already done it."

Isn't this the prayer of faith? Jonah speaks with as much assurance as if it were done already. He knows the mercy and power of God.

Are you drowning in the waters of the deep? After taxing your mind to the limits to find an escape route, are you convinced there is none? I live there today in some areas of my life. If God does not come through, there will be no life. Will you become a child of faith with me? Let's declare the reality of our deliverance as though it has already occurred. Jonah's voice doesn't have to be solo. His prayer can be heard in unison as we join him in faith.

Even though I see no evidence of deliverance, I rely on the truth of your character, Lord. You are merciful, slow to anger, and abounding in grace. Thank you for the rescue to come. Amen.

September 5

For the Right Audience

The Ninevites believed God.

JONAH 3:5

After Jonah repented in the belly of the fish, God sent him out again with the same orders. Arriving in Nineveh poorly dressed and weak from his journey, he hardly had the look of a diplomat coming to make an important national decree. Yet this one man, a stranger in Nineveh, went to the streets proclaiming God's message.

People began repenting, weeping for their sin, and pouring ashes over their heads. Even the king heard about Jonah's message. Knowing it was from heaven, he rose from his throne and laid aside his royal robe, signifying he had forfeited his throne and robe to God's justice. The results of Jonah's preaching were historically amazing.

What a contrast to the Israelites then. God sent them prophets proclaiming similar messages of coming judgment for unconfessed sin. Yet the outcome was different. They chose to harden their hearts and walk in rebellion.

Henry Blackabee, who wrote the well-known Experiencing God series, says God's will for us becomes evident when we see where he is already working and join him there. Was he at work in the hearts of those in Israel? Not at that time. Was his Spirit bringing revival in an unsuspected place by an unsuspected prophet? Absolutely.

Many of us beat our heads against the wall reaching out to churches that seem unaffected by the kingdom message. Perhaps God wants to redirect our efforts to those perishing for lack of knowledge. There a little truth and the love of Jesus blossoms immediately into new faith. Nineveh's sons and daughters are waiting.

Show me where the harvest is, God, and where the ground is fertile for your truth. Shine your light on my path so I may be led to a receptive audience. Amen.

September 6

Unthinkable Mercy

"You have been concerned about this vine. . . . Should
I not be concerned about that great city?"
JONAH 4:10–11

*T*hough Jonah's ministry in Nineveh yielded great spiritual fruit, he
is angry and goes to sit on a barren piece of land to process his
feelings. It is hot during the day, cold at night, and there is no relief
from either extreme. He is at the mercy of the weather.

But God has mercy. He makes a vine grow and cover Jonah's head
to shade him from the heat of the day. Jonah becomes attached to the
vine. The vine, rather than God, becomes his comfort.

God cannot remain idle when we turn to idols. He taught Jonah
a lesson by causing the plant to die. The heat became so scorching that
Jonah begged to die. God asked, "Do you have good reason to be
angry?" Jonah replied, "Yes." His passion overruled his conscience.
Then God said, "If I had destroyed the nation, 1,200 infants who had
committed no sin would have perished. Not to mention the livestock,
which is more valuable to me than a plant! The vine that you pitied
perished in the night. But the souls of Nineveh, created by me,
are immortal."

We don't know the rest of Jonah's story. But the lesson for any of
us with enemies is this: There is one God over all, and it is his will that
none should perish. Jesus highlighted this truth by instructing us to
pray for our enemies.

Oh, for the grace to obey when we might have more compassion
for our pet than for a friend who has betrayed us, a spouse who has
been unfaithful, or a political enemy who has committed acts of cruelty.

Father, help me mature so I can understand your great mercy. Amen.

September 7

The Veil of Religiosity

"These people come near to me with their mouth and honor me with their lips, but their hearts are far from me."

ISAIAH 29:13

Oh, the joy of worshiping in a family of believers who enjoy a deep and vibrant relationship with God. Nothing can compare. Yet it took me many years to discover why God is often hidden in religious form. He is veiled by rote performances given for the sake of preserving tradition.

I've tried to find meaning within the church walls
Sometimes I just can't see it there
Your face is well hidden in stained-glass décor
It's shadowed by dishonest prayers
We use these to build a religion of pride
We're slaves to our worn-out clichés
Help me tear down those idols that keep me from
    You
Help me leave them behind and just
Realize You're more than our standards and codes
You're more than what hands find to do
Your face must be seen at the core of a soul
That's tender with touches from You.
I want to know You; don't let my heart play a
    game
I want to know You and feel a joy just hearing
    Your name
I want to know Your words so I can find Your
    heart
Your soul is my treasure; I feel I'm just starting to
    know You
And knowing is loving You, Lord. [2]

Reveal yourself to me, Lord. Awaken my heart. Make me fully alive to you, apart from religious trappings. I thirst for you. Amen.

[2]Written by Christine Wyrtzen. Copyright © 1987 Eloise's Music Box.

September 8

Inside Out

"Whoever believes in me, as the Scripture has said, streams of living water will flow from within him."

JOHN 7:38

*J*esus speaks of a phenomenon I long for! I want my whole being to overflow with the refreshing waters of his Spirit. That river will heal many who stand in its flow. The words will bring healing and peace to another's torment. The prayers will transform the core of a friend when change looks impossible. The wisdom will bring enlightenment when options seem elusive. The encouragement will build another up when self-hatred is all that they know.

Compare that with King David's description of another kind of person, the one whose throat is an open grave. What a powerful metaphor. Every word coming out of their mouth results in injury and ultimate destruction. These are the people of whom we say, "If they have nothing good to say, they should say nothing at all!"

David says that this kind of person has nothing reliable to say. Do you interact with anyone like that? A critical boss or a parent who is never pleased and dispenses words that destroy your spirit? Perhaps you have an adolescent child living away from God, and the child's speech is full of profanity and broken promises.

What can we do about another's spiritual condition besides pray? Not much. What can we do about the condition of our own heart? A lot. God promises each of us a transformed inner world as we spend time with him. If we are open to the complete work of the Holy Spirit, he will reveal to us truth that replaces stagnant water with life-giving streams.

Teach me to listen to my own words today, Lord. Show me what is coming from stagnant water. I want your Spirit to grow in me, producing a well of living water. Amen.

September 9

Trapped in Silence

Give ear to my words, O LORD, consider my sighing.
PSALM 5:1

*M*any live in a world of private thoughts. They are afraid to speak. Thoughts, dreams, and deepest hurts are trapped inside a vault with a steel door. They remember the day, perhaps, that they decided to shut their heart away. They know that unconditional love is the key that would unlock it. However, they cannot find that kind of love. The cancer of loneliness eats away their soul.

I know. I remember the day, when I was seven, that I decided to stop talking freely. I made up new guidelines for speaking. I would only share my thoughts (1) if they would be interesting to someone, (2) if I sensed I would be believed, (3) if I could turn my long story into a concise one, and (4) if I could finish talking before the person listening crossed the line between interested and bored. Life wasn't fair. My new rules didn't bring peace. Yes, my heart was safer, but the loneliness was unbearable.

God delivered me from silence. He led me to understand that he was not part of the grandstand of disinterested listeners. He knocked on the door of my steel vault, revealed that he had the key, asked me if he could come in, and then joined me in my prison. He nudged me to begin to talk and I've not stopped since. Little by little he called me out into the open spaces where words can be plentiful and love is extravagantly given.

In this world we are often not believed. People fail to take us seriously. Our views are often judged. But we are not citizens here. In God's kingdom our voice is welcomed and authenticity is celebrated.

Only you can open my prison doors. If you knock, Lord, I will let you in. Amen.

September 10

Giving Up Too Early

Why are you downcast, O my soul? Why so disturbed
within me? Put your hope in God.

PSALM 42:5

I cannot begin to imagine how difficult it was for Jesus to come to
an unjust world. He suffered unfairly at the hands of his own
creation. He made the men who crucified him. What an insult to the
Creator. What betrayal of power. Could any story be sadder than this?

I picture the last few moments of Jesus' life, prior to the victory
that was won. What were his thoughts? I can imagine that he ached for
righteous resolution, when the keys to hell and death would forever
be redeemed and injustice would be placated. Things looked darkest
right before he proved victorious. Though hope was elusive and it
appeared there was none, it was to be revealed momentarily. Outcomes
can't be predicted by the darkness of our times.

I conclude from watching Jesus' life and death that my own
ultimate redemption is closer than I might think. For now it can seem
that I am frozen in time. I wait suspended beneath the loud ticking of
the clock. There are moments when I wonder if Jesus understands and
plans to act beyond mere compassion. But I know he does and he will!

My longing for deliverance introduces me to an ache for eternal
glory. It turns my eyes upward and encourages me to trust the One
who will eventually even the score, right all wrongs, and bring all
things into the light of his truth and holiness. Though my life appears
to hang in the balance, I am cradled securely in the eternal purposes
of God.

*I can't see around the corner. I'm hurting. Lord, you are writing a
glorious future and leading me by the hand. Amen.*

September 11

Missing the Whole Point

In love he predestined us to be adopted as his sons
through Jesus Christ, in accordance with his pleasure
and will.

EPHESIANS 1:4–5

*F*ifteen years ago a counselor encouraged me to express what I felt
the Christian life was all about. What I ended up putting on paper
was revealing. My writing was full of lies and I couldn't even discern
the distortions.

I share from my journal.

> God looked at the condition of my fallen
> heart and was grieved. He could not look upon
> sin. He adopted me and loved me for what I
> could become in him. The cross is simply a
> way for me to daily rid myself of all he finds
> disgusting in me. The Bible is the measuring
> stick by which I determine what needs to be
> changed. So far I have not found his words to
> be life. They are law. The concepts of the
> Christian life, which sum it all up, are disci-
> pline, conscientiousness, servanthood, and
> death to self. I feel ultimately trapped in this
> way of life. I hate this existence, yet I dare not
> throw it all away. For I do believe there is a
> God, and a judgment, so the cycle continues.

What was missing? Love. Mercy. Grace. The very foundations of
the gospel. Now, years later, I know that God is a person to be
experienced, and once he is experienced, there is joy unspeakable. In
his presence are pleasures forevermore. May our good deeds and the
decision to put away sin stem from a joyful response to having been
loved deeply by the one who paid the ultimate price to make us his.

*I haven't given up anything to be yours, Lord. You gave up every-
thing to give me the privilege. You made me to know joy. Amen.*

September 12

I'm an Adopted Child

He predestined us to be adopted as his sons through
Jesus Christ, in accordance with his pleasure and will.
EPHESIANS 1:5

*T*he heart of God is a Father's heart. He instituted the father/child relationship at the time of creation. In fact, we are called the children of creation!

When Adam and Eve sinned and the fall of man occurred, our status as God's children changed. Our sin brought about spiritual death. It required atonement so that our relationship with God could be restored. The process of adoption was conceived and began to take shape. On the cross, Jesus paid with his life for the privilege of adopting children and bringing them home. Because of him, we can exchange families. Though we were born as children of the devil, we were destined before the foundation of the world to be daughters of God. Our identity was rewritten the very moment we repented of our sin and came home by way of Jesus' death and resurrection. We know this story well, but it often fails to live in the deepest part of who we are.

Adopting a child is a wonderful experience. The wonder of that day when new parents bring them home in their arms doesn't fade with time.

Yet, for years I have known the truth that I am God's adopted child. Perhaps he's the only one who rejoiced; it was a party for one, for I failed to enter into the joy of it until a few years ago. I kept defining myself by everything *but* my new status as God's royal daughter. Things have changed. I am learning to trade every garment of shame for a robe of honor.

You've adopted me, yet I keep living like an orphan. I stretch out my arms to you, Father, and ask that you do whatever you must to make yourself real to me. Amen.

September 13

Choosing Truth

God raised us up with Christ and seated us with him
in the heavenly realms in Christ Jesus.

EPHESIANS 2:6

My flesh battles with my spirit every day. My flesh tells me one thing and my spirit, reborn in Jesus, tells me another. The voices of my world preach their own peculiar gospel, but God has revealed the true gospel. Which voice I choose to listen to will determine what I think, how I feel, and what choices I make today.

Becoming a daughter of almighty God introduces me to a sharp learning curve of spiritual truths. I learn that I am totally forgiven. God chooses to put my sin behind his back and not hold it against me. This is difficult to accept, for every day I am prone to recite all my sins, failures, and shortcomings. God chooses to forget yet I so easily choose to review. How paradoxical.

I also learn that because of Jesus God sees me as perfect. My spirit is already seated in a place of great honor with my Father in heaven. But here on earth I feel I am only worth my contribution to society. I am loved for my gifts. It's so easy for my flesh to believe the lie that my value is based on society's criteria.

God says, "Because my child loves me, I will set her securely on high." This is my reality today. I am honored, anointed, and declared worthy because of Jesus. No matter what I encounter today that contradicts these spiritual realities, I can rehearse the truths of God that shape eternity.

May I see myself from your viewpoint, Father. Allow me to see my spirit high above the earth, seated with you, so I may be strengthened for the battles with my flesh. Amen.

September 14

Burying Myself

We are God's workmanship, created in Christ Jesus to
do good works, which God prepared in advance for
us to do.

EPHESIANS 2:10

*W*e are women of grace, loved and anointed. However, sometimes in our lives we make choices that do not reflect our
privileged status. Instead of living freely as dearly loved daughters, we
live in the bondage of others' choices for us.

Do you have a hard time saying no? Do you feel you always have
to be accommodating? When you must decline, do you feel guilty?

A prosperous businessman said, "I may not know the formula for
success, but the formula for failure is trying to please everyone." One
of the prime reasons we fail when we live for others is that we neglect
to find our security in God. We, like the chameleon, have adapted so
radically to fit everyone's expectations that we no longer know ourselves. That special woman is buried under numerous self-inflicted
makeovers. After living in servitude, we slowly shut down emotionally
to our deepest desires and original dreams.

We are God's workmanship, uniquely designed to work in the
areas he planned for us before our birth. We're only going to be deeply
fulfilled when we choose the pathway he designed. All others will lead
to frustration and futility. Saying no to anything else takes courage,
but let us keep in mind that even Jesus didn't make a move without
asking for his Father's instructions. If he needed momentary direction,
I certainly do. People can't make those choices for me.

*Your smile and nod of approval are all I need, Father. Help me
remember to pray before I accept another's request. All the good things
I'm asked to do can't be your plan. I'm just one person. Give me
wisdom. Amen.*

September 15

Stuck in Our Head

They are darkened in their understanding and separated
from the life of God because of the ignorance that is in
them due to the hardening of their hearts.

EPHESIANS 4:18

*I*n our contemporary church culture, it is easy, perhaps even instinctive, to be lulled into spiritual mind games. If we're candid with each other, much of what passes for our Christian experience amounts to little more than exercises in behavior modification. Many of us know about God but fail to understand that God is also a person to be known.

I have talked with many Christian women about spiritual development, and it is evident to me that relationships with God are often one-dimensional, based solely on head knowledge. Tragically, this precludes deep personal change. God is elusive, causing us to feel that we've done something wrong to make him stay at arm's length. You, friend, are a whole person. God wants you to experience him in a way that impacts all of who you are! He wants to touch your mind, heart, and spirit. He encourages you to align your belief system with his truth, engage your heart as a result of interacting with him, and exercise your spirit by applying his life-giving principles.

What are the results if we embrace the God of Scripture with our mind, heart, and spirit? We become fully alive and we're able to know spiritual truth, understand matters of the heart, and exercise our spirit by walking in childlike faith as a daughter of promise.

My head is full of knowledge but my heart feels lifeless and sterile. Lord, transform my faith. Make each part of me alive unto you so I may know abundant life. Amen.

September 16

Standing Tall in Our New Identity

. . . to be made new in the attitude of your minds . . .
EPHESIANS 4:23

I need to be in the process of claiming my spiritual inheritance and legacy. Doing that will engage me in the process of renewing my mind. Inner transformation will impact not only my thoughts but also the way I feel about others and myself.

What happens when I fail to claim my inheritance? Though I'm anointed and cherished, I may still feel deep down that something is wrong with me. I'm convinced that I'm the exception to the truth that God loves all people. I wear the badge of shame. My thoughts are distorted and Satan loves to move in and cement those distortions. He prompts other wounded people to reinforce those lies, making sure I stay in bondage and never move into the joy and freedom God intended for me.

Scripture speaks often about the need to own the truth about myself as God defines it. He says that when I choose to accept his words by faith, whether or not I feel as though they're true, I am on the road to freedom.

If I wait for people to show me my value, I set myself up for disaster. I can't depend on people to accurately reflect to me God's truth about who I am. I live in a world in which the beautiful, talented, and privileged are adored. Not in God's kingdom. The more tragic my story, the more powerfully I experience his healing, and the more profound my platform becomes as I reach out to others on his behalf. God never wastes pain but instead maximizes it as a means of redemption.

I want to stand tall, Father. I am your child and you have given me a new name. Amen.

September 17

Dressed in Graveclothes

Put on the new self, created to be like God in true
righteousness and holiness.

EPHESIANS 4:24

We have a new identity. We're loved and forgiven of all our sins.
The Lover of our soul calls us to an intimate relationship. But
do we feel the joy of this good news?

Our enemy loves to deceive. He's good at it. We've fallen into his
web and we're not aware that we've been tricked. Satan rubs his hands
with glee as we cling to our erroneous perceptions of God. He chuckles as we twist Scripture, take verses out of context, and view them
through the lenses of our own faulty paradigms.

I used to excel in the art of hiding. I didn't understand that my
need to hide was proof that Satan had won. I couldn't see that while
God desired to dress me in his robe of righteousness, I had allowed
Satan to dress me in rags. Embarrassed over my wardrobe, I made my
Christianity an intellectual exercise while I died in shame. I was
entombed by lies of condemnation.

Satan danced on my grave while the graveclothes, not fitted for
any daughter of promise, outfitted my being with nuggets of truth
dipped in errors and distortions. Satan was happy to define my
identity and become my personal tailor. There are many daughters of
Jesus who never know any reality other than this.

Today Satan is looking to see if we're undressed. He inspects us
carefully, without respect for our boundaries, until he finds out where
we're vulnerable. Then he fashions a garment that feels as if it fits. Jesus
died to give us a new name, a new robe. We have to take the old one
off first.

I'm sick of graveclothes, Jesus. I'll be defined by you. Amen.

September 18

Who's Talking?

Do not let any unwholesome talk come out of your
mouths, but only what is helpful for building others
up according to their needs.

EPHESIANS 4:29

*D*on't you wish people were consistently encouraging with their
words? We can carry one nasty comment with us for years, but
our future can also be shaped for the good by a few words of praise.

Oftentimes the negative things we hear from others confuse us.
When do we know if we're hearing the truth about ourselves? It seems
to me that we need a grid for sifting what goes into our ears before it
enters our hearts.

How about some initial questions, like these:

- Who's doing the talking?
- Does this person really care about me?
- Would this person be happy if I succeeded in life?
- Does this person have the reputation for being a cheerleader or a discourager?
- Is there anything this person can gain by putting me down, such as power or control?
- When I see this person coming, do I think, *Oh no, now what have I done?*

When I've run through this list, if I still feel the comment could
be true, I talk to God about it. I ask his Spirit to confirm it through
prayer, Scripture, and people I trust. If he does not, I disown it.

God is not the Master Tormentor. He does not bring a word of
correction without giving us quick resolution and freedom of spirit. If
we find ourselves wallowing in despair and failure because of someone's criticism, we may be hurting for nothing. Satan may have used
another's wounds to hurt us, for he loves to destroy the joy of our
calling and cause us to walk crippled.

I believe you above everyone else. Give me discernment, Lord. Amen.

September 19

Childlike King

"O LORD my God, you have made your servant king in place of my father David. But I am only a little child and do not know how to carry out my duties."

1 KINGS 3:7

Solomon, the wisest man to ever live, trembled at the prospect of kingship. He suspected his own inadequacy. In contrast, Absalom, a fool, wished himself to be a judge. He presumed honor and strutted his power until he self-destructed.

Solomon is a role model for any of us who feel ill-equipped or inadequate. He reminds us that even one who possesses great amounts of wisdom is intellectually poor compared with God, whose mind is infinitely vast.

Absalom provides a mirror for us in our arrogant moments. Unfortunately, I can recall the last time I strutted my stuff. I knew it the moment the words came out of my mouth. My insecurity won the minute I spoke.

Genuine humility is very becoming. It does not presume advancement. Solomon expressed his humble heart when he reminded Yahweh that he was just a little child. From this springs his next prayer: "Of all the gifts you could give, grant wisdom!" God gave wisdom because Solomon asked, and riches because he didn't ask. God rewards those who make spiritual things their treasure. Arrogance, on the other hand, is unbecoming. Who are we that we think we can excel without God? Can we see into the future? Can we read others' minds? Do we not know from where our gifts and abilities came?

Mimicking Solomon's humility yields spiritual prosperity. Avoiding Absalom's arrogance saves us from defeat.

Lord, I come humbly. I am not capable of handling life without you. I am as a little person, needing your wisdom that transcends my capabilities. Amen.

An Oil Business

"Your servant has nothing there at all . . . except a little oil."

2 KINGS 4:2

The widow of a prophet fell on hard times and was in great debt. She thought her only choice was to allow her two sons to become slaves to pay it off. The thought of this made her despair. She asked Elisha what she should do.

He inquired as to what assets she had in the house. She answered, "Only one pot of oil." He knew God could use this. He told her to go throughout the neighborhood gathering empty pots, then to go home, close the door, and pour the oil into the pots. She did as he said, and as long as she kept filling the pots, the oil kept flowing. When she ran out of empty pots, however, there was no more oil. When she told Elisha what happened, he instructed her to sell the oil and pay off her debts first with the profits.

There are three principles here for me to consider. First, what do I have in my hand that God can work with, though I consider it insignificant? Second, perhaps God is calling me to faith as he plans something seemingly ludicrous. (If the widow had only acquired two empty pots, there would merely have been enough oil to fill them. However, the oil flowed long enough to fill as many pots as she'd had faith to gather.) And third, I should pay off debts with the first of my profits.

Elisha is a reflection of Jesus, for when the widow felt hopeless, Elisha had the answer. Jesus is never out of options. Though we, in our best attempts, try to explore avenues that will bring us relief, Jesus' answers are usually ones that never would have occurred to us.

What is in my hand, Lord? I am incredulous at your answer, but anything you empower can become a mighty thing. Amen.

September 21

Fear of Hope

"About this time next year," Elisha said, "you will hold a son in your arms."

"No, my lord," she objected. "Don't mislead your servant, O man of God!"

2 KINGS 4:16

A woman from Shunem was a friend of Elisha's. She and her husband had added a small room to their home so Elisha would have a place to stay whenever he came through their town. He knew them both well.

Every home has heartache and this one was no different. This woman's womb was barren. Elisha was touched by her grief and offered to pray that God would give her a son. The woman, though she knew Elisha was a man of God, was skeptical. She knew that the only thing worse than barrenness was hoping for a miracle and then being disappointed. It was better to not expect anything than to hope in vain.

I've been her, knowing that God is true to his promises, but still afraid to reach out for just one of them. My petitions were stuck in my throat. My arms hung limply at my side. The flicker of hope was housed in a room with stale air. I had long ago closed the door, thinking it was for my protection, but in doing so, I prevented the wind of the Spirit from having access to the flame. I doubted that things could ever be any different for me. All I knew was the past, and the past kept repeating itself.

How glad I am that I decided to hope for change! The Shunammite woman did, too. She allowed Elisha to pray, and a short while later she held her newborn son in her arms. Her barren womb was touched by the Giver of life.

Hear my whispers, Lord. See my hands raised in expectation. Touch my place of hopelessness. Amen.

September 22

Poised for a Miracle

She went up and laid him on the bed of the man of
God, then shut the door and went out.

2 KINGS 4:21

*T*he Shunammite woman's son, the child of her dreams, was dead.
She was in shock. How could this be? His health had been perfect.
There had been no sign that tragedy would strike. But unexpectedly
that morning he had held his head and moaned in agony, "My head,
my head." His mother had sped to attend to him, but he died minutes
later. It seemed that what God gave, he took away cruelly.

However, perception is everything. Instead of preparing him for a
funeral, this mother carried her son to the prophet Elisha's room. Elisha
was a friend of the family. He visited their house so frequently that he
had his own bedroom. The mother laid out her son on Elisha's bed, a
place where the living slept. She awaited a miracle, hoping that the son
God had miraculously given her would breathe again.

Miracles unfold for those who make preparation for them. If the
mother had buried her son instead of sending for the prophet to come
and intervene, there would have been no resurrection.

There have been many places in my life that needed deliverance.
But as long as I assumed a posture of defeat and grieved a seemingly
unnecessary loss, I missed what could have been a miracle. God's
victories are cooperative. We do our part by believing that a victorious
outcome is possible and bring our hopeless situation to the prophet's
door rather than the coroner's office. We ask for a miracle by faith.
God does his part in faithfulness.

*I smell death in the air, Lord, but you are the resurrection and the
life. I await your arrival. Amen.*

September 23

Radical Intervention

He got on the bed and lay upon the boy, mouth to
mouth, eyes to eyes, hands to hands. As he stretched
himself out upon him, the boy's body grew warm.

2 KINGS 4:34

*H*ow big a crisis does it take for me to lose all inhibitions and risk
everything? Pretty big, usually. I am not a risk taker by nature.
I usually play it safe, feel out the environment, and gather all the facts
before I commit myself to doing something out of the ordinary.

I should take lessons from Elisha. A young boy had died, the
cherished son of his friends. He had been their son of promise, their
long-awaited pride and joy. Elisha was the one who had prayed for
his conception.

Now the boy was dead. Elisha was filled with grief as he stood by
his bedside. What was Elisha's proper role now? Would he be the
comforter to the family? Or perhaps the man of God who would recite
Scripture at the gravesite? Both would have been appreciated. Either
would have been accepted.

Elisha's faith surpassed normal expectations. His belief that God
could and would heal through the most bizarre and unconventional
methods prompted Elisha to do something very unusual. He stretched
out on top of the boy, mouth to mouth, eyes to eyes, and hands to
hands. The boy's body began to grow warm. He was brought from
death to life by an outrageous act of love.

Who needs me to be an Elisha today? What act of love,
forgiveness, or mercy could I extend that might resurrect another soul
from the brink of despair? Though I may look like a fool in the process,
to that one who needs it my gesture will be lifesaving.

Make me an Elisha. I need courage, Lord. Amen.

September 24

Unexpected Godliness

He sacrificed his own son in the fire, practiced sorcery
and divination, and consulted mediums and spiritists.

2 KINGS 21:6

*J*osiah inherited a tragic legacy. His grandfather, Manasseh, was a wicked king who sacrificed one of his sons in a satanic ritual. How much lower can you go? Your conscience has to be seared to put your own flesh and blood to the torch.

Amon, another son of Manasseh, eventually inherited the throne. He wasn't much better. He reigned two years before being assassinated. His son, Josiah, was eight years old when he was crowned king. He reigned for the next thirty-one years and instituted the most sweeping godly reforms in all of Israel's history. How could such purity emerge from an evil legacy?

It astounds me because "Like father, like son" is too often my belief. Though the adage is usually true, it does not take into account a God who can do the impossible. Can our Father preserve the spirit of a young child though he lives in proximity with evil? Absolutely.

If you are married to an alcoholic, your child is not doomed to become one himself. Prayer can deliver him. If your child lives in a neighborhood where gangs rule, your son need not become a member. Prayer can deliver him. If your dear children suffered abuse at the hands of a family member or baby-sitter, you may fear that their life is ruined because they witnessed evil firsthand. Oh, not so. Prayer can deliver them.

We cannot conceive that there might be a core of innocence left, yet the Spirit of God sealed off the heart of your child and declared it untouchable. Though there are memories, there is freedom. Though there is grief, there is still innocence.

Make my child a Josiah, Lord. Amen.

September 25

Know Yourself

The law of the LORD is perfect, reviving the soul.
PSALM 19:7

I received this note recently:

> Christine, help me understand what's wrong with me. I'm a Christian. I know God's Spirit lives inside me. He is supposed to be enough to satisfy me, but I crave what people refuse to give me. What's the matter? I know all the answers in my head, but my heart fails me.

She's empty. She admits it. Good for her!

The first thing any of us must do to access the power of the Spirit is explore our own emptiness. I'm learning the fabric of my brokenness so I can understand how and where I need God. Without that knowledge, I don't know how to pray for myself nor recognize the gifts God has to give me. I began to experience abundant life when I learned the truth about God, learned the truth about myself, and then allowed the truth of God to impact the truth about me. I needed my Father to interact with me, instruct me, and enlighten me.

I believe that much of the malaise of the church occurs because we study God and his truths until our minds are saturated, but there is still spiritual illness. The weak and wounded serve in the trenches. No wonder women are telling me, "What I'm doing isn't working! I feel empty." We have not been taught that throughout Scripture God places importance on understanding our own heart—how it self-deceives, how it is bent, and why we need what we do. We can't fix a broken bicycle unless we know where it's broken. The same principle applies spiritually.

Lord, please show me where I am empty and why. Help me see myself through your eyes. Amen.

September 26

Lighting My Spirit

The spirit of man is the candle of the LORD.
PROVERBS 20:27 KJV

I read this verse the other day, loved it, and ended up writing a song inspired by it. I am charmed by the idea that my spirit can be a candle of God's light and glory. This gives me profound purpose for living.

How can you and I become the brightest of candles? By understanding that light becomes magnificent when seen against the backdrop of utter darkness. Light a match in daylight and it doesn't have much pizzazz. Light it in a cave and it's lifesaving.

I wonder why my spirit fails to radiate the glory of God more brilliantly? Perhaps it's because I'm fearful of allowing his light to shine amid the darkest places of my soul, the corners where disappointments fester, failures are recounted, sins condemn, and others' betrayals eat me alive. It's more convenient to leave those tangled cobwebs alone and to live with my back turned toward them.

When I face myself at the core of my inner darkness, I see how much I need God. I'm confronted by the challenge of giving up my rights to all these private obsessions, of abdicating my right to be jury and judge over myself.

God is asking me to turn over the darkness to him for redemption. Every corner of my spirit begs a visitation of the Light. I ache to glow. Just as hope is sweetest when we feel despair, and peace is a treasure when there is chaos, his light shines brightest in my darkest places.

I want to be set on fire, Lord. Shine your light where you wish. Give me the courage to see what is revealed. May your glory reign in every corner of my spirit. Amen.

What Forgiveness Means

"Forgive all our sins and receive us graciously."
HOSEA 14:2

Every person struggles with the issue of forgiveness. We have a list of folks who have failed us. The hurt can be overwhelming. We often get stuck and never move beyond the pain of the wounds. We choose to live in the bitterness of the memories.

Doesn't it seem unfair to have to forgive those who might not deserve it? Yes. Was it unfair that Jesus forgave me when I didn't deserve it? Yes. Therefore I must consider this: If I really believe that God loves me perfectly and that his ways are life-giving, I must believe that forgiveness is for my good. He has prescribed it for a journey of freedom and joy. God never asks us to do something impossible. Why then are we frozen in unforgiveness? I believe we misunderstand forgiveness.

Forgiveness is not excusing someone else's behavior or minimizing the gravity of their sins. Jesus asks us to acknowledge the full extent of the damage.

Forgiveness is not the same as reconciliation. We can always forgive, for that is between God and us. Reconciliation, however, is not possible unless both parties are operating in truth.

Forgiveness does not mean forgetting. We can forgive another though in this lifetime we might never forget what they've done.

Forgiveness is not natural. Revenge is. Forgiveness is supernatural in that I allow God to detach my emotional responses from painful events. I step out from the past into the present. I relinquish my rights to be king of my world and administer justice. I put the matters of others' wrongs against me into his hands.

Forgiveness is a way of life, not something that happens once and I'm done with it. Lord, help me to be a forgiving person today. Amen.

September 28

Perverted Justice

You have turned justice into poison.

AMOS 6:12

*F*or any of us with the gift of discernment, our dilemma is not recognizing what is right but knowing when to speak. Without sensitivity to God's timetable, we can become reckless spiritual police. We gain a reputation for badgering others with the truth.

My crusade for justice turns poisonous when it is fueled by personal pain. My need to be right, my need to control, my need for fairness, or my appetite for revenge is the breeding ground for toxic justice. No wonder Paul was so clear on the issue of speaking the truth with love. Truth without love alters the very nature of truth. God's messages to us are always wrapped with the colors of mercy and grace.

Is there anyone in your life whom you're trying to change? Are there policies in your church or company that you're trying to institute? Are you being successful? Do others see you as one who is wise and temperate? Or when they see you coming, do they mutter, "Here she comes. Get ready for trouble."

Of course, truth must be proclaimed. I want to be faithful to speak when God nudges me. However, when presenting truth in an atmosphere of resistance, I need to examine my motives to make sure I have God's heart for those who listen. I need to engage in warfare, coming against the enemy, who loves to distort truth and cause others to hear it through a faulty grid. And finally, I can ask the Spirit of God to prepare the soil in others' hearts so when the seed of truth is planted, it will take root.

Lord, help me handle the truth wisely, sensitively, and with humility. Amen.

September 29

For Jesus' Sake

Being found in appearance as a man, he humbled
himself.

PHILIPPIANS 2:8

One of the prevailing themes of Scripture is God's judgment
against those who trample on or forget the weak, widows,
orphans, and anyone else who is feeble-minded. This provokes God's
anger faster than anything.

Are you working through childhood issues? Are you seeking love
from those who are now old and feeble? It can be frustrating. You want
resolution in your lifetime, before the older adults die.

In the meantime it is too easy to defame them, shame them, and
ridicule their weaknesses to friends and family members. Mistreating
the elderly and dishonoring them is grievous to God. It creates a
powerless Christian experience.

It is important to realize that though the love given was anemic,
in many instances the adults truly did love, but only within the framework they understood and could generate on their own. Yes, the love
may have been limited, but they didn't know what was lacking. They
probably believed they loved you well. It's easy to moan and complain,
try to expand their understanding, but they cannot get it.

It's time to move on. They are old, frail, fear-bound, and—
probably most importantly—people who have never been loved
intimately so they can understand love. They can't give away what they
have not first possessed.

As a child of God, I'm not given the luxury of picking and
choosing who I want to love. God wishes to call these difficult people
to his heart and may use me to do his wooing. Jesus wore the cloak of
humility to serve his enemies. May I choose to wear the same garment.

*I love your mercy, Father. But words are cheap if I don't give mercy
to others who I think are undeserving. Give me grace to be like Jesus.
Amen.*

September 30

Teamwork

"I sent you to reap what you have not worked for. Others have done the hard work, and you have reaped the benefits of their labor."

JOHN 4:38

I am a bit of a perfectionist in a few areas of my life. Not bad, though, and God is helping me work on the parts that are left.

It's not much fun to work for a perfectionist. I've done that. They can easily think that if a job is going to be done well and done right, it will only happen because of their solitary effort. Playing martyr and being perfectionistic often go hand in hand. Oftentimes the ones who try to help are driven away because their work is never considered good enough.

Perfectionists find it hard to work as a team player. Yet God wants his people to understand that while our work in his kingdom is important, given to us for our pleasure, kingdom fruit does not result because of any isolated effort. Many who raise their hands at a crusade event to become God's child are doing so because others faithfully prayed for them, perhaps tearfully, most likely for years.

And no one should discount the work God himself did to bring about their journey home to his heart. His Spirit worked to till fertile spiritual soil that produced the sweet fruit of salvation.

Being able to team up with God is a privilege. He does all the hard work and is gracious enough to give his children the joy of harvesting the crop. That kind of gift reminds me of a mother who measures all the ingredients of a cake, gets it ready to mix, and then tells her child to stir the batter. The child believes he made the cake.

You finished the work, Lord. But thank you for giving me the joy of harvesting. Amen.

October

October 1

No Man's Land

The Son is the radiance of God's glory and the exact representation of his being, sustaining all things by his powerful word.

HEBREWS 1:3

*I*n the decades that followed the death and resurrection of Jesus, Jewish believers floundered. They were in no man's land. Their own people shunned them because they abandoned the work of the Law. The Gentiles rejected them because they failed to embrace the culture of the day. They suffered intense persecution. All they had was a faith in Jesus but that faith was tenuous. They began to doubt that they really knew truth. Had they given up everything for nothing? Was Jesus who he claimed to be? Was the way of grace God's way? Maybe they'd been misguided and their suffering was for nothing.

A nameless man wrote the book of Hebrews to strengthen them. He reviewed who Jesus was, lest they doubt it. Their persecution moved his heart. Their physical suffering was difficult enough without this crisis of faith. With both, the people of God were brought to the breaking point.

I identify with the writer of this magnificent book. I reach out to those of you who feel you are in no man's land. You've taken a stand for your faith, perhaps even alienating family members, but you wonder if it's all worth it. You've embraced Jesus at great cost yet your connection to him seems weak. Your heart lacks confidence. The joy of your salvation is a distant thing.

Jesus sustains all things, including your faith, by the power of his word. He from whom truth was derived before the creation of the world holds you securely in his grip. His very word spoke you into existence and you are sustained by its power.

My arms are weak, Lord, but the important thing is that yours are strong. Amen.

October 2

Tattered Earth

In the beginning, O Lord, you laid the foundations
of the earth, and the heavens are the work of your
hands. They will perish, but you remain; they will all
wear out like a garment.

HEBREWS 1:10–11

*H*ave any old clothes hanging in your closet? Just this week I
weeded out my wardrobe and made a trip to a nearby secondhand store. I passed on misshapen dresses, shirts with limp collars, and
jeans with knees that had grown thin and threadbare. These were all
signs that my clothing was wearing out. While they were once new
and made a decent presentation, time and overuse relegated them to
the back of the closet. What was once a dress shirt became a paint shirt.
Old jeans became gardening clothes. You know the kind.

The earth is wearing out like clothes, according to God. What was
once his sterling presentation has slowly been defiled over time. The
landscape is littered. Acid rain covers the Rocky Mountains. The most
pristine environments show the wear and tear of the long-term effects
of the Fall. It is hard to imagine that lakes and rivers were once so pure
that a person could cup hands and drink from them without fear of
pollution.

I must not allow myself to get too attached here. This world will
continue to deteriorate. My hope, my treasure, my investment is in
my future home, the one that will not pass away. In God's presence
there is no aging. We will bear the image of the one who is glorious and
who changes not with time. His radiance is the same today as
yesterday. Though my flesh and everything around me withers, my
soul has only begun to prosper.

*I am a citizen of your kingdom, Lord, a place where beauty never
dims. Thank you. Amen.*

October 3

Making Sure I Remember

We must pay more careful attention, therefore, to
what we have heard, so that we do not drift away.
HEBREWS 2:1

Sometimes I can't recall information easily. While talking to a
friend, a book comes to mind but the title escapes me. Or I'll tell
of a certain pastor whose words impacted me, but suddenly I can't
remember his name. I have also gone to the store, thinking I
committed a grocery list to memory, but forgotten the last two items.
The mind can be a wonderful tool. It's capable of storing much
information but we have to intentionally reinforce what we want to
recall later.

Whenever I'm confronted with something I know I'll want to
remember down the road, I take care to commit it to memory so the
information will be there when I need it. I'll review it over and over
again in my mind. I'll say it out loud several times. I'll write the
information down, sometimes in several places, to make sure it's not
lost. I might even ask a friend or family member, "Help me remember
this, okay?"

Oftentimes I have failed to handle God's Word with care. I didn't
realize its power. Now I do. I print out beautiful portions of Scripture,
frame them, and display them. Keeping them in front of me nudges
me to meditate on them. Other verses are handwritten on a three-
by-five-inch card, laminated, and carried like a credit card in my
wallet. Currently the top of my desk displays a favorite passage from
the book of Hosea, typed out in an elegant, italicized font and
combined with a favorite piece of artwork. God's Word, which
safeguards my mind and sustains my heart, is worth any investment of
my time.

Your words live forever, Lord. Help me make time for them. Amen.

October 4

Powerless to Change Truth

> If the message spoken by angels was binding, and every violation and disobedience received its just punishment, how shall we escape if we ignore such a great salvation?
>
> HEBREWS 2:2

God always speaks the truth. That is great news for me, provided that I value truth and am open to receive it. If I humbly approach my Father with a teachable spirit, his words will bring freedom, guidance, comfort, and inspiration.

Truth becomes bad news the moment I choose to ignore it, however. If I happen to dislike the essence of it because it grates against my self-made philosophy, I'm in trouble. I can begin to think that I chart my own course. Though I acknowledge that some of God's truth is valid, I think I will be unaffected by what I decide to reject. It simply won't apply to me. I can nullify God's principles by lack of application.

Not true! Truth is truth whether I embrace it or not.

Jesus came to set captives free. Some will look to him for the key to their prison door. Others will whine in their captivity, having rejected the nail-pierced hand that offered them the way out. More will perish for lack of knowledge. We must bring the truth.

Jesus came to give a garland for ashes. Some will give up their rights to their pain and anger and find his healing. Others will carry on with bitter tears, rejecting the way of God's deliverance. More will drown in their tears, not knowing there is a "man of sorrows, acquainted with grief." We must bring the truth.

I am faced with choices throughout this day. Truth does not change for me. I will change as I submit to it, for submitting unleashes its power. Change becomes almost effortless.

You are the truth, Abba. I bow to you. Pour my heart into your Son's mold. Amen.

October 5

I'm a Gift That Makes Jesus Rejoice

"Here am I, and the children God has given me."
HEBREWS 2:13

*C*hildren are a gift from the LORD," Scripture tells us. Any of you who have held your newborn child know that feeling of wonder. Babies come gift wrapped in pastel hues. "Fragile" marks the package, and it is adorned with the most exquisite array of ribbons. Parents unwrap the gift of a child over a lifetime.

When we were spiritually adopted through Jesus, God gave us to him as children. We are the gift, the reward for his suffering. He unwrapped each of us, one package at a time. We came gift wrapped in scarlet hues, clothed in the garments of forgiveness. "Fragile" marked our package, and it was adorned with the ribbons of royal color. Our spiritual potential is being unveiled over a lifetime.

Jesus spent thirty-three years here, showing us how to live. Because we are under his care, he mentors us as he tells us to follow his lead.

"See how I love those who don't deserve it?" he asks. "Do as I do."

"See how much I commune with my Father? You need him, too," he enlightens. "Notice my tears? They are for those who are still lost. Love them and bring them to me," he pleads. At each turn he parents us, leading by example.

Do you question your worth today? Consider this: You were the priceless gift God gave Jesus at the conclusion of his suffering. When Jesus washed you clean at your spiritual birth, he rejoiced when he discovered it was you. A party was thrown in heaven. You will never be an orphan again. You belong to the one who will one day present you as a gift, yet again, to his Father.

I stand tall today, Jesus, and carry no shame. Amen.

Merciful and Faithful

For this reason he had to be made like his brothers in
every way, in order that he might become a merciful
and faithful high priest in service to God.

HEBREWS 2:17

*I*s anything more difficult than confession? Seeking out a high priest,
securing his attention, and saying, "Look what I've done. I've
sinned" can be humiliating. Especially if we hear, "You did what? I'm
disgusted. I can't believe you did that!" We will take our sins underground and hide in shame rather than risk such embarrassment.

Jesus lived among us so I would be comforted that he knows what
it's like to live my life. He faced the same temptations. He was
presented with the same sinful options that visit my front door every
day. He felt their allure and understood how easy it would be to fall.
Though he never sinned, he understands why I do. He is so committed to rescue me from the slavery of it that he gave his life to secure my
freedom. He is my high priest.

When I bring my offenses to his attention, I sense his grief over the
ways sin has hurt me. After all, I'm his child and he aches over the ways
sin corrupts my soul and torments me. I will never hear words that
communicate disgust and repulsion. Instead his mercy causes him to
exclaim, "Oh, I'm so glad you've come to me. I can forgive you."

I also need never fear that I've sinned one too many times. Though
I might have fallen yesterday, his mercies are new every morning. Just
as he told me to forgive others "seventy times seven," he models that
kind of faithful forgiveness toward me. He offers me a new beginning
with each sunrise.

Jesus, I'm relieved I don't need to hide from you. Amen.

October 7

The Remedy of Encouragement

Encourage one another daily, as long as it is called
Today, so that none of you may be hardened by sin's
deceitfulness.

HEBREWS 3:13

I want to be your encourager, a voice that cheers you on to believe
that God is who he says he is and that walking in his ways will
prosper your soul. There's a lot at stake. Without personal encouragement we begin to lose sight of the goal. We get lost in the isolation of
making so many choices. The days blend into one another and we
slowly lose perspective. To complicate matters, the voices that offer
false promises are too alluring to refuse.

No wonder God told us to whisper the truth in each other's ears,
because sin is deceitful. It lies. It makes promises it can never deliver
in the long run. Initially sin feels good. An affair is exhilarating.
Controlling others is empowering. Taking revenge feels therapeutic.
Building a bigger house is an anesthetic to the pain. Gossip makes us
feel better about ourselves. Fighting for our rights massages the pain of
unfairness. The list goes on.

The longer I choose to believe (and act on) the false promises of
sin, the harder my heart becomes. If I sin today, I will be more
hardened tomorrow. I'll be even less likely to be affected by the truth.
God's voice will be more unwelcome. The purity of his ways will seem
more perverted.

Let's put our arms around someone who is struggling with
critical choices today. Let's remind them that God's ways are worth it.
He delivers what he promises: peace, confidence, eternal rewards, and
the joy of living in the light of his love.

*Keep my heart soft toward you, Father. I embrace your truth even
though it is the harder choice. Amen.*

October 8

Longevity Pays Off

We have come to share in Christ if we hold firmly till
the end the confidence we had at first.

HEBREWS 3:14

I've been privileged to meet some great people. I'm not referring to
the famous kind necessarily, but "great" in the context of
"Christlikeness." Most of them are old. They've walked with Jesus for
a lifetime, and the companionship they have shared with him has paid
off. Their eyes sparkle. Their handshake has purpose and passion. Bad
news never shocks them yet they are not cynical. Their words are few
but they impart courage with a simple phrase. They breathe wisdom.
(I wish I'd written down everything I've heard them say.) They don't
seem to be thrown off balance by tragedy. They don't minimize it but
instead simply state the need to go to prayer. Nothing shakes
their foundation.

I want to be like them when I grow up. I won't achieve this
overnight, because the writer of Hebrews reveals that longevity is the
key to this kind of spiritual greatness. The mysteries of Christ unfold
with the years. There are no shortcuts to getting to know him. Time
with Jesus, through the good and the bad, deepens my relationship
with him in a way only time can. Our relating will slowly resemble
that of a well-seasoned marriage.

I can easily miss the meaning of today's verse by thinking that the
reward for longevity with Jesus is stability, wisdom, and faith. Not true.
The reward is an irreplaceable knowing of Jesus. The byproducts of
that are stability, wisdom, faith, and joy! Jesus shares the most poignant
parts of himself with those who have walked with him the longest. Oh,
the joy that awaits for any of us who hang in there!

I commit myself to you till the end, Lord Jesus. Amen.

October 9

Passing Over a Treasure

The message they heard was of no value to them,
because those who heard did not combine it with faith.
HEBREWS 4:2

I was given a gift recently, an antique vase. I didn't care for it. I smiled politely when I opened it but I thought it was rather gaudy. I immediately thought of selling it at my next yard sale, but my perception changed when I found out its history and value. I couldn't recognize it for what it was. It was hand-painted. The process the artist used to give it its intricate design was painstaking. After I heard the story of the piece, its appearance began to change. It now sits on my desk, with roses in it.

At first glance God's ways don't appeal to me, either. They seem repulsive to my taste buds. "Lose my life to find it?" "Love my enemies?" "Give up my rights and surrender to his plan?" "Lose my independence and become childlike?"

I'm like a moth drawn to a flame, pulled toward my own demise, without the awareness that I can't recognize what's good for me. Faith helps me see the difference between good and bad. When I hear a spiritual truth that is difficult to believe, I must exercise faith and say, "God cherishes me and only gives good gifts. I choose to believe that this principle is a nugget of wisdom. I'm acting on it though I don't understand it."

At that point it begins to lose its sour quality. I must "taste and see that the LORD is good," not merely cruise by the banquet table and make an assessment from a distance. Otherwise I'll be wrong every time.

I won't discard your wisdom, Lord; I'll treasure it. Amen.

First Things First

The word of God is living and active. Sharper than any double-edged sword, it penetrates even to dividing soul and spirit, joints and marrow; it judges the thoughts and attitudes of the heart.

HEBREWS 4:12

If I want to know how well a piece of clothing is made, all I have to do is turn it inside out. I'll be able to see if the seams are finished on the inside, if the stitching is precise, if the garment is lined for extended wear, and if it is double-stitched to give a crisp, professional, finished look. Though two garments may look the same from the outside, their difference in value is readily apparent by comparing them from the inside out.

God's Word is powerful. It is meant to shape our outward behaviors through exposing the depths of our inner life. Many use the Bible as a guide for behavior modification only. Scripture becomes nothing more than a code of conduct. Hearts are never transformed, though outward performance appears impeccable.

Oh, that my outward behaviors would change as a result of allowing God to turn me inside out first. Scripture will do that if I allow it. It takes the thoughts, feelings, and contents of my heart and lays them out on the table for me to examine. Though humbling and oftentimes shocking, it gives me an opportunity to really know myself and discover just where I need God's regenerative touch. As he changes me at the core, outward signs slowly become visible to those who know me. Putting on one's best Sunday clothes in an attempt to look holy has never been God's way. He desires inner changes wrought by experience with his extravagant love.

My soul is laid open to you, Father. Amen.

October 11

Showcasing a Jewel

We have one who has been tempted in every way, just
as we are — yet was without sin.

HEBREWS 4:15

*G*od's thoughts are not my thoughts. If I had been the Father of
Jesus and planned to send my Son to earth, it would have been
a grand event. He would have been born into royalty, lived in palatial
estates, and enjoyed the privileges due him. Jesus would have been
protected from harassment by the mere power of his office, enabling
him to devote himself to his ministry. Though this sounds like a good
plan to me, it didn't to God, who decided to showcase his Son's life in
completely different textures and colors.

Jesus was born to poor people, birthed in the most unlikely place,
a stable! He was nearly killed with all the other infant boys and became
a fugitive as an infant. He had no home, owned nothing, and enjoyed
no prestige. The backdrop of his life was suffering and betrayal. Against
the threads of darkness Jesus' light shone brightly.

A jeweler knows that the success of selling precious gems depends
in part on how he chooses to showcase them. If the customer is to
appreciate their beauty, they must be viewed against draperies of black,
crimson, or dark green velvet.

Jesus, who is light and glory, was framed in the darkness of his
times. The victory of his resurrection was showcased against the
seeming defeat of the cross and the cruelty of the crucifixion. The hope
he promised was posed within the context of human betrayal and the
darkness of humanity's deeds. It was against these dark threads of
tragedy that the power of his love was cast.

*Let me take comfort that you also showcase your glory against the
dark threads of my life, Lord. They are not wasted! Amen.*

October 12

Trusting the One Who Understands

We do not have a high priest who is unable to sympathize with our weaknesses, but we have one who has been tempted in every way, just as we are — yet was without sin.

HEBREWS 4:15

God understands our pain, because he made us. But I am often skeptical, wondering if the one who fashioned me with his hands and wired me cognitively and emotionally really understands what it feels like to be human and live in this world. Sure, he created me. But the one who draws the blueprint of the house doesn't know the feel of the house with his eyes closed unless he takes the time to live in it. Unless he calls it home for a period of time, he won't be able to maneuver up and down the stairs in the middle of the night. He won't know where the creaks in the floors are, nor will he be able to unlock the outer doors in the dark just by the feel of the key. All this comes from experience, time spent in the surroundings.

It's hard for me to believe that God truly knows what it is like to live in a confusing world. Oh, but wait. With the entrance of God on earth in human form, he acquired a new platform of credibility. Now besides saying, "I understand you because I made you," he also adds, "I understand because I've lived it. I've experienced it, too. I am one who has also been wounded. I understand frailty, limitations, betrayal, and abandonment."

Ah, this feels different to me. When I run to Jesus, I need to know he has felt the stings of this life, too.

Jesus, I entrust myself to you. You've earned the credibility to dry my tears. Amen.

October 13

A Throne Unlike Others

Let us then approach the throne of grace with confidence, so that we may receive mercy and find grace to help us in our time of need.

HEBREWS 4:16

I consider the "thrones" I have approached in my lifetime. They were usually preceded by a message. "Your dad wants to talk with you." "Please go to the principal's office." "The board of deacons would like to ask you some questions." "The boss wants to schedule a time to review your yearly performance." What was my visceral reaction? A churning stomach.

To know that I can approach God's throne without dread is a great relief.

If I come as a penitent prodigal, I will receive mercy. I won't hear that I've used up all my chances. I won't be condemned and banished from his presence. No matter what I've done, I will receive mercy. The punishment I deserve will be withheld because of what Jesus did for me. He was condemned in my place, giving me the right to forever approach his holy Father without fear.

If I come emotionally broken, I will receive grace. I won't hear that he's tired of my cries for help. I won't be judged for being too needy. He won't brush me off by telling me there are people with more severe problems for him to care for. I can expect empathy, understanding, and grace to cushion me for the duration of my trial.

God's throne room is decorated with the colors of mercy and grace. They are the policies of choice. While I should never take either gift lightly, since Jesus paid with his life to make them available to me, I can come confidently.

When I cross the threshold, Lord, I hear you say, "You've come. How wonderful! What is it you need, mercy or grace?" Thank you. Amen.

325

Poor Students

He is able to deal gently with those who are ignorant
and are going astray.

HEBREWS 5:2

*T*eacher's pets are born when students reveal an aptitude for the
subject being taught. They have no trouble eliciting praise from
their professor. It comes to them effortlessly.

The ones who need the encouragement are those who rarely raise
their hand, the ones who can't quite grasp the concepts. The material
is a step ahead of them. They operate within a defeated mind-set.

Is the art of learning a contest between the gifted and the
unintelligent? Not necessarily. A slow learner might not be lacking in
aptitude. He might suffer from a learning disability or be distracted
emotionally by a chaotic home. If we knew the real-life stories behind
many below-average students, we'd have a lot more compassion. We'd
understand that the student at the head of the class might quickly lose
his position if he battled the same destructive elements behind the
scenes as does his struggling classmate.

Likewise, the church can easily delight in those who learn quickly,
those who exhibit signs of rapid spiritual change. They're held up as
models, and the ones who can't keep the pace of the advanced become
discouraged when they go one step forward and three steps back. They
sense others' disappointment in them. Spiritual leaders need to deal
gently with those who frequently stumble. It is not always due to
spiritual slothfulness.

I know. For nearly four decades I couldn't grasp the love of Jesus
on an emotional level due to the multifaceted elements of my life story.
Jesus was a patient bridegroom. Undaunted by the obstacles, he slowly
awakened my heart to the reality of his love. Now he helps me reach
out to those who limp in their spiritual walk.

Help me see others as you see them, Jesus. Amen.

October 15

Trust, Praise, and Forgiveness

Although he was a son, he learned obedience from what he suffered.

HEBREWS 5:8

I wasn't born with a bent toward obedience. Once I became aware of a rule, I wanted to break it. When I was told, "Whatever you do, don't open that cupboard," I couldn't wait for the grown-ups to leave the room so I could go sneak a peek. My heart thought of creative ways to rebel. Pain, however, became a great motivator to change.

One of the positive outcomes of personal suffering is that it has reformed my appetite for obedience. In submitting to God's plans for me (which include opening my heart to accept his extravagant love), I have found joy.

For example, God has told me to trust him. I won't be inclined to obey until I'm in so much discomfort that I can't find my own way out of my dilemma. I'll learn that I can't trust myself. Faced with no options, I'll consider trusting God.

God has also told me to praise him. A rebellious heart is a self-centered one. Praise for anyone besides myself doesn't occur to me. I won't think of praising God until I hurt deeply enough. If I'm abandoned, I'll praise God for his faithfulness. If I'm trapped, I'll praise God for his deliverance. If I lack discernment, I'll praise God for his wisdom. Praise is born through the birth canal of pain.

And God has told me to forgive. I won't think of obeying unless I have experienced the long-term effects of unforgiveness. If my body and soul have been ravaged by years of bitterness, I'll entertain the thought that perhaps God was right all along. Forgiveness *is* a gift I give to myself.

Father, I am refined by fire for obedience. Make my heart still and submissive. Amen.

October 16

Confused by Good and Evil

Solid food is for the mature, who by constant use have
trained themselves to distinguish good from evil.

HEBREWS 5:14

Scripture is multilayered. Each time I read it, I never cease to
discover new riches of truth. Internalizing it over a lifetime pays
off. My spiritual skill of discernment is sharpened. What might have
looked like something distasteful to me as a baby believer is perceived
as something of value now that I'm farther down the road. Abba is
training me to distinguish between good and evil.

For instance, in my earlier years I used to believe that every prayer
should be answered immediately. "Good fathers come running as soon
as their children whimper," I reasoned. When my prayers seemed to go
unanswered, some for a decade or more, I wondered at God's
goodness. This was childlike thinking. I failed to realize that a good
father does not rush in and rescue too soon. A greater lesson can be
learned by withholding the answer and letting me discover it on my
own. Lessons of endurance and problem solving can't be taught any
other way.

I am not always able to recognize and label what is good and what
is bad. God's actions or inactions that appear cruel, passive, and
uncaring today will be revealed as loving in the long run. It was for my
best. My Father is the perfect father, driven by love and a wisdom that
takes me a lifetime to begin to understand. However, with each
passing day I am being trained to repent of snap judgments against
God's character. As soon as I label his behavior toward me as unfair,
unloving, or distant, I know that my discernment needs a major
tune-up.

You are good, Father. Keep teaching me about good and evil. Amen.

October 17

Payoff of Wholehearted Investment

We want each of you to show this same diligence to
the very end, in order to make your hope sure.
HEBREWS 6:11

*I*nvesting in most anything involves risk. The stock market, a new
friendship, a business venture, an entrepreneurial dream—none of
these can unequivocally promise a good return. The only investment
that is sure to yield more than what I initially lay out is an investment
in eternity. There's a no-risk guarantee. In fact, the writer of Hebrews
assures me that the more I risk, the more hope I'll enjoy.

If I give my time, my heart, my trust, or my money to God half-
heartedly, my level of hope will be affected. Hope is proportionate to
the degree that I open up my heart and tenaciously pursue the things
of God by faith. I don't have to fear that my investment has been made
in vain. My hope rests on the nature and character of God.

God set the pace by giving us his Son. Jesus is not reserved with
me. He risked it all, spent his life, shared all of his inheritance, and
threw open the door to his heart so I could enter into a relationship
with him fully and completely. He has not held back anything from
me, having made the awkward first move in our relationship. He gives
me the courage to come to him with no reservations, because he was
vulnerable first. I just have to find the courage to respond in kind.

Jesus makes it possible for me to write a check for any amount in
the bank account called hope. My confidence gradually becomes
unshakable. Diligence pays well.

*Jesus, what is important to you today? Show me. I'll work together
with you. Amen.*

October 18

"You Promised!"

After waiting patiently, Abraham received what
was promised.

HEBREWS 6:15

*M*aking a promise is a serious thing. When I was a kid, I knew
the seriousness of someone giving me their word. I was in
the sixth grade. A friend had promised to let me play shortstop in our
next softball game. She was team captain and had the power to make
such choices. When it was time for her to assign positions during our
next gym period, she chose another girl over me. I was hurt. I later
told her, "But you promised!" She shrugged her shoulders, not upset in
the least by what she'd done. I learned then that some speak carelessly.

God is the promise keeper. Intellectually we know our theology.
However, life is messy and complicated. Often the length of time that
passes between the point when a promise is given and the fulfillment
of it can span years. While we wait, our faith in God's character is
tested. We begin to wonder, "Is God like other people in my life? Does
he speak carelessly or simply forget what he promised to do? And if
reminded, will he shrug his shoulders, too?"

What has God promised you? Are you discouraged? Do
circumstances seem to indicate that the promise is more intangible
today than it was yesterday? You might sense you're moving away from
its fulfillment rather than closer. Perhaps your confidence in God is
shaken to the core.

If we were fortunate enough to have a conversation with Abraham
today, he would put his arm around our shoulders and tell us to trust
God and be patient. A fulfilled promise is only half of God's agenda.
The building up of our faith while we patiently wait is as important to
God as the promise itself.

I won't give up on you, Lord. Amen.

October 19

The Promise Keeper

Because God wanted to make the unchanging nature
of his purpose very clear to the heirs of what was
promised, he confirmed it with an oath.

HEBREWS 6:17

*H*ow many promises have you made? Were you careful to make
only promises you knew you could keep? Do the ones you've
broken haunt you? I've broken some, and though I apologized,
sometimes the results were devastating. A broken promise is like a
cancer that can eat away another's ability to trust.

God loves to make promises! He has made tens of thousands yet
has uttered none in haste. He speaks wisely and joyfully keeps
his word.

There is nothing more heartbreaking than to be promised
something, only to decide after careful evaluation that the person who
made the promise was untrustworthy. Especially if the individual not
only broke their word but shows no regret. Then we feel like a fool for
having trusted. I have known betrayal like this in my lifetime. At first
I blamed myself: "How could I have been such a bad judge of character?"

God is unchanging. He is the great "I AM" from everlasting to
everlasting. He is the perfect promise keeper. He is still keeping
covenants made centuries ago. He never wavers nor second-guesses the
wisdom of his past promises. His words are perfect and his
commitment to his covenants is unchanging.

Wherever your footsteps take you today, and whatever your need,
God will be there to fulfill every promise that is yours to claim. Oh,
the tragedy of unclaimed covenants. There's a spiritual bank account
with your name on it, full of promises ready to be spent.

*I'm motivated to know your word better, Lord. I want to claim all
the promises that are mine and live with joy as I see you keep them.
Amen.*

October 20

Wasted Promises

Because God wanted to make the unchanging nature of his purpose very clear to the heirs of what was promised, he confirmed it with an oath.

HEBREWS 6:17

*G*od is a promise maker. He loves to make covenants. Yet he doesn't do it carelessly, nor does he take his promises lightly once he's spoken. Every word he delivers is true at the time, weighted with meaning, and remains true until the end of time.

Who are the recipients of the promises? Family. If I am Abba's daughter, the promises are for me. If I am not his child, I'm like an orphan peeking in the windows of the home of a loving family, watching their interactions and wishing such a family were mine.

May I never lose the wonder that I was once that child on the outside, but through Jesus I've been adopted. I live inside the house. Royal blood now courses through my veins. The loving words spoken by the Father are now for me. How many promises do I know? How many more exist that I am unaware of because I haven't taken the time to go looking for them? And of the ones I am familiar with, how many do I tend to discount because they seem too good to be true? I may struggle to see my worth in God's eyes, so I can't believe they are for me. I may still feel like the orphan on the outside even though God has given me a key to the front door and made a place for me at the table.

Promises are part of my inheritance. Unless I intentionally excavate each one from Scripture, they will remain as undiscovered gold. They deserve to be mined, pondered, and treasured.

A promise made is love given. I accept your love, Lord. Amen.

October 21

Holiness Made Easy

Let us draw near to God with a sincere heart in full assurance of faith, having our hearts sprinkled to cleanse us from a guilty conscience.

HEBREWS 10:22

If you are God's daughter, chances are you want to live a holy life. It's important to you because the pursuit of holiness pleases our Father.

Could there also be less-than-ideal reasons for pursuing a holy lifestyle? I believe so. I grew up in a Christian home, attended a Baptist church, went to a Christian college, and have been involved in ministry since my teen years. If you had pinned me down along the way and asked me why I was trying to live a holy life, I would have answered, "Because God wants it and I feel guilty when I don't!" Does this ring true with you?

I have discovered that my foundation was wrong. Scripture says, "If you love God, you'll keep his commandments." I used to think that I needed to work hard to act holy to prove to God that I loved him. Purity was a lifestyle of good works I churned out from mere discipline. I failed to see holiness as being influenced by Someone who is holy.

As I have learned to spend time with God and really get to know him, my love and admiration for how he thinks, acts, and speaks is affecting me. An amazing thing is occurring. Holy living is coming naturally. It isn't work anymore, for it's boiling down to a daughter emulating a Father she adores! Imitation takes practice but it's a joyful exercise, done intuitively as I live with my hand in his.

In my frantic performing, I forgot to get to know you, Lord. Help me see that knowing and loving you will make me into someone more holy. Amen.

October 22

Appealing with Power

Let us consider how we may spur one another on toward love and good deeds.

HEBREWS 10:24

*A*re you an advocate? Perhaps you are appealing for the good of your child, showing your partner better ways to build bridges of love and communication. Maybe you're trying to persuade a sister or brother to handle an aging parent differently, or you have decided to confront an alcoholic in your family. Chances are, you've made speeches, even nagged, and as you're reading this, you are weary of arguments and excuses. Time to give up and let others be, right?

Paul asked Philemon to do something difficult—take back a slave who had once stolen from him. Though Paul knew Philemon well, he introduced himself as "a prisoner of Jesus Christ." Paul could have pulled rank, reminding Philemon that he was his pastor and overseer of the church. But he chose instead to introduce a touchy subject by framing his credentials with vulnerability.

How do we adapt that principle as we approach a friend, spouse, or church leader and try to persuade them to make changes and do the right thing? I can't remember who coined the phrase "wounded healer," but it proposes that each of us who attempt to bring healing will be more successful if we come as one whose wounds have been or are being healed. We show that we don't walk ahead as one superior, or behind as a supervisor; we walk beside as an equal. Our wounds unite us, bringing us together with humility, with an expectancy of God's gracious, healing touches.

It would be easy, Father, to pretend to have humility to manipulate others to do what I want. Deliver me from that. Work in my life to make me genuinely humble. Amen.

October 23

Wasted Panic

Do not throw away your confidence; it will be
richly rewarded.

HEBREWS 10:35

John tells of a wealthy nobleman coming to Jesus on behalf of his
terminally ill son. The man walks fifteen miles to plead his case
in person rather than send a servant. He is breathless and panicked.
We know who Jesus is, so what's the urgency? Even if his son dies, Jesus
can raise the dead!

Jesus says to the man, "Unless you see signs and wonders, you
simply will not believe." Doesn't this seem harsh? But perhaps Jesus is
tired of our fickle trust. Not because it offends him but because we are
hurt needlessly by the lies that cause us to distrust him.

There are days when I look in the mirror and see this man's weak
faith looking back at me. An old saint said, "If God be not worried,
why should I?"

We need a lifestyle of faith, one that believes the truth of who God
is when circumstances shout otherwise. When his hand cannot be
traced, he is quietly at work behind the scenes, preparing people and
circumstances for movement. We must not doubt him nor condemn
ourselves for God's silence.

What is your crisis today? Is the smell of death in the air? Cry out
for help, certainly. But between the cries and the answer, stand in faith.
God is loving and merciful all the time. God's plans for you are for
good and not for evil. God is accessible and active on your behalf, even
when out of sight. God chooses intervention rather than passivity,
though your eyes may see no proof in your circumstances today.

*I am engraved on the palm of your hand, Lord. I'm never out of your
sight. I'm always in your grasp. Amen.*

October 24

Day Seven Awaits

By faith the walls of Jericho fell, after the people had
marched around them for seven days.

HEBREWS 11:30

I want you to imagine that you're an Israelite. You've been ordered
by God to march around the city of Jericho for seven days. The
first day of this adventure you rise optimistically out of bed. You're
looking for a miracle. You can't wait to get out there, for certainly each
time you march around the walls, you're going to see God move in a
mighty way. Right?

But the first day, first time around, nothing happens. On the
second day, you rise hoping again for some display of God's power.
But again the heavens are silent. Simultaneously, those who watch you
circle the city find this quite humorous. By the fifth and sixth days, it
is quite apparent to the onlookers that you serve an impotent deity.

Hindsight tells us what happened at the end of the seventh day,
but here's my point: How many of us are walking in places that
resemble days one through six? The miracle hasn't happened yet. We're
marking time, exercising faith muscles, and cradling eternity in
our hearts.

I don't know exactly when day seven will happen for you or for
me. But I do know that much of our life can be characterized by the
seeming silence and inactivity of God. While I do not pretend to know
the whole of God's agenda, I do know that prior to day seven it's time
for us to grow our faith, cradle those infant mustard seeds, and ask
God to blow his Spirit across the frail shoots of new growth. May we be
tenacious, unmoving, and looking ever upward for our final deliverance.

*I don't want to lose hope, God. Day seven is coming. May your Spirit
cup his hands around the flame of hope in my spirit. Amen.*

October 25

The Sacrificial Gift of Praise

Let us continually offer to God a sacrifice of praise.
HEBREWS 13:15

*H*ow about taking time to praise God today? Is the idea appealing? Perhaps it's a shocking suggestion. You may be saying, "Christine, praise God? For what? The way my life is going, that's the last thing I want to do!" I understand. For most of us praise may not even be in our spiritual vocabulary when we're stressed out.

An interesting phrase in Scripture is "a sacrifice of praise." What does this mean? We know that a sacrifice is a gift that costs the giver a lot; the gift may even be priceless. I believe that a sacrifice of praise is giving God a gift of praise from our lips that we don't feel like giving. It's choosing to praise when our circumstances indicate that it is ludicrous to do so.

What could motivate us to praise anyway? God says, "Look at how much I love you. Didn't I sacrifice my only Son's life? I know that your life is hard today, but if you'll praise me, I'll bless you for it in ways you cannot imagine."

Praise tore down the walls of Jericho. Perhaps praise from our lips will tear down the very circumstances that made us reluctant to praise in the first place. Does God require it because he's greedy for glory? No. Like prayer, we do it for our benefit, not God's. Our Father knows that the offering of praise will help us keep our spiritual perspective.

I've been stingy with praise, Lord. I admit it. But when I think about your many gifts to me, starting with your forgiveness, I realize that I am a rich person in spite of my circumstances. I praise you for being everything that I need. Amen.

October 26

No Obstacles

We have this hope as an anchor for the soul, firm and
secure. It enters the inner sanctuary behind the curtain.
HEBREWS 6:19

I know what it's like to hope in vain. Hope was tenuous because I
didn't have a relationship with the one of whom I needed something. I wrote a letter perhaps and just hoped it would get read. Or I
requested an interview but my letter got lost in the paperwork. There's
nothing more frustrating than needing an appointment with the
person whose intervention would mean everything yet being stopped
at the door by a secretary.

Today I come to God with many needs and concerns. The battle
is raging. I need to know he cares. I ache for compassion and mercy. I
need time to tell my story. I have hope and my hope is well founded
because Jesus tore in two the veil that separated God and me. Because
of that I have intimate access to him. I need no appointment. He will
not struggle to remember my name, nor will I need to jog his
memory to recall the elements of my story. Not only does he know
me, but also he longs for my company all the time.

I am more than fortunate. The only One who is powerful enough
to calm the storm is the very one who welcomes cries for help. The
One with the answer openly receives those who need enlightenment.
The One who extends mercy delights to give it to the ones who beg for
mercy. The One who knows my name and counts the hairs on my
head is waiting for me, though I live in a world in which a social
security number characterizes my identity.

*There is no veil, Father. I'm so relieved that I can step into your
presence and know you'll give me what I need. Amen.*

October 27

God, the Commodity

In righteousness I will see your face; when I awake, I
will be satisfied with seeing your likeness.

PSALM 17:15

*D*o you ever tire of feeling needed? Have you ever wondered if
your value to others lies in what you give them? If you were in
a nonfunctional state due to illness or emotional stress, how many of
your significant relationships would survive?

I discovered at a young age that my value to some people lay in my
talent. They would use me to avail themselves of it. The price I paid
to give them my gift was often unnoticed and unappreciated. What
mattered to them was that they got the performance they wanted.

I understand Jesus' weary sigh as he knew that multitudes followed
him because of the wonders he performed. When the miracles ceased,
his supporters disappeared into thin air. People were fickle then and
still are today.

Who is your dearest friend? The one with whom you sit and
appreciate a piece of music or the beauty of a sunset? You feel no
pressure to perform. That friendship is rare but precious. God wants
the same from us. He's grieved when he is only pursued for what he
can give.

While God has challenged me to ask for what I need because he
delights in my active participation in the "family business" through
intercession, I believe he is most thrilled when I am smitten with him.
Like Moses, I feel I just have to glimpse his glory or I'll be incurably
dissatisfied.

We who dote on the gifts but miss the heart of the Giver are
spiritually poor.

*Jesus, if all I did for the rest of my life was behold your beauty, it
would be enough. For you have already done more for me than I
ever deserved. Amen.*

Created to Praise

From the lips of children and infants you have ordained praise because of your enemies, to silence the foe and the avenger.

PSALM 8:2

Were you ever hired to do a job for which you were ill-prepared? You gave it your best but it was not in an area in which you were gifted. You probably hated every minute of it.

Right after we were married, I needed to work to put Ron through college. I took a job as a dental assistant. I knew nothing about dentistry and I shouldn't have been hired! Imagine my shock when my first experience was to assist our fine doctor in putting in implants (slitting the gums, drilling into bone to insert prosthetic teeth). Enough said. I lasted a week and it was most humbling.

Doing what we were created to do fulfills us! However, most people live in ignorance of the reason for their existence. God tells us that our purpose for living is to praise him. We were created to praise. Since that's true, when we're not praising, we're missing our greatest joy. (Like spending our lives in dentistry when we were made to be musicians!)

Just as we set a timer to take medications, so we must intentionally take God's prescription daily. Our bodies need vitamin C. Our spirit needs to praise or it's sickly. Our teeth and bones need calcium. Our spirit needs to worship God or it is blocked from knowing joy. How tragic to live and die and miss the point of life.

By the way, there's an added benefit. Satan flees in an atmosphere of praise. He is completely crippled and retreats in defeat.

I always thought you wanted the praise. I had it wrong, Lord. You want me to praise because that's how I will know joy. Amen.

October 29

Re-Creating Our History

You created my inmost being; you knit me together in my mother's womb.

PSALM 139:13

A baby's life should begin when two people bond. It should evolve from a beautiful act of intimacy and the sacred experience of connectedness.

Many were conceived, though, in an atmosphere of violence, friction, or in the confines of a loveless relationship. Intuitively they know the nature of their conception, even if no one told them the story. Though they weren't there to view the encounter, they sense the holes in their spirit. Perhaps their mother never told them what it was like when she carried them. Perhaps she failed to relate that she treasured the life inside her. Many know their date of birth, their weight, and their length. Period. They dare not assume that there was joy at their arrival or that there were happy tears shed when their mother and father held them for the first time. They may sense they have no history of value being attached to them.

Ah, but they do. Each of us can allow our Father to re-create it for us. Though the conception might have been loveless, the breath of a loving God formed our being. He lovingly knitted us together. Angels danced at our birth and danced again at our new birth. Each of us has the loving history we seek. We have been held, rocked to sleep, and sung to by the Master Musician.

The one who creates life has the right to define our value. Many thought it was their parents, so perhaps they considered themselves worthless. But God is the life-giver. He is our Father and has declared us worthy, and we live and die by his loving hand.

I see myself in the womb under your care, Lord. Re-create my history within my spirit. I am your cherished creation. Amen.

October 30

Faith's Edge

Be still before the LORD, all mankind, because he has
roused himself from his holy dwelling.

ZECHARIAH 2:13

*T*he Christian life is one of faith yet most of our lives are lived without it. We think we can manage everything by ourselves. Taught
from infancy how to be in control of our world and take care of
ourselves, we gained a false sense of power. We must watch out.

Somewhere down the road a crisis will come. It will be a time
when we are helpless to affect the things crushing us. It might be a
medical diagnosis or an unmanageable child. It may be the helplessness
of unemployment or the betrayal of a friend. We'll kick and scream.
We'll hate facing the reality that we're powerless. Yet it will bring us to
the very edge of faith. We'll be forced to say, "There is no way I can do
this on my own. Solutions escape me. I place my hand in yours, God.
Unless you come through for me, I'm cooked!"

We'll finally have the awareness that our problems seem to be
God-sized, not human-sized. Can God help? Does he hear? You bet!
In fact, he waits, poised for that moment when we come to the end
of ourselves.

Zechariah speaks of God being aroused from his holy habitation.
In other words, God is mobilized into action by our cries for help. He
rubs his hands with great anticipation of the ways he will lovingly
intervene and cause us to experience his power and his presence. He
relishes the thought that we will encounter him in life-changing ways.
Look up! If you're crying out for help, please know that cries for help
are welcome.

I face a mountain I can't climb, Lord. Help! Amen.

October 31

A Party for Prodigals

"See, I have taken away your sin, and I will put rich garments on you."

ZECHARIAH 3:4

Do you like to look at the "before and after" pictures of a woman who has had a makeover? I do. Most of us do. We might like to be that woman and be able to don a fresh face, updated look, and new attitude. God makes us an unbelievable offer. He offers us a makeover on the inside.

Remember the prodigal son? He came home humiliated. He was dirty and desperate. What was his father's reaction? "Get the best robe in the house and put a ring on his finger." Not because he deserved it but because unconditional love marked the nature and character of the father's heart.

Unfaithful, weary, and needing renewal and restoration, we prodigals come to God expecting disappointment and rejection. What we encounter instead is a celebration to welcome us home. We can almost hear, "Get the best robe in heaven. Put my ring on her finger." It's a party in our honor.

Can you feel the weight of the robe around your shoulders today? Can you feel the velvet against your skin? Dressed in finery, you can walk out to live in this world. Your dress may get dirty and you may be called names, but you know where to go home to feel better, don't you? After all, you're not a native but a foreigner. You can stand a little taller and live out of the reality that you are royalty.

You can have that new look—from the inside out.

I cannot fathom the kind of love you offer, Father. When I came home, I deserved your condemnation but you offered me your kingdom. All because of Jesus. Amen.

November

November 1

Foresight Versus Faith

Trust in the LORD with all your heart and lean not on your own understanding; in all your ways acknowledge him, and he will make your paths straight.

PROVERBS 3:5–6

Ever get frustrated because God gives so few details? I often do. I believe that if God outlined a detailed plan for me to follow, I'd be able to jump in and execute it faster. Doesn't God value productivity?

I've only been given one piece of God's call. I feel like Abraham. God called out to him and said, "Pick up your family, your belongings, and leave for a place I'll show you." He didn't provide much of a road map yet Abraham went.

Many hundred years later Jesus called out to Simon and Andrew while they were fishing and said, "Come follow me." Leaving everything, they followed. Loving order and structure, I probably would have asked Jesus, "Follow and do what, exactly?"

Many years ago God woke me up in the middle of the night and spoke to my heart. "You are to have a ministry called Daughters of Promise. Every morning I will unveil what that means for you that day." If you were to ask me what I'd like to see happen with Daughters of Promise over the next ten years, I would reveal my dreams. However, I am aware that it might not be what God has planned.

Today I breathe this prayer: "These hours are yours, Lord. Reveal your intentions for me moment by moment." God rarely lets us see down the road. Rather he wants us to stretch out our arms in dependence and faith, living one day at a time.

Your plans for me are simple, Father. Today you'll show me what to do. Help me be content with such childlike faith. Amen.

November 2

Joyful Shouting

When the LORD brought back the captives to Zion,
we were like men who dreamed. Our mouths were
filled with laughter, our tongues with songs of joy.

PSALM 126:1–2

I have a difficult time digesting these verses. Captivity I understand, but when the passage takes a drastic turn and speaks of joyful shouting, I struggle. Though I have known deliverance and have even seen dreams come true, I struggle with the idea of expressing joy with such abandon.

God is showing me that my experience of him can be so great that my soul can know a way of life that includes radical joy. Instead of enjoying isolated moments of pleasure, I want this kind of joy to inhabit my lifestyle. The nation of Israel so radiated joy that even the neighboring nations said, "The LORD has done great things for them." Their joy was simply not of this world, and others who watched them knew it!

For any of us who are still held captive—captive to shame, financial debt, a difficult marriage, ill health, or habits and addictions—the message is full of hope. God is the deliverer. He hears the cries of his children. He is not passive. His deliverance, whether in this life or hereafter, is complete and resplendent. So much so that holy laughter and contagious joy follow. Let's not resign ourselves to anything less. Let's keep dreaming, asking, crying, and pleading. We have a Savior who advocates and a Father who intervenes at the perfect time. We can count on what follows, for deliverance precedes joy unspeakable.

Father, I admit that I struggle with stoicism. I weep and express joy with reserve. I need freedom. Help me to experience every dimension of the emotions you created. Amen.

November 3

Help! I'm Drowning in the Mundane

Whoever can be trusted with very little can also be trusted with much.

LUKE 16:10

God never entrusts great responsibility to the inexperienced. Preparation for the calling is everything. An employer scrutinizes the resumes of prospective employees, and God is concerned with my spiritual resume. My Christian education and experiences in the trenches provide a foundation from which I'll successfully live out his highest plans for me. I'm being trained to know him, hear his voice, and obey without second thoughts. I'm learning I need to be faithful in little things so he can trust me with bigger tasks. My Father is ever at work in me. In the daily stuff of life, I'm being prepared to take part in the redemption of his kingdom.

God called out to Abraham and said, "I will make your name great." He didn't say, "Your name is great." God had work to do to make Abraham's character match his assignment. Like Abraham, I must adjust my view of the mundane. Small assignments are not spiritually insignificant. How I handle them dictates to what degree God is able to trust me with something larger.

Be patient today as you work unnoticed behind the scenes. Perhaps you are the pastor of a church one-tenth the size you think you deserve, or you labor tediously at the bottom rung of your company when God has revealed to you he's preparing you for leadership. You are restless, discontent, waiting for your big break. Don't miss the truth that there's value in the process. Work patiently, thanking God for opportunities, being faithful in the little things. Handled well, today will be a building block for future leadership.

Forgive me for feeling entitled to greater things. I trust your leadership, Lord. Help me know you better right where I am. Amen.

November 4

Surprised by a Relationship

"Once more I will astound these people with wonder upon wonder."

ISAIAH 29:14

*B*eing saved and knowing Jesus are not one and the same thing. Many who have trusted Christ as their Savior haven't experienced him as a person. What a tragedy. Christianity does not equal fire insurance against hell. It is so much more than that. It is all about being reconciled to the person of God for eternity. It is a homecoming. It is being restored in holy union with our Creator.

Once anyone has experienced Jesus, they're never the same. Remember the rich young ruler who decided it was going to be too expensive to follow Christ? He counted the cost and felt it was too great. However, he went away different because of the encounter.

If we just become familiar with Jesus through reading his story, we've missed the whole point. Our minds may know the plot but our hearts can be sterile. It's a far different thing to say, "Ah, I know God is merciful, not because I read that he is but because he's been merciful to me!"

How can you experience him today? After reading a portion of Scripture, spend time being still. Ask God to reveal himself to you. Listen for him in your heart. He will speak to you. At first you'll think that you are merely hearing your own thoughts. But discern. Keep a journal. Compare what you think you hear with the truth of him in Scripture. Many times he speaks in scriptural phrases and brings to your mind a verse that you are to claim and rest in. He promises that any who search for him wholeheartedly will find him.

My heart is meant to be moved by you, Lord. Give me more than just an intellectual form of Christianity. Amen.

November 5

Taking Your Place Under God's Wings

Hide me in the shadow of your wings.

PSALM 17:8

King David often spoke of the place beneath God's wings. I have had to learn that this is not just an abstract, inspirational picture to help me feel better on bad days. It can be my reality. I can make it mine by nurturing my soul with spiritual truth. The shadow of God's wings is the place from which I can endeavor to live my life. When I do, the result is resiliency and strength.

Do you remember what it felt like to be hugged by someone big and powerful? Do you recall the wonder of being swept off your feet? If you remember that bear hug, you probably also remember a sense of safety. The hug was more real than what was going on outside the hug. Perhaps your ears were even covered, so sounds in the room were muffled.

I practice seeing myself tucked under God's wings, for he says I am. As when I'm being hugged, the voices on the outside are less real to me than the voice of my Father. What he says has far more relevance and impact. So what happens when earthly voices deliver harsh words? They are immediately held up against the truth of who my Father says I am. If the criticism is accurate, he'll gently confirm it as I rest in his embrace. If the criticism is not valid, I will sense my Father's nod to let go of the comments. What a vantage point from which to filter truth from lies.

Oh, Father, you are my shelter. While your embrace is not offered to help me escape from my problems, it is offered as a place to heal. Thank you for such faithful care. Amen.

November 6

A Love That Waits

"No eye has seen, no ear has heard, no mind has conceived what God has prepared for those who love him."

1 CORINTHIANS 2:9

*M*ary and Martha sent for Jesus to tell him that Lazarus was very ill. Jesus waited two days before responding. That interim put the women in emotional conflict. They had been confident of Jesus' affection. The message they sent to him proved it: "Lord, he whom you love is sick." But Jesus' failure to drop everything and come made them wonder, "Doesn't someone who cares respond immediately?"

Hindsight allows us to understand the two-day delay. The stage wasn't set. Jesus would have altered the powerful elements of the story had he arrived before Lazarus's death. His friend needed to be in the grave three days, showcasing the power of God and mirroring the coming resurrection of Jesus. Lazarus's miracle was just days before Christ's own death and burial.

Have you cried out for help? Are you still waiting for God to arrive on the scene? Are you in conflict due to his supposed inactivity? You may know in your head that he loves you, but his failure to arrive with measures of intervention seem contradictory to his claims of affection!

Be comforted by this story. His touch on your fallen world is not absent due to lack of love. The stage is simply not yet set for the unveiling of the miracle. The work being done by divine hands behind the scenes is not yet completed.

Jesus never slumbers nor sleeps. He is building the props to showcase your redemption. He is fastidious with the details of your freedom journey.

You work while I wait in faith, Lord. I can trust the nature of your heart, even when I don't see evidence of a miracle. Amen.

November 7

Poor Planning

Do you not know that your body is a temple of the
Holy Spirit, who is in you, whom you have received
from God? You are not your own.

1 CORINTHIANS 6:19

*A*s I write this, I am recovering from pneumonia. I guess I
pushed myself too hard this summer. I recorded a new album,
stayed up late too many consecutive nights, and did a fair amount of
traveling the rest of the time. Because of the resulting fatigue, my
immune system was compromised, which prevented my body from
fighting disease.

I hate being sick and I've concluded that I am ill because I really
haven't learned where my limits are. I am often out of tune with my
body and my spirit, making myself vulnerable to sickness because of my
poor lifestyle choices. I haven't done well at taking care of my temple.

Maybe you are currently making the same mistake. You're
pushing it. You feel on the edge of burnout and find it necessary to
engage your inner taskmaster to keep moving. If your thoughts could
be tape-recorded and played back, they would reveal a merciless drill
sergeant. God must cringe when we treat ourselves like slaves.

The author Vance Havner, now with the Lord, remarked that he
used to believe every request for a speaking engagement was an
opportunity given by God, until he received two invitations to speak
for the same night. Apparently, not all that we put on our calendar is
God's will for us, though it may appear so. Jesus never planned
anything unless he prayed about it first and received a directive from
his Father. Not everyone was healed. Not every crowd heard a sermon.
Often he chose rest and solitude instead.

*I give you permission to rearrange my calendar, Father. Show me
your lifestyle plan for my life. Amen.*

November 8

Limited Understanding

Now we see but a poor reflection.

1 CORINTHIANS 13:12

*T*he message of Jesus is paradoxical. We're told in the Old Testament that God will prosper his people, but in the New Testament we're informed that we share in the sufferings of Christ. "Which is it?" we ask.

Oftentimes we're inclined to pick the answer we like best, support it with a one-sided view of Scripture, and call it truth. Partial truth brings disillusionment. When God does not perform within the box we've made, our faith is shattered because we trusted our own spiritual apologetics.

Jesus rode into Jerusalem on a donkey and was hailed as king of Israel. People waved palm branches in his honor. Moments later, addressing the crowd, he spoke of dying. "When I am lifted up from the earth, I will draw all men to myself."

The crowd didn't want a dying king, so they did what many of us do when a portion of Scripture causes us to squirm. They argued, quoting parts of the Bible to support their case, without taking into account the whole of Scripture. They reminded Jesus of all the Old Testament passages speaking of the Messiah living forever. They ignored the passages referring to a suffering Christ pierced for the sins of the world. Jesus answered their questions by repeating the truth of his coming death and resurrection. When they objected again, he withdrew.

The gospel serves the interests of his kingdom, not mine. Though I may not understand spiritual mysteries, I must be committed to embrace all of Scripture, reading passages in context. I don't need to understand everything. I trust God, who knows it all.

Only a rebellious child needs an explanation before obeying. I honor you with my obedience, Lord. Amen.

Look Around—God Lives

We have this treasure in jars of clay to show that this
all-surpassing power is from God and not from us.
2 CORINTHIANS 4:7

*M*ost people are selfless in a crisis. The World Trade Center disaster proved that. God's character was showcased in the righteous deeds of people. Tales of heroism on the evening news pointed us to his heart. The stories were reminders that we are created in his image and therefore often rise to the occasion to model the one who fashioned us after himself.

Each of our heroic acts, though appearing larger than life to others, only reveals the slightest essence of who God is and what he has done for humankind.

Humanity has been in a crisis ever since Adam and Eve sinned many centuries ago. Our intimacy with God was destroyed. Our utopia was altered. Eden became known as the "real world" where we began to suffer the effects of the Fall. God never got over the grief of his loss. He cared so much about our plight that he enacted a plan to atone for sin, making it possible for us to be restored to his heart.

He sacrificed his Son to save us. His mercy spanned time. When the sympathy of people would have been exhausted, God commissioned his Son to die. He still seeks the lost and searches for any of us who want to be rescued. He calls us home through Christ. He gave up a Son so we could call him Father.

When we listen to the news with a lump in our throat, may we remember the great love with which we are loved.

Father, you were proactive in a crisis. You found a way for me to come home through the death of your Son. Thank you. Amen.

November 10

Green Redemption

If anyone is in Christ, he is a new creation; the old
has gone, the new has come!

2 CORINTHIANS 5:17

I sat in a friend's backyard the other day. Evidence of her green
thumb spoke of redemption. Her life has been one of heartache.
Her childhood was tragic. Her father was an alcoholic; her mother was
emotionally absent. Her dad died when she was nine, and an abusive
stepfather entered the picture. Having known only cruel men, she
married four times, each to a mean man. She became an alcoholic
herself before finding Christ as her Savior. Her last eight years have
been ones of rebirth and healing at the hands of her personal
Redeemer. Her face and her handiwork show it.

Her extensive garden reveals an artistic rendering of newfound life.
Numerous beds overflow with flowers, herbs, and vegetables. Ferns
spill over from pots, each one bright green and healthy. Her
redemption has worked its way outward. The beauty of it brought tears
to my eyes as I saw her soul interpreted in the greenery.

Her heart is rich now. She has finally met a Father who loves her
perfectly. "Abusive" does not describe his character. He is exquisitely
gentle, acting toward her with kind intention. That discovery spills out
through her hands.

She had a gift waiting for me. On my chair was a small wreath of
herbs and miniature roses she had grown, dried, and delicately wired
together. The wreath now graces my desk.

She's not a platform person, yet for each who sips tea in her lawn
chair, she is the ultimate evangelist. She brings her guests to Jesus and
doesn't even need words.

*My hands showcase your great work in me, Lord. May everything I
touch bring more evidence of you. Amen.*

November 11

Looking Grief in the Face

My eyes fail from weeping, I am in torment within,
my heart is poured out on the ground.

LAMENTATIONS 2:11

*T*he writer of Lamentations expresses what we often feel. He has done us a favor by sharing what could have been kept private. Instead, he took the time to chronicle his grief so that we might find comfort and companionship through his desperate admission.

Have you ever cried so many tears that it seemed none were left? I have. At such a point, grief is raw. Not only are tears inaccessible, but also finding the words to adequately describe the pain seems mountainous. It's as if language is crippled and we're driven to find comfort in the company of others who have traveled similar paths to ours; those who know enough to not offer petty condolences.

We also begin to understand the spiritual truth that Jesus is our only perfect companion. Not only because he was "a man of sorrows, and familiar with suffering" (Isaiah 53:3), but because his spirit lives inside of us. He knows our thoughts and understands our feelings. There is no emotion out of the realm of his experience and no experience out of the realm of his compassion.

Today, if you are crying out for comfort, don't fail to look into the deepest part of yourself to find the Christ who took up residence the moment you called him "Lord." Your Wisdom is within. Your Comfort is within. Your Companion lives within. Your Strength and Refuge is tangible and near. You need not fear abandonment when the fire gets hot. He, who is incapable of breaking promises said, "I will never leave you nor forsake you."

I know where to find you. You're deep inside, in that sacred place where only you live. I'm not alone now and never will be. I'm so relieved. Amen.

The Gift of Emotion

"Because of the oppression of the weak and the groaning of the needy, I will now arise," says the LORD. "I will protect them from those who malign them."

PSALM 12:5

*W*hen was the last time someone was angry because you'd been hurt, or cried because you expressed sadness? Most likely, you recognized the valuable gift they gave you.

We need people who will respond emotionally to the pain in our lives. Otherwise we can't get our hands around injustice, betrayal, anger, or hurt. Mere verbal responses fail to give a barometer reading for the extent of the travesties. Until we behold another's emotional reaction, we have a hard time emotionally processing the extent of the wrongs done against us.

Many live their lives crying out to those around them, "Why don't you love me with your heart?" Sometimes they never get an answer. Their loved ones simply watch their suffering, nod their heads and agree that it exists, but then give sermons and walk away.

It's difficult to experience the security of another's love if there is an absence of emotion when we've been threatened or hurt. If parents or spouses don't bristle, defend, and share our tears, how are we to know love? We need to see the pain in their eyes and experience the fierce, protective embrace that says, "No one will hurt you while I'm around."

God sees our oppression, hears our groaning, and before we ever cry for help, has planned our deliverance. Jesus, who showed us the face of God, wept with his friends at the death of Lazarus. He didn't stoically proclaim, "Oh yes, I see there's been a death. Everyone is sad." He entered into their grief.

When others are emotionally unavailable to me, you will meet the needs of my heart, Lord. Yours is a passionate love. Amen.

November 13

Tomorrow's Trouble

"Do not worry, saying, 'What shall we eat?' or 'What shall we drink?'"

MATTHEW 6:31

Jesus turned a small boy's lunch into a feast for five thousand people. The crowd was hungry, and he provided extravagant amounts. They ate until they were full. However, Jesus didn't give them enough for their next meal. He didn't put together a "take home" basket for each guest, like we might do after hosting a Thanksgiving dinner. Momentary provision has always been his way!

His Kingdom is built on the principle of childlike dependence. I live, breath, and move by the power of his hand. His gift of spiritual food is allocated daily. Just as I cook one meal at a time for my family, so God sustains me.

He gives me just enough wisdom, grace, strength, and perseverance to see me through today's challenges. If I worry about what might happen tomorrow, and then anticipate defeat because I see how ill-equipped I am at this moment to handle it, I suffer needlessly. The truth is, I am not ready now for the future! God teaches me to live one day at a time. When tomorrow comes, and if it overwhelms me, I can cry out for help and he will be there to give me what I need. If he supplied ample resources ahead of time, I might become self-satisfied and forget that all control belongs to him.

I am learning to rest in Abba's provision. He has never failed me. I have learned the hard way about obsessing about the future. I have been acquainted with panic. I have come to understand that worrying only hurts me. It serves no purpose. God lovingly offers you and me another way. He extends his hand and says, "Trust me today. I'll take care of you."

You hold yourself responsible to meet my needs. That means I can take the pressure off myself. Thank you, Father. Amen.

November 14

Today's Worries Are
Tomorrow's Forgotten Details

Seek first his kingdom and his righteousness, and all
these things will be given to you as well.

MATTHEW 6:33

*H*ow many times have you tossed and turned all night, worrying
about things in your life? While you may recall the tossing, the
troubles themselves are probably fuzzy or even vague memories by
now. Why don't we learn from that? Why do we let today's worries
become overwhelming? Why do we let today's concerns consume us?

Why cannot we grasp once and for all that our heavenly Father is
eternal? For him a thousand years is like one day. That's very hard for
us to fathom. In God's time frame, for example, perhaps he just parted
the Red Sea for Moses, the Crucifixion was yesterday, and Martin
Luther recently started walking the streets of heaven. The events of
history may be mere moments in time that occurred just prior to the
day in which we live.

Whatever overwhelms us right now will be a mere glitch in light
of eternity. Someday when we're in our heavenly home, our present
cares will seem like minor details in retrospect.

Today my spirit is already seated in heavenly places with Christ
Jesus. When I close my eyes and perceive the reality of the earth as a
speck in the universe, I see my problems in perspective. As I spend
time basking in the presence of my Father, where I taste the eternal,
everlasting love that prods me to let go of my time-bound anxieties
and fears, I remember Jesus' words, "Seek first the kingdom of God."

*Oh, Father, I'm tormented with anxiety. You see where I'll be one
year from now, though. You already know how you'll provide and
intervene. Comfort me with the truth that I am an eternal being
and I'm in your grip. Amen.*

November 15

Asking for Help

"If you, then, though you are evil, know how to give
good gifts to your children, how much more will your
Father in heaven give good gifts to those who ask him!"
MATTHEW 7:11

A child raised in a healthy home is not afraid to ask, "Daddy,
please leave the light on. I'm afraid."

For any who were raised in a stoic home, asking for anything is
probably cumbersome. We end up being abused because we appear to
be individuals who can do it all without needing much. We might even
refuse help, thinking it will stain our self-sufficient reputation!

God is different from those who expect us to shut down our needs.
We walk by faith. Knowing he cannot lie, we make a decision to
believe that he is not a God of deprivation. He loves extravagantly and
gives lavishly. Believing him and then acting on it is a choice!

This happens slowly. Just as we learned lies one at a time, God
helps us unlearn them one by one. Just as our heart gradually grew
cold and disillusioned, so it will gradually warm up as his Spirit brings
it back to life. Think of this process as you might think of a person in
an intensive care unit, receiving a life-giving IV, one drip at a time. If
the fluid were infused all at once, it would be too shocking. God is not
one who overwhelms. He knows our frame and takes us on this
journey at a pace that is best for us.

We can become the women God created. Free to need, free to ask.
We can be children in our Father's kingdom and know the joy of
extending our arms and anticipating the answers to our prayers.

*I relinquish my fear, Lord. I will begin to tell you what I need.
Strengthen my faith. Amen.*

November 16

Being Misjudged

"Only in his hometown and in his own house is a prophet without honor."

MATTHEW 13:57

*H*ow many people in your life take you seriously? Among those who have known you for the breadth of your lifetime, how many see God's deepest work in your soul and value what he has birthed in you? If you can name more than three, count yourself fortunate. It is most common to be discounted by those who are closest to us. I can't think of many things more painful than being misjudged or overlooked by others who think they know us but really don't!

Jesus knows the pain of being discredited. He who is wisdom was scoffed at. Yet Jesus was not surprised by others' blindness. He said, "No one comes to me unless my Father draws him." In other words, godly things are hidden to this world. They are only brought to light by the Spirit, who divulges kingdom mysteries. The deepest work of God in our lives will be veiled, especially to childhood friends and family.

If you feel lost, forgotten, that the most beautiful things in your soul are overlooked, know that you're not alone. God gave his precious Son grace to endure the effects of others' spiritual blindness, and he will do the same for you. Don't take their skepticism to heart, allowing it to erode the work of God in your inner world. His Spirit can validate this important truth to you today as you begin to doubt and condemn yourself. Embrace all he has re-created in you.

Lord, you know me. You see and delight in the work of your Spirit in my life. Give me the grace to endure others' blindness, and a peace that will sustain me till truth is revealed. Amen.

November 17

The Absence of Empathy

Jesus replied: "'Love the Lord your God with all your heart and with all your soul and with all your mind.' This is the first and greatest commandment. And the second is like it: 'Love your neighbor as yourself.'"

MATTHEW 22:37 – 39

I was watching a movie about the Nuremberg trials over the weekend. What struck me was a conversation between the head prosecutor and the appointed psychologist. After a Nazi video of the concentration camps was shown, the prosecutor asked the psychologist how the Nazis could commit such acts of evil. The psychologist responded that while he did not know the heart of evil, he did find one thing that the unrepentant Nazis had in common. They lacked empathy.

Empathy is choosing to put yourself in another person's experience. It is trying to understand what another person must be feeling. This instantly reminded me of some things Jesus said. The Nazis' lack of empathy was in direct opposition to how Jesus told us to live. They had so distanced themselves from their emotions that they could commit every indecent and vile act under the sun.

It is the same with us. We can choose to either empathize or not identify emotionally with others. Each of us lives only a few choices away from apathy. We are unwise to think that small actions of insensitivity do not matter. Though they may appear insignificant, indifference and coldness of heart are malignant cancers that eventually infect the totality of who we are. We need God's work of grace daily in our lives.

If you hadn't empathized with lost humanity, Father, where would I be? You loved me enough to intervene, to send your Son to bring me home. Thank you. Amen.

November 18

Beyond the Written Page

The LORD longs to be gracious to you; he rises to
show you compassion.

ISAIAH 30:18

Many times we study God as if from a fact sheet. The pages
in our Bible tell us that he is merciful, loving, fair, and holy.
They also outline his activity throughout the centuries. When we've
finished reading God's biography, we're warmed by it at best.

Is an intellectual exercise enough to get us through rough spots?
The bumps in the road, perhaps, but it is hardly adequate to provide
the vast support needed for the deeper tragedies in life. I've learned
there is a big difference between knowing about God and knowing
God personally.

I contend that just obtaining facts about God brings distant
enlightenment, but knowing God through personal experience brings
passion. It is the difference between getting to know someone
secondhand, through someone else's perceptions and descriptions,
versus carving out a relationship with that person on our own. There
is power in a firsthand encounter.

For the sake of illustration, let's pretend that we have decided to
play matchmaker.

We're going to select a mate for our daughter on the Internet. After
a careful search we find a suitable match. The information about our
choice is glowing. When we present our stack of data to our daughter,
will her heart be stirred? Will she experience an intimate relationship
with her prospective spouse by reviewing his bio sheet?

Many Christians study Scripture forensically without ever
experiencing the heart of their Father firsthand. Daughters of Promise
was raised up to teach women how to connect to the heart of God,
helping them bring into balance factual truth and experiential reality.

Sometimes I feel as if my relationship with you is only intellectual.
Break free into my heart, Lord Jesus. Amen.

November 19

The Ishmael Project

And Abraham said to God, "If only Ishmael might live under your blessing!"

GENESIS 17:18

God promised Abraham a son through his wife, Sarah. She was old but Abraham believed. For a while, at least. After more than a decade, he couldn't seem to sustain his faith in God's promise. He might have feared that he dreamt such a revelation or perhaps he concluded that God was impotent. Whatever the reason, he took matters into his own hands. He slept with Hagar and produced a counterfeit blessing, Ishmael. When God appeared again and reminded him that an Isaac would be coming, Abraham pleaded with God to bless Ishmael instead. He wanted God's endorsement of what he had perpetrated in the flesh. God will never cooperate with such petitions. Not because he is in ogre, but because his dreams for us are for an "Isaac." Nothing less.

I want love. It is found in God, yet I have often circumvented him and settled for Ishmaels. Too much expectation was placed on people, rather than the One who promised me all of his heart.

I want fulfillment. A ministry was promised to me long ago, yet I was inclined to generate one through my own ingenuity. Stationery was printed, logos were designed, and pretty songs were written about God. My Ishmael produced scanty spiritual fruit compared to the harvest of my present day ministry. Now, I taste of God's promise. Isaac was born; Daughters of Promise bears the witness of the glory of God. It's all about him and little about me, other than daily submission to what he unfolds.

An Ishmael will always produce a cobweb of pain and disillusionment. An Isaac brings pure joy. Today, I purpose to wait on God for his perfect gifts. No matter what. No matter how long it takes.

You are a promise-keeper, proven through the ages. I trust you, Father. Amen.

November 20

Thanksgiving Review

I was once a blasphemer and a persecutor and a
violent man.

I TIMOTHY 1:13

One of the prevailing themes of Scripture is "remember and review." "Remember where you came from. Remember what you were like before God loved you. Remember and tell your children."

Are any of you ashamed of what you used to be? If so, do you hide your dirty laundry in the closet, wanting never to reveal the extent of your brokenness? It's a desire we all fight. If anyone had reason to be ashamed of his past, it was Paul. Yet he did not give in to the urge to make himself appear better than he was, which is a temptation for all of us.

Remember the story of the prostitute who came to see Jesus? She poured her most expensive ointment on his feet, wept, and wiped his feet with her hair. The disciples were disgusted. "Who is this woman?" they asked. Jesus commended her act of worship and forgave her sins. She was simply told to go and sin no more. In trying to teach the disciples about kingdom love, Jesus said this: "She loves me much because I have forgiven her much!" This woman would never forget who she used to be and how Jesus' love transformed her life.

I am the first to sing songs about Jesus coming to save sinners. Yet I can spend the rest of my time trying to hide my sinfulness. Make sense? Not in the kingdom, it doesn't. I choose to remember the good, the bad, and the ugly, for the sake of humility and gratitude. I will love you more if I remember how lavishly I am loved! What a great way to enter Thanksgiving.

In your mercy, Lord, you rescued me. I'm grateful. Amen.

November 21

The Model Shepherd

He tends his flock like a shepherd: He gathers the
lambs in his arms and carries them close to his heart.
ISAIAH 40:11

*J*esus surpasses all other shepherds in the tending of his flock.
Other shepherds can be so wrapped up in their own lives that
they become oblivious to the whereabouts of their sheep. The needs of
the sheep in their care can go unnoticed. Insufficient care and
attention can compromise a flock's well-being. After a while the sheep
learn to fend for themselves the best way they can. They also learn not
to expect much.

Jesus, however, never fails to notice the one who is sick. He hears
sighs of discouragement and cries of hunger. Before the first pang of
hunger is felt, Jesus has already picked out green pastures for relief
and repose.

He knows when just one sheep is missing, and will go in search of
it at the expense of his own life. Bringing back even one lost sheep to
the fold is worth any sacrifice.

The Great Shepherd values the individual and is never tempted to
lose his perspective with group thinking. His agenda is not driven by
productivity. While he loves to see Christians work together in unity
on kingdom projects, he values each person within the system apart
from what he or she produces. Intimacy is far more important than
any accomplishment. The joy of cooperation is what it's all about. The
end product is beside the point.

If a sheep is injured, Jesus carries it against his breast until there is
complete healing. Being in his fold, hearing his voice, and following
in his footsteps brings a security that is not of this world.

*Lord Jesus, I rest in your care. Your love for me brings me such joy.
Amen.*

November 22

God As a Warrior

The LORD will march out like a mighty man, like a
warrior he will stir up his zeal; with a shout he will
raise the battle cry and will triumph over his enemies.

ISAIAH 42:13

*T*he most gentle of fathers can be aroused to make war. Just put his child at risk and you will see the transformation from nurturer to warrior. No sacrifice is too great to save the one he loves.

While God is a gentle Father who delights in holding his creation in the shadow of his wings, he is also ready to roll up his sleeves to intervene for our protection and healing. I used to despair because I believed God was more passive than active. I pictured him as a Father far more concerned about others, only watching me from afar. If I were at the end of my rope, he might throw me a crumb or two.

It was impossible to draw close to the uncaring God of my own design. The problem wasn't God's inactivity but my fear of daring to believe the truth about his love for me. I couldn't see that he was different from a few other authority figures who had often seemed oblivious to my heart. Until I stopped linking him with them, I was stuck.

Every problem I had with God came from my distorted eyeglasses. Satan ground the lenses in his laboratory. He adjusted the eye chart so that when I put on the glasses, things appeared to be clear. But I've learned finally that any lens that keeps me from enjoying intimacy with God is the wrong prescription.

Father, your Word needs to be my new eye chart. Heal my eyes and align my vision accordingly. Amen.

November 23

A Princess

"Fear not, for I have redeemed you; I have summoned you by name; you are mine."

ISAIAH 43:1

I have an old doll at home. I found her in a church nursery while on tour in the Midwest. I was the guest artist and I was sent to change my clothes in the nursery, the only private room the church had with an adjoining bathroom. I finished dressing and was waiting for the pastoral staff to arrive for prayer when I saw her.

The doll was lying facedown in the corner of the room. She was naked. Her hair was matted and there were bald patches on the top of her head. Black scuff marks marred her appearance. It looked as if she had been thrown there, just discarded. I picked her up for a closer look and realized I related to her. She had been around the block a few times. She was streetwise, I was sure. It was hard to imagine that once she had been new. A thing of value. A gift that lit up some young girl's face.

I said out loud, "I know you! I feel like you tonight. I'm empty. I don't even like myself!" When the pastor arrived, I asked him if I could buy the doll. He looked at me strangely and said, "Just take her!"

She sits in my office now. Oh, there are moments now and then when I feel like her, but overall I have been healed from my shameful identity. While I used to dread the thought of Jesus' appearing and would have done anything to stall our intimate reunion, now I ache for his arrival.

Lord, I used to keep our covenant relationship contractual and impersonal, but the love in your eyes has taken away my shame. I love how you say my name. Amen.

November 24

Reunited with Prophets

"See, I am doing a new thing! Now it springs up; do
you not perceive it? I am making a way in the desert
and streams in the wasteland."

ISAIAH 43:19

I've heard many Christians say that they look forward to spending
time with the apostle Paul when they get to heaven someday. He
is their mentor and they identify with his personality and his gifts.

Perhaps you have your trip home planned as well. I do and I have
to tell you that I'll be looking for the prophets. They've become like old
friends these past few years as I've spent nearly all my devotional time
in their writings. They paid such a price for carrying out their mission.
Isaiah, for instance, was sawed in two because he dared give the message of Yahweh a voice. Far too often I have read his words without
appreciating his courage and his faith. His example serves to expose
the times when I've been tempted to sit on my gifts because I might
be misunderstood. God is in the process of growing my faith to the
proportions of Isaiah's.

If he had never written anything except today's Scripture, this verse
alone would have been enough, in my opinion. How gracious of God
to say, "Don't wallow in your past mistakes, the ones for which you've
already repented. Walk in the faith of my forgiveness. I will do something new. I'll carve a roadway in the wilderness of regrets and make
rivers in the desert."

I'm glad Isaiah listened to the Spirit of God. I rejoice in his life
and pattern my own after his example.

*I am eager to meet Isaiah, Lord. But in the meantime thank him for
me, for being obedient to your call on his life. Amen.*

Paradise Found

"I will pour water on the thirsty land, and streams on
the dry ground."

ISAIAH 44:3

We were born with a dream. We knew what we wanted, whether
it was love, fulfillment, romance, or adventure. Our desire for
them keeps us alive. We are exhilarated by the thought that what we
seek is nearly in our grasp.

Somewhere along the line desire can wither. Loss, love gone
wrong, and dreams thwarted by friends and loved ones convince us
that it's too painful to continue to dream. We drive our longings
inward. We settle into a life characterized by a cynical rhetoric that
says, "C'est la vie!"

May we remember the paradise God created in the Garden of
Eden. The Garden included lush floral colors, romance, intellectual
fulfillment, and perfect intimacy with God. No week at the finest spa
in the world could begin to equal it. In the Garden, there was no desire
that was not culminated in total enjoyment.

Jesus reminds us that paradise is not lost. His kingdom is paradise
and in that world we live forever, starting now. His teaching exceeds
our appetite for mere knowledge, for his language drips with an
invitation to want, to long for, and to desire. Let's not become numb
in response to a world that has seen terror and evil. Let's not simply
mark time, living out our days on this earth with broken dreams.
Paradise is where the Spirit of God is, and since we are his temple, we
only have to look inward for that place where desire is fulfilled.

*I am like the king in exile who longs for home. It is this hope that
keeps my soul alive. My face radiates with the memory of home and
the thought of you, Lord. Amen.*

November 26

Treasures in the Dark

"I will give you the treasures of darkness, riches stored
in secret places, so that you may know that I am the
LORD, the God of Israel, who summons you by name."
ISAIAH 45:3

The book of Isaiah is pregnant with words of eternal life. Many
promises of God were revealed through prophets, and this one
paid with his life to record God's thoughts for us. Today's verse is one
of my favorites.

I used to believe that darkness holds only pain. I was shocked to
read that there are treasures to be found in the place I least suspected.
I don't know why it surprised me. After all, God is love and love is
redemptive. Redemption seeks a way to bring good out of bad at
all costs.

God, through Isaiah, is letting each of us know today that there are
riches hidden in the dark places of our lives. We won't see them without divine light. Without God's illumination, the darkness is
pervasive and obscures everything. When God enters, however, his
glory reveals what our eyes could never discern.

We begin to unwrap layer after layer of wisdom. Our griefs, our
sin, and our mistakes provide the foundation upon which we begin to
understand God's precepts more profoundly. Our experiences allow us
to digest them at a deep level. Personal pain opens our eyes to a
suffering Savior in ways we hadn't understood before. We are able to
bond with him more intimately because we have shared some of his
agony. We review his life and death with new interest and with a
fervency born from our need to connect and be one with him. Such
intimacy is the greatest of all treasures.

*The darkness loses its sting when treasures are found. Don't let me
miss one, Father. Amen.*

November 27

Beauty Is in the Eye of the Beholder

He had no beauty or majesty to attract us to him,
nothing in his appearance that we should desire him.

ISAIAH 53:2

saiah was saying, "At first glance Jesus is not attractive. There seems
to be nothing in him you'd want or need." But a redeemed heart
changes all that. I know firsthand. Jesus is more than I ever hoped for.
My heart longs for more of him. I often say, "Lord, I don't want to
miss anything of you!" Is that your heart's cry today? When your passion for knowing Jesus becomes evident to others, do they shake their
head in bewilderment?

Those who don't know him can't understand what makes our
hearts alive to him. Why are we passionate about an ancient book?
Why would we want to cultivate a lifestyle of prayer? Why are we
interested in reading about old kings, patriarchs, and dead disciples?
It makes no sense to them. Our lifestyle choices seem as restrictive as
a straitjacket.

If skeptics live around you, be reminded that God has allowed it
to be this way. Only his children know that Jesus is precious and worth
dying for. Only we recognize his beauty and treasure the wisdom of his
ways. Only we know that obeying his precepts brings joy and freedom.

How might we pray for others who don't understand? Let's ask the
Holy Spirit to take the blinders from their eyes. Let's cry out to a
merciful God to release their hearts, minds, and spirits to recognize
the truth and understand him for who he is. Once their eyesight is
illuminated by the power of the Spirit, they'll never be the same.
May your love for Jesus be radiant against the backdrop of stares
and skepticism.

*By your mercy, Lord, bring those I love to you, that they may
discover your beauty. Amen.*

November 28

The Oak Box

"With everlasting kindness I will have compassion on you," says the LORD.

ISAIAH 54:8

I recall painful periods in my life. Times when I wrestled with all my options and felt trapped. Times when my dreams disappeared. Times when the green light of opportunity turned to red, and I was left waiting and wanting. Times when loss and betrayal were too numerous to digest or process. I strained to see the heart of my heavenly Father. But the greater my pain, the more elusive he seemed.

That's when I closed my eyes and remembered a certain man. His tender spirit and acts of kindness reminded me of God's heart.

He was soft-spoken, rarely at the top of anyone's guest list. He was a person you might forget to invite, in fact. At a social gathering he would not be described as the life of the party. Most likely, he would be seen talking quietly with someone in a corner of the room. His kindness and acts of love are legendary, however.

Some years ago he bought some oak pieces, sanded them to perfection, and constructed a small box with a lid. He applied a coat of polyurethane and when it was dry, fitted plush green velvet on the inside. He delivered it to his granddaughter's house. Maybe she thought the box was a keepsake in which she could store her favorite jewelry. But no. The box was for her to use to bury her favorite pet hamster, which had just died.

This man's children and grandchildren have had no difficulty understanding the heart of their heavenly Father, because they've seen it in him.

Lord, so often you show us who you are through the hands of your children. And to think you are more kind than this earthly grandfather! Thank you. Amen.

November 29

Common Gifts

Has not God made foolish the wisdom of the world?
1 CORINTHIANS 1:20

*T*he walls of Jericho collapsed after the children of Israel marched around them for seven days. It's a story many of us heard when we were children, yet it's good for us to review these stories as adults. Scripture is multidimensional and no matter how many times we review it, there are facets yet to be revealed. The Bible is a layered piece of literature. Over time the Spirit of God peels away layer after layer, introducing us to nuances we've missed before.

A new aspect of the Jericho story hit me this morning. The priests were told to sound the trumpets as they marched around the city walls. Have you ever pictured their instruments? In our world of religious fanfare and well-dressed cathedrals, I imagined trumpets of the most brilliant silver or gold. Not so. In fact, God told them to carry trumpets made of hollowed-out ram's horns. He intended for them to perform on the basest of instruments so the glory of the victory might be ascribed to him.

More often than not our gifts are common. We feel we don't have much to offer, but we fail to realize that this is God's plan. He doesn't want there to be any mistake that the power is not in the instrument but in the One who empowers it. For any of us who have silver trumpets, by all means let's sound them for God's glory. But far more of us possess a gift we consider mediocre. May our song, played on a ram's horn, no longer make us feel ashamed.

Today I've caught the message of the ram's horn, Lord. Little is much when you are in it. Amen.

The Path to Freedom

Create in me a pure heart, O God, and renew a steadfast spirit within me.

PSALM 51:10

*M*any times our quality of life is restricted by a compulsion or habit or a bent toward behavior that seems impossible to change. It can be frustrating to know in our head how powerful Christ is yet have a hard time finding his power for the places in us that need change or deliverance.

There is hope for us. But there are steps we need to take to start walking from bondage into freedom. Jesus rarely delivers us as a result of one prayer. Freedom is won through a cooperative effort. He wants us to understand how we are wired and what led us to our vices.

First, we need to pray for discernment of the root problem. If we try to break free from a behavior, even repenting of it, but have no idea why we engaged in it in the first place, we'll be putting a Band-Aid on a surgical wound. It's important to understand what drove us to the crutch initially.

Second, it's imperative to remove all provisions that would enable us to continue in harmful patterns. If there are things around the house that make it easy for us to slip back into old ways, we need to get rid of them. Supportive friends can help.

Third, it's critical that we ask God to defeat the missions and assignments of the enemy, who desires to keep us in bondage. We need to make sure we are taking advantage of all our spiritual weapons, including Scripture, the armor of God, music, and prayer.

Nothing is impossible to change. Lord, reveal to me the hidden roots that feed my thoughts and actions. Bring freedom and change at the core of my heart. Amen.

December

December 1

Blinded by Beauty

"You corrupted your wisdom because of your splendor."
EZEKIEL 28:17

*S*atan was once a magnificent angelic being who lived in God's presence. He became self-impressed and failed to worship God. He was his own idol. His wisdom became corrupted. His story offers me a warning sign.

God has invested a lot into me. He sacrificed the life of his Son to make me his. He deposited his Holy Spirit inside me, giving me greater potential to think, feel, and act like Jesus. Humility and an awareness of my need for God is the key that unlocks more of his power in my life. As I remove all barriers to my soul and give him full access to my thoughts and feelings, wisdom is born. It takes root, begins to grow and flourish, and expresses itself through my actions.

I am God's creation, fearfully and wonderfully made, created to house his glory. My splendor is peaked only when I function according to God's design, when he fills and empowers me to do heaven's work. Seeing the fruit of that is exhilarating.

If I experience that exhilaration long enough, I can begin to think that the results are due to my own ingenuity. If enough people tell me I'm great, I can become self-impressed. I can forget that the harvest of spiritual fruit is not because of me. It begins and ends with the God who empowers me.

May I never buy into the lie that I am better than others and more enlightened than most. I will live to see the tragic results. The jewel of wisdom will begin to corrode. What I need most will begin to slip from my fingers.

Father, help me run the race well. I humbly acknowledge that everything good in me is birthed by you. Amen.

December 2

God Never Ignores 911

The righteous cry out, and the LORD hears them; he
delivers them from all their troubles.

PSALM 34:17

When was the last time you felt God's intervention? God
intervenes for all of us far more than we ever realize. There
are times, though, when we can trace his hand.

Some years ago I made a nine-hour trip with my children on a
winding mountain expressway. Coming down a long stretch, our car
simply quit. We prayed as it rolled to a stop just ten feet from an
emergency phone booth. An hour later a tow truck came. The driver
hooked our car, with us still safely inside, on the back of his truck and
started off. What a sensation to move at fifty-five miles per hour but
have no control!

A benign adventure turned threatening when the driver of the tow
truck got sleepy. He began weaving over the lines as we looked on with
terror. One wrong turn and we would go over the guardrail,
catapulting hundreds of feet down the mountain. I couldn't blow the
horn or roll down the windows to yell, because everything on our car
was electric. All we could do was pray. I yelled, "Jesus help! Wake him
up now!" Within two seconds the kids and I watched him jolt, shake
his head, and roll down the window to refresh himself! We drove safely
to the gas station.

Our family has never forgotten how seriously God takes a simple
cry for help. He was there instantly to intervene. Whatever crosses your
path today, God is not surprised nor is he wringing his hands
in helplessness.

*I find such comfort in knowing that you are not passive when I cry
for help. You are an active Father, involved and invested in the care
of your children. Thank you. Amen.*

December 3

It's Me Again, Lord

He has not despised or disdained the suffering of the
afflicted one; he has not hidden his face from him but
has listened to his cry for help.

PSALM 22:24

*A*re you experiencing difficult times? Perhaps you've been in
these circumstances for a while. Your need is ongoing and
you've stopped asking for support from your friends, because you sense
their fatigue.

I know what it's like to be in pain over a long period of time. I
know how it is to raise my hand in prayer meeting to share my request
one more time, or call the same couple of friends and tell them I need
them yet again. It feels bad. My heart knows it's risky.

I understand people's limits. We all have them. Each of us has a
limited reservoir of compassion, energy, and interest. There's only so
much we can do in our attempt to help. We can communicate God's
heart but our contribution is only meant to be ancillary. The deep
needs of those who are hurting will only be met when they take hold
of the resources of God. Our love simply shows them the way home.

Our heavenly Father is tireless, though! King David reminds us of
this in today's Scripture. People are merely human beings. Though they
are usually sincere, they are limited and may fail us. But God is God!
He always loves; he's always interested and eager to help and comfort.
He is untiring in his devotion and commitment. In the midst of our
pain we can find great joy in this. Perhaps that is why we are told to
rejoice in all things. Our joy is rooted in the faithfulness and depend-
ability of our loving Father.

*It's me again, Lord. Thank you for not sighing in weariness. I rejoice
in your unfailing love. Amen.*

December 4

Trading Answers for a Person

Wait for the LORD; be strong and take heart and wait for the LORD.

PSALM 27:14

*D*uring my spiritually immature moments, I wish I could coerce God to act according to my wishes. If he'd only behave more predictably, there would be no mystery. I'd never have to squirm again over any of his words or actions. I'd never be forced to stretch outside the religious box I created.

I might think I'd be happier, but I'd know nothing of the true God and what it means to live by faith. God will not be confined. His ways exceed the logic of my finite mind. To be in relationship with him requires faith. I have to trust God when he provides no tangible answers for the things that perplex me. When all circumstantial evidence appears to prove that God's intentions toward me are anything but good and kind, he calls me to trust him anyway. In the midst of uncertainty he offers me himself.

Any of us who have been parents know that there were times when, for the good of our child, we were called to do something that at the time seemed cruel to them. They misunderstood us and we felt their pain. Their distrust from their limited perspective made sense to us. Amid their anger and tears, though, we put our arms around them to try to comfort them anyway.

In essence God is the parent who tries to calm our emotional tirades with his embrace. He whispers, "I know you don't understand. Someday you will but I'm here until then. You can trust Me. Rest."

God, I am discovering that you are enough. I have a lot of questions but you hold the answers and one day I will understand. Comfort me while I wait. Amen.

Running from the Obvious

"In him we live and move and have our being."
ACTS 17:28

*G*od intends for me to live with a sense of completeness, fulfillment, and purpose. There are days when I falter and lose touch with it all, though. When life dumps its circumstances on me, I tumble into an introspective mood and become self-absorbed. I lose my way momentarily.

I'm learning that anything that disturbs my connection to Jesus must be dealt with at once! The solution is always simple. It is an answer that even the smallest child can understand and apply. The remedy is remembering to do what Jesus told us to do. He said, "Come to me."

I was hurt this morning by someone close to me. I expected something better of that person but was horribly let down. I wallowed around in the pain for a while. Instead of running to Jesus and taking him up on his invitation to go home to his heart, I brooded and rehearsed the incident. I played it over and over again, as one might rewind a video and repeatedly watch a movie scene.

I decided a little later to call an end to my pity party. The very thing I needed to do was the thing I had run from all morning. My choices hadn't made much sense.

Only as I learn to live my life from the shelter of God's wings can there be joy. Only as I spill out my hurts to him and find healing in his perfect love will I be able to rebound with peace instead of torment.

Forgive me for always making you my last resort, Lord. Teach me to run to you first instead of last. You are my refuge. Amen.

December 6

Shy or Just Fearful?

Boldly and without hindrance he preached the kingdom of God and taught about the Lord Jesus Christ.

ACTS 28:31

I used to be a shy person. I never gave an insight unless asked. I rarely disagreed with the consensus. I was a peacemaker. But I've come to realize that hiding was due not so much to the nature of my personality as to a lack of personal development. Once I encountered Jesus and was able to receive the healing of his love, I finally discovered who I was. I found myself unable to stop talking about this life-changing journey. As I was led to tell the story, I could not hide the radiance of my joy. It is contagious, so I'm told.

Some of you have preceded me in this discovery. Others of you are following me. Malaise, whether spiritual, physical, or emotional, can be healed. And when it is, there will be a personality shift so astounding that it will shake up one's world.

It casts new light on the verse "By their fruit you shall know them." Just as acts of rebellion give us a reading on another's spiritual thermometer, so apparently does joyful confidence. I'm not talking about an assertiveness rooted in arrogance, for this is not of the Spirit, but I speak of the passion born of a joyful, transformed life.

Tell your story, and if you are still in the healing process, know that you will have one to tell! It will be powerful and full of glory.

You've helped me realize, Father, that it's one thing to be an introvert but another thing to live in fear of people. Please redeem all the years I hid to limit rejection. As you allow me to grow in the environment of your love, give me the courage to walk freely and unafraid. Amen.

December 7

Too Many Sad Songs

Sing to him a new song; play skillfully, and shout for joy.
PSALM 33:3

*M*usic shapes a society one person at a time. What any person listens to over time affects the way he thinks and feels. We need only examine the music of our times to discover that too many artists release one sad song after another. Their lyrics reveal plots of revenge, adultery, suicide. Even the arrangements enhance the message of hopelessness and cynicism.

Satan's scheme throughout history has been to trap musicians, since he knows the power music has on a spiritual level. Because he has put artists into bondage, the sad songs roll off the tongues of the "King David's" of our times. Rather than writing joyful songs to reveal the love of their Creator, they compose laments of futility. Musicians are using their creativity to express their life view. Whatever is in their heart permeates the spirit of their songs. While no one would argue that many of these artists have talent, they house a spiritual gift gone awry. They have little knowledge of God's purpose for them; thus the music of their soul speaks death instead of life.

I am moved today to pray for fellow musicians who hear only music that showcases the tragedy of life in this fallen world. They sing the stories of their lives. But how wonderful when the song of God's love is composed in the life of an artist. That artist's creativity will begin to tell his own redemptive story with a sense of celebration, joy, and hope.

How do I use my gift, Lord? Does it reveal your beauty? Are others drawn to you through it? Help me know you better. Purify me so my gift is a more true expression of you. Amen.

December 8

Discovering My Purpose

It is God who works in you to will and to act according
to his good purpose.

PHILIPPIANS 2:13

A woman said to me the other day, "My life is flat! Yes, I'm a
Christian, but days just seem so mundane!" I've been
thinking about her comments, and I have come to realize that much
of our Christian teaching proposes that our purpose as God's children
is to evangelize, love others, live holy lives, and be spiritually
productive. It is tied up in doing, suggesting that the mundane of life
is of little spiritual value. In fact, if all we know for days on end is the
mundane, we often feel guilty. We battle a sense of insignificance in the
kingdom, feeling we owe God much more than this!

God has revealed that I was created for a relationship with him.
Pure and simple. Life, whether made up of mundane or significant
moments, can consist of a continuous inner conversation with him.
Profound interaction becomes commonplace because the Spirit of my
Father is my companion.

My mundane activity is infused with spiritual empowerment.
Trivial things are transformed as I talk with God and perceive his
response. A five-minute exchange with my son can be pivotal for both
of us. Setting the dinner table with prayers for meaningful
conversation turns mealtime into a divine appointment.

For what purpose was I made? To be someone's daughter or
mother? To be Mrs. Ron Wyrtzen? To enjoy the ministry of writing,
speaking, and singing? None of these is my primary calling. Nothing
sung or spoken will have eternal significance if it does not spring from
my God-given purpose, which is to know and enjoy God.

*Change my perspective about the mundane, Lord. I awaken to this
new revelation that my life revolves around knowing you. Amen.*

Unforgettable Night

> I want to know Christ and the power of his resurrection and the fellowship of sharing in his sufferings.
>
> PHILIPPIANS 3:10

*P*aul lived in uncertainty, never knowing if his next moment would reveal the power of God or the sufferings associated with following Christ. Like us, he lived a life characterized by both suffering and deliverance.

Some years ago I made a trip to a small town. I had a sense of foreboding before going. This was unusual for me. I committed it to prayer but unfortunately the fear only grew stronger.

I made the trip, checked into my hotel, and was given a key to my room. When I reached my door, I noticed a small black X just below the room number. It looked as if it had been made with a marker. I thought, *Could my room be marked?*

I called some people for prayer. Part of me felt silly. Here I was, in a strange place. Who were my enemies? Why would there be people out to get me?

I went to bed with my clothes on. I dozed fitfully. Around one o'clock in the morning, a car pulled up outside my hotel window and awakened me. A group of men got out, slammed the doors, and pounded on my window. One announced, "She's in here. Let's go get her." I fell to my knees, asking God to miraculously save me. I waited. Nothing happened. About two minutes later I heard them get into their car and leave.

Perhaps God posted an army of angels at the entrance. I'll never know the story until eternity. Truly, that was a "power of his resurrection" day. It might have been a "fellowship of his suffering" experience, but God turned the tide.

Whether today holds deliverance or suffering, Lord, may I know you better. Amen.

December 10

The Tragedy of Settling for Less

I press on toward the goal to win the prize for which
God has called me heavenward in Christ Jesus.

PHILIPPIANS 3:14

I want to ask a tough question today. Are you settling for less than what God desires for you? That's a tragic thought, since God designed us for great things. You're not the first to give up exploring God's best, however.

Some of the children of Israel wanted to stay by the Jordan River rather than enter the Promised Land. They argued that it would be a perfect dwelling place because it was lush and green. The path of least resistance no doubt seemed attractive to them because of what they had been through. Haven't we been there?

If God had permitted them to settle there, just think what they would have missed. They would never have experienced the miracle of crossing the Jordan. They wouldn't have conquered the giants in the land or come to grips with their own powerlessness. They would not have seen that God was more powerful than their formidable enemies. Also, because they had not yet experienced Canaan, they did not have a reference point for knowing that the honey there would be sweeter than any they had ever tasted, or that their sense of well-being would be more profound than anything they had ever experienced.

This journey comes at a cost. If we want what God ultimately desires for us, he will ask us to confront our fears, admit our powerlessness, and exercise our faith. Only then will we begin our journey into uncharted territory.

God, I'm marching ahead. I'll be so sorry later if I don't. Faith is a gift, so as I walk forward, grant me the faith to believe you'll conquer the giants. Amen.

December 11

Parenting with God

From heaven the LORD looks down and sees all mankind.
PSALM 33:13

*M*y daughter called home from college one day, all excited. "Mom, every time I open the Scriptures these days, it's like they were written just for me." My heart felt so good. My day was filled with meaning and significance.

None of us knows how our children are going to turn out. Usually during their teen years we are on our knees, worried deeply about seeds of rebellion and strokes of independence that could take them in the wrong direction. After all, our children are individuals and no matter how great a job we do at parenting, some will make choices against God.

Are you a mother who loves God, and have you tried with all your strength to instill that hunger for him in your children? Is your child away from God's heart right now? Is your relationship with your child strained?

You might be asking, "Does God understand?" Yes! God, the perfect parent, nevertheless raised rebellious kids, because we also had the gift of free choice and chose to rebel. Does he know what it's like to ache to see that heart connection restored? Absolutely. He knows the relief and the joy of hearing one of his children say, "I've missed you. I'm coming home!"

Please know today that God has a vested interest in your role as a parent, and even more than that, he cares about that wayward son or daughter. Run to his arms for comfort and never give up praying for the return of your prodigal. God's love keeps reaching, no matter how long it takes. Our love needs to resemble his!

You love my children even more than I do, Father. Your heart aches to have them close to you. Show them the pathway home. Amen.

Relationship Between Light and Bread

A tabernacle was set up. In its first room were the
lampstand, the table and the consecrated bread.

HEBREWS 9:2

*I*n the outer room of the tabernacle, two things could be found. A
lampstand with a light that burned continuously, and a table with
the showbread on it. The tabernacle was windowless, therefore very
dark. The only way a priest could find his way to the table with the
showbread was with the light the candles provided. Light and bread
were connected.

They still are. Nothing has changed. The Bread of Life can only
be found today when the Light of the World shows me the way. I live
in darkness. There are no windows to eternal life. I've been left
wanting, aching, and longing for meaning beyond what's here. My
soul is hungry but my eyes are blinded and unable to recognize the
bread that will satisfy my hunger. I won't see Jesus for who he is until
there's illumination. I won't be attracted to spiritual food until he
shows me that he is what I've been seeking. The Bread of Life will not
appear palatable unless the lamplight of his Spirit reveals it as the
banquet it is.

After all, Jesus was a suffering servant. He was continually
misunderstood. He preached humility and repentance. He commanded his followers to forgive, seventy times seven times. He
encouraged his friends to love their enemies. Such spiritual food
would appear to taste sour. I might even think I had stumbled onto
the wrong meal. Until divine light shines on the showbread, I will
not dare to partake. Ah, but when my eyes can finally see, I behold
delicacies that are not of this world.

*I am hungry for you, Jesus. Illumine my spiritual meal for today.
Amen.*

December 13

Treasuring the Word

Your love is ever before me, and I walk continually in
your truth.

PSALM 26:3

*D*o you love to read the Bible? Be honest. Is it something
you look forward to, and when you do it, are you sad when the
time is up? What a tragedy that the Bible is often misused and
therefore misunderstood.

Many women have commented in private to me, "I don't know
how to study the Bible." "I don't know how to read it and have it mean
anything." I applaud their honesty and quite frankly, I shared their
feelings until some years ago. The problem is, we have heard that the
Bible is a rule book, a guidebook of sorts. "Have a problem? The Bible
has the answer!"

If we only look to the Bible for formulas so we can be happier,
we've missed the whole point. The Bible is all about knowing a Person.
Our greatest need as women is not to be loved but to love God by
getting to know him through the words he spoke and inspired.
In doing so, we will be changed. By loving God, we will be in the
presence of Love.

So today pick up your Bible, hold it to your heart, and pray, "Oh,
Lord, remove my old glasses. Help me see you in this book. As I open
the pages, reveal yourself to me in all your splendor, in all your mercy
and unspeakable grace." That will be the moment God begins to live
in the pages. As you can't help but treasure his words, you will know
a profound sense of well-being. I hope you'll do this. Since I prayed
that prayer, my life has never been the same.

*I hold your words to my heart, Lord, for by them you have re-created
me from the inside out. How can I ever thank you? Amen.*

December 14

Receiving

Though my father and mother forsake me, the LORD will receive me.

PSALM 27:10

*W*e were born with a need to connect deeply with others. Even as adults we find ourselves aching to do just that! Fears prevent others from engaging us at the level we crave, and insecurities hold us back from asking for it. Parents are afraid to connect with their children, and children are taught not to ask for more than they're given.

Some parents don't have the wholeness of heart to bond with their children. There's no intimacy. No snuggling. No kisses, tickling, squeals of laughter. The souls of their children grow up empty until later in life, when they can embark on the relentless pursuit of finding God as father and mother. Abba, Father, becomes the one who makes their heart sing.

Jesus was "born unto his own and his own received him not." For any who have been emotionally deprived, there's rest in the knowledge that Jesus knows what it is like not to be received. He who made the world should have expected a welcome. "Ah, the Creator is coming. Let's throw a party." But they didn't even recognize him.

It is even sadder that Jesus is still coming to his own but is still not received. Our soul is not laid open to him. When Jesus comes, he is ushered in the front door but is left standing in the hallway with his coat on.

The story can be different for us and for him. Yes, we're often deprived emotionally. Daily we ache for more. But we know where to go get it, don't we? Oh, the rewards when we dare to need Jesus and let him cross the threshold with no reservations.

I need connection, Father. You know that and made my soul to fit in your Spirit. I'm coming to you, all the way. Amen.

December 15

Action Brings Reaction

I sought the LORD, and he answered me.

PSALM 34:4

Do you have trouble asking for help? I know the feeling. I have had trouble asking for anything. It's something I've had to work at overcoming.

Anyone who was raised in a stoic home and shamed when they asked for what they wanted will struggle. I know those who nearly keel over before requesting a drink or to use the rest room.

This fear cripples a relationship with God in heaven, too.

God says he has good gifts for us, but for him to give them to us, we must ask. He gave us the platform to do that by adopting us into his family. We are his daughters of promise. As we delight in him, God says, he will give generously as long as we ask for generous amounts.

The spiritual principle he hopes we'll hear today is that there must be an action by us to bring his reaction. There must be a question to bring an answer. There must be our expressions of need to arouse his response. God is saying, "In many respects you don't have what you need because you have not asked." What are we waiting for?

"We don't deserve it," we say. No, we don't. But the nature of God is to give anyway.

It requires humility and trust to ask for and receive those things that we did absolutely nothing to earn.

You are unlike a father or mother I've ever known, Lord. You are aware of my needs before I am. Give me the courage to ask you for the good things you have for me. Amen.

December 16

The Pain of Detachment

The LORD is close to the brokenhearted and saves
those who are crushed in spirit.

PSALM 34:18

I was in an airport early this morning and watched an old man say
good-bye to his middle-aged daughter. She whispered, "See you
next summer." He nodded, seemed detached, and didn't appear very
sad to leave her. Something was missing. Attachment. There was no
tugging of the heart. They could have been mild acquaintances. That
got me thinking about families in which there is little emotional
bonding. Oh, the sadness of that!

Maybe you could have been that daughter I described. Your parents are stoic, or perhaps another child was preferred over you, and all
the loving emotional responses were saved for that sibling. I closed my
eyes in the car on the way home, and God spoke to me about that
woman. He said, "Oh, I've not forgotten her! She does know me and
is learning to bring her broken heart to me! I miss her when she is out
of my presence for just one moment! And wait till she sees the reunion
I'm planning for her when she finally comes home."

I opened my eyes in amazement. Yes, that's it! That's the answer for
any of us who find our relationships here less than satisfying. Sure, it
would be nice if there were always intimacy between parents and
children. God wishes it were so. But he wants us to know that when
others make choices in favor of distance and estrangement, our hearts
don't have to remain empty and alone. He's accessible. Go to him today
if you feel the ache of abandonment. He'll never leave you wanting
or disappointed.

*Others may walk away from my heart, Lord, but you never will. I
am safely tucked away with you for eternity. Amen.*

December 17

Giving Yourself a Gift

"Lord, do not hold this sin against them."

ACTS 7:60

God has delivered me from bitterness. The freedom I have found through discovering the secrets of forgiveness has given me taste after taste of living water. I know great measures of contentment, joy, and peace. It has been hard work but worth it. The journey to freedom commenced when I began to explore my own emptiness. I asked God to show me when, where, and how I had been broken.

When I began to examine my fractures, I was confronted with a list of those who had failed me. Day after day I relived those bitter memories. As I licked my wounds, it seemed unfair to have to forgive those who didn't deserve it. But it was also unfair that Jesus forgave me when I didn't deserve it. This realization gave me the courage to move beyond the pain.

If we really believe that God loves us perfectly and that his ways are life-giving, we must believe that forgiveness is for our good. God, the loving Father, does not ask us to do something difficult in order to watch us squirm. He does not take pleasure in seeing us groan under the pressure of carrying out difficult requests. Abba asks us to forgive, not just to be like him, but because that is what allows us to live freely and unencumbered. As soon as I forgive, I am no longer controlled by the past or my emotional responses to past events.

Though biblical forgiveness is widely taught, it is rarely extended. The act of forgiveness is so rare that when Stephen was being stoned and publicly forgave his executioners, Jesus rose to his feet at the right hand of God to behold such a scene.

Living in unforgiveness hurts me most of all, Jesus. By forgiving I give myself a gift. Help me obey the principles of your kingdom. Amen.

December 18

An Ancient Mentor

"I have found David son of Jesse a man after my own
heart; he will do everything I want him to do."

ACTS 13:22

*T*he walls of my son's room display the posters of NBA basketball
stars. They are his role models. We all have them, people about
whom we say, "I want to be like you when I grow up." King David is
a role model for me, for many reasons.

His heart for God set him apart at a young age. His boyhood
calling to be king caused jealousy among his brothers, and his
adolescence proved difficult because of his anointing.

David was a musician. His harp became a form of God's voice, for
when David played, people heard the whispers of Yahweh. King Saul's
inner torment gave way to peace as David's music washed over his soul.

David was authentic. He provided a window through which we
could partake in both his grief and spiritual ecstasies. We are
privileged to share in the extent of his agony and the depth of his
praise. Though many of his writings began with words of despair, they
ended with words of faith.

His response to sin was simple. David said, "Wash me and cleanse
me from this guilt. Let me be pure again, for I admit my shameful
deed." Many times I have failed to respond as David did. I've been
defensive and terrified of being wrong.

What made David "a man after God's own heart"? I believe the
secret to his greatness was his passion for God above everything else.
Though he fell into sin and bore the consequences of his mistakes, his
legacy of faith continued to breathe life for generations that followed.

*David is with you, Father. Tell him how much he has impacted my
life. Amen.*

December 19

The Stigma of the Calling

"You will be with child and give birth to a son."
LUKE 1:31

*H*as God ever led you to do something for which you were seriously criticized? Perhaps you paid dearly for it. We often think freedom from harassment is a sign of blessing.

Mary, the mother of Jesus, could tell us otherwise. God didn't ask her if she wanted to give birth to his Son. He just informed her that this was to take place! The stakes were high. The price of exposed harlotry was being stoned. God's calling meant that she would not only live with this threat but risk the misunderstanding of her fiancé and family.

There is an element missing in the Christmas story. Mary's fear. Nothing reveals that she was in emotional turmoil. She seemed to understand that she had been chosen, and she trusted God despite the uncertain outcome.

God's calling and stigma go hand in hand many times. Just ask the prophets. Isaiah prophesied for fifty-five years without seeing any of his prophecies fulfilled. He was eventually martyred for his life's work. We have been duped into believing that blessing equals prosperity and popularity. When multitudes flock to God's messenger, we call this proof of his calling. Let's remember Mary. The most significant kingdom work is often done in obscurity. A prayer offered at a kitchen table. The message of Jesus shared in the Middle East, with no visible results.

No amount of acclaim can outshine the peace that comes from feeling the hand of God on our shoulder. The world is a fickle friend. The grandstand, once full of supporters, empties fast at the first sign of controversy. Is God's favor most important to me?

Father, may I be like Mary, who faithfully carried the seed of her calling at great price. Amen.

Common Name, Uncommon Maiden

The virgin's name was Mary.

LUKE 1:27

*P*icking a baby's name is a long process. We usually try it out for days and see how it rolls off our tongue. Most of us purposely bypass the common names of our day to choose something unique. Our hearts swell with meaning when we call our child by name for the first time. I remember the initial months after my children were born. I used their first and middle names when talking to them, because it was fun.

Mary is the Hebrew form of Miriam. It is a common name yet Mary was anything but common. Though she lived in an obscure place, one that would fail to bring her respectable credentials, the God of the universe noticed her. What she possessed was rare indeed and it qualified her, in God's eyes, to mother baby Jesus. She possessed an unwavering faith in the God of her ancestors. There was no questioning of his ways. He was God, she was not. When the angel appeared and told her that she had found favor with God, she didn't respond with a sense of entitlement. "Well, it's about time!" Her humility holds up a mirror to my own expectations of blessing. Mary's gratitude reminds me that favor is a wondrous thing and can't be earned.

Being chosen had its own set of risks as well as blessings. Mary's faith and her ability to trust in spite of great obstacles made her journey bearable. For when God revealed his plans for her, they were bigger than what she could manage on her own. While there was joy, there were also public stigmas and threats on her baby's life. Without faith she would have crumbled.

I feel so common. Thank you for bestowing undeserved favor upon me, Lord. Amen.

December 21

I'm Carrying Your Baby

She was found to be with child through the Holy Spirit.
MATTHEW 1:18

Two people who are deeply in love dream about the day when they will create life together. As a woman thinks of carrying her husband's child, she is deeply moved. When a baby finally grows inside her, she will touch and bless her swollen abdomen with whispers of affection.

I wish I could go back about two thousand years and be Mary's friend. For now I can only guess what she might have spoken to her unborn child and also to the Father of her child. It's one thing to carry the baby of the one you love, but quite another to carry the baby of the one you worship! Was her relationship with God heart-oriented before he chose her to birth his Son? If not, carrying Immanuel certainly revolutionized the dynamics of their relationship.

It is the handiwork of God that forms all children in the womb, but how much more was God invested in the prenatal development of his Son? What did Mary feel during those nine months? Did her worship deepen? What did she say to Jesus as she placed her hand over her womb? Might we have heard her whisper toward heaven, "I can't believe I'm carrying your child!"

Today each of us carries the Spirit of God inside. He moved in at our conversion. His growth is either encouraged or stunted, according to how well we nurture that new life within us. Are we consistently aware of his presence? Are we in awe of the privilege of being chosen to house divinity? Do we whisper words of affection to the life inside? "I can't believe you are being birthed in me!"

Don't let me lose the wonder of your intimacy with me, Lord. Amen.

Righteousness and Mercy

Joseph her husband was a righteous man.

MATTHEW 1:19

When Judah found out that his daughter-in-law, Tamar, had played the part of a harlot, he sentenced her to be burned. When Joseph discovered that his fiancée, Mary, was pregnant, he reached out to her in love and mercy. Joseph was a righteous man and righteousness reaches out with mercy first, whereas humanness pronounces judgment. Joseph really knew Mary and wrestled with the issue of her pure heart and her circumstances. He knew that Mary's chastity and her pregnancy were incongruent. Only God could ease his torment by revealing the truth about her conception.

Without God's work of redemption in my heart, there is something sinister in me that loves gossip. Getting the dirt on upright people can be enjoyable. Shooting arrows of condemnation at them can be cathartic as I try to make myself believe that I'm not as bad as I thought. Jesus' standard of selfless, agape love burns brightly and eats holes through my self-righteousness. He reminds me that love is loyal and believes the best till proved otherwise.

A person can live righteously for forty years, mess up once, and people are quick to erase his good track record. All that he has been and done is wiped from his credentials. Where is our merciful response, the one that we would want if we were in his shoes? "Christine has done what? That doesn't sound like her. If it's true, I wonder what happened to Christine to make her act like that?"

"Mary pregnant? That can't be. Mary has a heart for her God and has proved herself faithful to me. There must be more to this story." And for Joseph there was.

You delight in righteousness, Lord. Left to myself, I delight in another's downfall. Make me like Joseph, not Judah. Amen.

December 23

Something's Different About You!

> When Elizabeth heard Mary's greeting, the baby leaped in her womb, and Elizabeth was filled with the Holy Spirit.
>
> LUKE 1:41

Can you imagine being Mary? She knows she carries the Son of God in her womb, but whom can she tell? She's blessed but such good news is trapped inside. She is experiencing the most profound revelation of God but finds there are no ears around to take in such an account.

Do you know what it is like to be a Mary? Some mornings after reading the Bible, after hearing God's Spirit speak to me, my heart is overcome. I want to call twenty people and say, "Stop everything. I've got to tell you something." But when it gets down to it, there are only a handful of people who have the spiritual eyes to see God's work in us. For Mary, Elizabeth was one of those people.

As Jesus grew inside Mary, we don't read of her talking about it to her family or even to Joseph. She travels a great distance to visit Elizabeth, and before Mary even tells her story, Elizabeth knows something is different. She could tell by Mary's hello that a radical shift had taken place inside Mary's soul. The Holy Spirit inside Elizabeth recognized the Spirit of God inside Mary. Upon that recognition there was leaping for joy.

Does such a phenomenon happen today? Yes! Those who cultivate the things of the Spirit and are rich with his presence recognize the Spirit in another immediately. Two strangers join hands, look deeply into each other's eyes, and sigh with pleasure at the recognition of who it is they treasure. No words are needed to confirm it.

Thank you for letting me experience the joys of your kingdom, Lord. My heart can hardly contain it. Amen.

December 24

Simply Beside Ourselves

When they saw the star, they were overjoyed.

MATTHEW 2:10

*A*t an airport gate recently, I saw a mother with five children. They were in high spirits and dressed in their Sunday best. Two boys sported navy blue suits. Three girls wore dresses with petticoats, white lacy socks, and black patent leather shoes. Their hair was fixed in French braids, with ribbons to match their dresses.

They were glued to the window. They studied each plane as it approached the gate, hoping it would be the one they were waiting for. "Mom, here comes one! Maybe it's his plane!" they said each time one approached. It was obvious that whoever was arriving was someone of utmost importance. I envisioned a grandparent from far away who hadn't seen his grandkids in quite some time.

A plane finally pulled up to our gate and the jetway door opened. All five kids were poised at the door. The intensity of their excitement was contagious. Finally a man emerged. The kids erupted into screams. "I see him. I see him!" The gentleman was mobbed. He reveled in it. Giggling, he kissed each child. I guessed he was their father.

I tapped him on the shoulder. "My goodness," I said, laughing, "how long have you been gone?"

"Two days," he said. Everyone around me roared.

Kids teach us about loving with abandon. I was struck that they were unconcerned about the commotion they made. They acted from their heart without second thought.

On Christmas morning I hope you will join me in expressing at the manger, "Oh, it's you. It's really you!" May our expression of worship be free.

Awaken my heart to experience life to the fullest, Jesus. May my love for you know no limits. Amen.

Bethlehem, the Unlikely Beginning

He came to that which was his own, but his own did
not receive him.

JOHN 1:11

*J*esus was born in Bethlehem. So was David, the man after God's
own heart. Such poverty marked that place. David learned to
shepherd there over a thousand years before Jesus graced this earth.
From the lessons David learned alone on the hillside, he became
qualified to shepherd a nation.

No wonder God planned his Son's birth in the place of shepherds.
From his lowly beginning Jesus would grow up to introduce himself to
us as the true Shepherd.

There are some differences between David and Jesus, though.
David was born in a home in the land of his father. Jesus wasn't. He
was born in a stable because his parents arrived in Bethlehem for the
census, only to find the local inn filled to capacity. Though Jesus was
born and lived in the Roman Empire, he never considered it home.
He knew that his real home was with his Father in heaven. Jesus
models the spiritual truth that we who follow him are also sojourners.

I pray I will continue to learn to avoid amassing worldly goods
here. May I not spend my time patting my world into place with
self-satisfaction. I desire to hold all things loosely, keeping my life
uncluttered and my focus homeward. I am a foreigner following the
pattern of my spiritual ancestors. The Great Shepherd, who was
not even offered a bed for his newborn head, most beautifully
modeled this.

Jesus leads by example. The name Bethlehem is sweet on my
tongue. Though unpretentious, this little town was truly significant to
the plan of heaven.

*Father, I don't bring power, influence, or wealth to your kingdom.
But I take comfort. From simple beginnings you raised up servants
who changed the world. Jesus proved that and I willingly follow in
his footsteps. Use me. Amen.*

December 26

Spiritual DNA

. . . being made in human likeness.

PHILIPPIANS 2:7

*W*hen children are born, parents quickly look for familiar features. "She has my eyes! Look, her mouth curves just like Grandpa's." Children are made in the likeness of those whose love created them. It doesn't take too many years for us to also recognize that a child has our temper, our strong will, our sensitive spirit, or a knack for the arts.

If a DNA test had been done on the baby Jesus, what would it have revealed? One thing is certain. Jesus' spiritual DNA was unlike anyone born before or since. He was God. He was perfect. There were no temper tantrums and no sulking in the corner until he got his way. Though he might have cried when he scraped his knee, or ached from the loneliness of adolescent rejection, or even overturned tables in a temple that had become commercialized, he never sinned.

We who have been spiritually adopted into his family are undergoing a metamorphosis. We are being fashioned into the likeness of Jesus. Our insecurities are being healed in his embrace. Our shame is disappearing beneath the robe he placed around our shoulders. Tempers are melting in the presence of the one we can trust. We are learning to cry but not manipulate, feel angry but take no revenge, and ask for companionship without becoming codependent. Jesus is our brother. He made his Father our Father. His royal blood is beginning to course through our veins and change the very nature of who we are.

I want others to know of your power, Father. May those close to me say, "Her spiritual adoption is changing her!" Amen.

December 27

Infant Martyrs

When Herod realized that he had been outwitted by
the Magi, he was furious, and he gave orders to kill all
the boys in Bethlehem.

MATTHEW 2:16

*M*others wept over their slain children. Wailing was heard
beyond the boundaries of Bethlehem. Herod's rage had
caused him to strike with a broad stroke. Every male child age two and
under had been murdered. The king's act was preposterous. He was
seventy years old. If an infant child were to grow and assume the
throne, it wouldn't be in his lifetime. Jesus was no threat to him! But
Herod wasn't out to protect his reign of power; he was out to exact
revenge. A mind-set bent on revenge inhibits rationality.

It's easy to focus on the miracle of Jesus' deliverance. His life was
spared because his parents had been warned in a dream about the
coming danger and had fled to Egypt. Yet the losses of these other
families arrest my attention today. Parents of these slain children had
no perspective on their loss. They did not know that their sons were
martyrs, slain for the cause of Christ. Their sons died so Jesus could
one day hang on a cross, lose his life, and give them all something
greater. Redemption.

Time brings perspective. I can look back at my life and say in
retrospect, "Yes, I lost that, but later God gave me this." We grieve
without hope unless we embrace kingdom principles. The stories of
our spiritual ancestors teach us that our weeping is not in vain. We can
pursue redemption, trading our losses for something infinitely greater.
Spiritual riches surpass the weight of our tears.

*Weeping is a part of life. But I do not cry without hope. Jesus, you
promise to redeem my losses. I look to you, for you write the future.
Amen.*

December 28

Silent Night

"My people will live in peaceful dwelling places, in secure homes, in undisturbed places of rest."

ISAIAH 32:18

*R*ecently I took part in a Christmas concert given by the Billy Graham Association for the city of Asheville, N.C. What a beautiful event! It was so soothing and worshipful in the midst of the driving chaos of the holidays.

Toward the end of the program Cliff Barrows and I performed "Silent Night" together. He played his harmonica and I played my flute. We did it a cappella, without any instrumental background. We took it slowly, at a wonderfully relaxed tempo. I thought of how many times I'd sung "Silent Night" throughout my life, but rarely did I experience the silent or holy part of Christmas. Overall it was a lifestyle problem, not just due to choices I made during the month of December.

I've made changes in the past decade. The tempo of my life has become more contemplative. If I miss time with God, I begin to notice unwelcome things in myself. My spirit becomes brittle and I'm not very gracious. Solitude, however, breeds elasticity in my spirit. It allows me to live my life out of the spiritual overflow.

I don't have it all licked. My cat Dickens is on my lap. He wants my attention but my arms are trying to maneuver around him to type. Apparently, he's annoyed. He just huffed in disgust, reached out, and bit my wrist. I'm laughing. Can I say that even he, like God, craves my undivided attention, not some token stroking as I rush by.

My goal for the coming new year is to nurture my inner world so my service is spiritually empowered.

The whole reason you created me was to spend time with you, Lord. I hear you calling. Amen.

December 29

Merciless Enemy

Your enemy the devil prowls around like a roaring
lion looking for someone to devour.

1 PETER 5:8

God warns us that Satan is clever, active, and merciless in his
attempts to destroy what God loves, his daughters! He is not out
to ruin our day; he is driven by the pleasure he receives at the thought
of destroying us. We are wise if we understand how he fights, so we
can be on guard.

What is your spiritual gift? Chances are, Satan has already tried to
undermine your confidence. Perhaps you've experienced your greatest
criticisms about the very thing God has empowered you to do.

Where have you been deprived? And what lies about life did you
adopt because of that deprivation? If your father was emotionally
absent, Satan will try to convince you that God is also an absent father.
If you grew up having to fend for yourself, Satan will attempt to
reinforce the lie that you are your own provider and God's care cannot
be trusted.

Do you have a tender heart? Satan will try to destroy that tender
and teachable spirit, for it is the very thing that allows you to
recognize and obey the voice of God. He'll use the wounds caused by
other people to assault it and cause you to hide it away.

Do you have a genetic physical weakness in your family line? Be
assured that Satan will attack there too. He loves disease and pain and
rejoices when it causes us to embrace hopelessness.

Our loving Father has not left his daughters defenseless. We have
everything we need in Christ to defeat the plans of our enemy. But
let's be street-smart. We must be armed with spiritual weapons that
will protect us. We can walk in victory and joy.

I'm living offensively with your words on my tongue, Lord. Amen.

December 30

The Unchanging Rock

"I the LORD do not change."

I'm so fickle. One day my spiritual appetite is alive and well. I read a passage of Scripture and my heart swells with the meaning of it. The next day the words fall flat. This used to scare me but I've since realized that the ongoing battle between our flesh and spirit is a curse from the Fall.

Abba, our Father, is the only one in our lives who is unchanging from day to day. If we want to know who he is today, in Scripture we can explore who he was yesterday. We can read accounts of his heart and character from several thousand years ago. What he said and did and what moved him then is the same today. That's a great comfort.

Do you know anyone who is the same as they were ten years ago? I wrote a book over a decade ago called *Carry Me*. At the time it was a reflection of who I thought God was, what I knew of myself, and the things that were important to me. Since then I've changed a lot, and I'd write a vastly different book now.

We're all evolving. Not God, though. You may have married a man who is simply not the man you dated. God stays the same. You may be watching painful changes in your children. God stays the same. Faithfulness, power, love, and gentleness are his hallmarks, and they have remained constant through the ages. No wonder Scripture calls him the rock upon which we stand. He provides a platform for truth that stands the test of time.

Everyone around me keeps changing. Friendships change and marriages change. Where can I go for stability? You, Abba. Thank you for always being the same. Amen.

December 31

Destroying to Rebuild

The LORD builds up Jerusalem; he gathers the exiles of Israel.

PSALM 147:2

*A*ny student of the Old Testament recalls the instances when God brought judgment on his people, wiping out entire cities. After they repented, he helped them rebuild. Perhaps, like me, you've struggled with the severity of God's dealings with his children. Often it was the next generation who experienced his blessing. The time that elapsed between judgment and blessing seems unreasonable to one viewing history at a glance.

I was the person through whom God birthed Daughters of Promise. Though I have been in ministry more then twenty-seven years, Daughters of Promise is just six years old at the time of this writing. To create something new, God allowed what was old to be put to death.

A well-known evangelist calls that the "death of a vision." The very thing God calls you to, he puts to death to resurrect in a purer form. Once it is rebuilt, there will be no doubt that he was the one who fashioned it. The glory will be his.

These past few years, I have felt labor pains as Daughters of Promise emerged from the womb of God's creativity. While that process has been exhilarating, the demolition of what once was has been painful. The dismantling process has felt like death. I've watched God disassemble former things piece by piece and wondered if he would ever bring his dreams for me to pass. But he did!

It's been a rigorous lesson of faith. I trust his heart, even when my limited view of his plan tells me otherwise. What feels like the end may only be the doorway to a new beginning.

Lord, your plans for me are for good, not for evil. Your plan always involves redemption. As you take away what is not good for me, I trust you. Amen.

Biblical Principles of the Cabin

Abba Offers His Children Rest

> There remains, then, a Sabbath-rest for the people
> of God.
>
> HEBREWS 4:9

> "Come to me, all you who are weary and burdened,
> and I will give you rest. Take my yoke upon you and
> learn from me, for I am gentle and humble in heart,
> and you will find rest for your souls."
>
> MATTHEW 11:28–29

God Provides a Place Where Our Soul Can Safely Live

> Turn your ear to me, come quickly to my rescue; be
> my rock of refuge, a strong fortress to save me.
>
> PSALM 31:2

> Be my rock of refuge, to which I can always go; give
> the command to save me, for you are my rock and my
> fortress.
>
> PSALM 71:3

God Calls Us by Name

> "You have said, 'I know you by name and you have
> found favor with me.'"
>
> EXODUS 33:12

The LORD said to Moses, "I will do the very thing you have asked, because I am pleased with you and I know you by name."

EXODUS 33:17

The Beauty of Nature Displays God's Creativity and Power

Praise the LORD, all his works everywhere in his dominion.

PSALM 103:22

The heavens declare the glory of God; the skies proclaim the work of his hands.

PSALM 19:1

God Is the Father Who Embraces Us

Keep me as the apple of your eye; hide me in the shadow of your wings.

PSALM 17:8

How priceless is your unfailing love! Both high and low among men find refuge in the shadow of your wings.

PSALM 36:7

Time Ceases in God's Kingdom

A thousand years in your sight are like a day that has just gone by, or like a watch in the night.

PSALM 90:4

Do not forget this one thing, dear friends: With the Lord a day is like a thousand years, and a thousand years are like a day.

2 PETER 3:8

God Knows Our Story

> You discern my going out and my lying down, you are familiar with all my ways.
>
> PSALM 139:3

> My frame was not hidden from you when I was made in the secret place. When I was woven together in the depths of the earth, your eyes saw my unformed body. All the days ordained for me were written in your book before one of them came to be.
>
> PSALM 139:15–16

> I will be glad and rejoice in your love, for you saw my affliction and knew the anguish of my soul.
>
> PSALM 31:7

Peaceful Sleep Is God's Provision

> I will lie down and sleep in peace, for you alone, O LORD, make me dwell in safety.
>
> PSALM 4:8

> He grants sleep to those he loves.
>
> PSALM 127:2

> When you lie down, you will not be afraid; when you lie down, your sleep will be sweet.
>
> PROVERBS 3:24

God Is a Musician Who Delights in and Sings to His Children

> "The LORD your God is with you, he is mighty to save. He will take great delight in you, he will quiet you with his love, he will rejoice over you with singing."
>
> ZEPHANIAH 3:17

He brought me out into a spacious place; he rescued me because he delighted in me.

PSALM 18:19

God Is Always Available

"I will never leave you nor forsake you."

JOSHUA 1:5

"Call to me and I will answer you and tell you great and unsearchable things you do not know."

JEREMIAH 33:3

Scripture Index

We want to hear from you. Please send your comments about this book to us in care of the address below. Thank you.

GRAND RAPIDS, MICHIGAN 49530 USA

WWW.ZONDERVAN.COM